THE TUDOR PARLIAMENTS

STUDIES IN MODERN HISTORY

General editors: *John Morrill and David Cannadine*

This series, intended primarily for students, will tackle significant historical issues in concise volumes which are both stimulating and scholarly. The authors combine a broad approach, explaining the current state of our knowledge in the area, with their own research and judgements; and the topics chosen range widely in subject, period and place.

Titles already published

THE TUDOR PARLIAMENTS

Crown, Lords and Commons, 1485–1603

Michael A. R. Graves

LONGMAN
London and New York

LONGMAN GROUP LIMITED
Longman House, Burnt Mill, Harlow
Essex CM20 2JE, England
Associated companies throughout the world

*Published in the United States of America
by Longman Inc., New York*

First published 1985

BRITISH LIBRARY CATALOGUING IN PUBLICATION DATA

Graves, Michael A. R.
  The Tudor parliaments : Crown, Lords and
  Commons 1485–1603. – (Studies in modern history)
  1. Great Britain – Parliament – History
  2. Great Britain – History – Tudors, 1485–1603
  I. Title   II. Series
  328.42′09   JN525

ISBN 0-582-49190-8

LIBRARY OF CONGRESS CATALOGUING IN PUBLICATION DATA

Graves, Michael A. R.
  The Tudor parliaments.

  (Studies in modern history)
  Bibliography: p.
  Includes index.
    1. Great Britain. Parliament – History. 2. Great
Britain – Politics and government – 1485–1603. I. Title.
II. Series: Studies in modern history (Longman (Firm))
JN521.G73 1986   328.42′09   84–27858
ISBN 0–582–49190–8 (pbk.)

Set in 10/11 pt VIP Times

Produced by Longman Group (FE) Limited
Printed in Hong Kong

CONTENTS

LIST OF TABLES

ABBREVIATIONS

B.I.H.R.   *Bulletin of the Institute of Historical Research*

B.J.R.L.   *Bulletin of the John Rylands Library*

E.H.R.   *English Historical Review*

H.J.   *Historical Journal*

J.B.S.   *Journal of British Studies*

T.R.H.S.   *Transactions of the Royal Historical Society*

Chapter one

THE HISTORIOGRAPHY OF THE TUDOR PARLIAMENTS: A CRITICAL ANALYSIS

'Revisionism' has become an accepted and familiar term in both Tudor and early Stuart historiography. As far as Parliament is concerned it represents a reaction against the politically-orientated, Commons-weighted history of Parliament, which has held the field for most of this century (and which, in the following pages, is styled the *orthodoxy* as a convenient shorthand description). It rests upon two premisses: that Parliament was both bicameral and a trinity (king, Lords and Commons); and that its functions, procedures and business, not politics, should be our prime concern – after all, politicking was no more than the art of achieving a desired end and the end-product of Parliament, its business, was legislation. The essence of the revisionist approach can be summarised thus:

(1) King, Lords and Commons were co-equal partners in the legislative process and the assent of all of them was necessary to make statute. However, this requires some qualification. The Crown presented measures for Parliament's consideration and, in most sessions, it requested financial aid. Thereafter its formal role was confined to the assent or veto of those Bills which had passed the two houses (though, as we shall see, in practice the Crown continuously used privy councillors to supervise the progress of Bills and it frequently intervened to check or smooth their passage). The Lords and Commons hammered out the final form of Bills which were to be presented to the monarch at the end of the session and they enjoyed an equal right to reject, amend or assent to Bills before them. However, their roles in relation to any particular Bill differed, depending on which house was the initiator (or 'proprietor') of it (see Ch. 2, p. 33). The Commons alone had the right to initiate grants of lay taxation. The Lords could reduce the amount of money voted but not increase it. However, in practice it often pressured and coerced the lower house to act speedily and generously; in 1593 it virtually seized the initiative. Moreover, as the assembly of a noble élite, it exercised, an additional, invisible social influence in

1

the Commons, which made it a formidable power within the parliamentary trinity.

(2) Parliaments were a conjunction, a 'coming together' of Crown and governing class. In so far as their existence – both their summons and dissolution (or prorogation) – was determined by the monarch, they were meetings of a royal institution. They were called to equip the monarch with the new laws and additional revenue – also enacted in statutory form – which would enable him to govern effectively. When a Parliament had performed those functions satisfactorily, its life was terminated. In practice, however, it satisfied more needs than this. Parliament was an occasion for the Crown to state its intentions, declare its policies and test public opinion, and for the governing class to express its views, present its grievances and raise matters of general concern. It was also a platform on which ambitious men could attract royal favour and, above all, it was a means of satisfying the legislative needs of the governing élite.[1] Most parliamentary Bills were introduced not by the government but by lords spiritual and temporal, knights and burgesses who were promoting their own interests or those of kin, friends, neighbours or of the communities which they represented. Therefore in terms of law-making – the prime function of Parliaments – the success of any session must be measured by the quality and volume of the laws which it passed, in other words by its productivity: did it give the Crown what it needed and, in some measure, satisfy the legislative aspirations of members of the governing class?

(3) Parliaments were co-operative ventures. In any assembly of aggressive, self-confident 'governors', who were accustomed to giving orders and to being obeyed, there were bound to be clashes of personality, opinion and interest. It would be unrealistic to expect any Tudor monarch, his episcopate and peerage, and a sizeable representative sample of the gentry and urban oligarchies, to work together in perfect harmony throughout a parliamentary session. Yet the fact remains that, for most of the time, they were in general agreement on fundamentals. Hot-heads, brabblers and praters, men of extreme views or profound conviction, the bold and the tactless were always to be found: those who spoke out in 1523 against heavy taxation consumed in futile wars and the acquisition of 'ungracious dogholes' in France; Sir George Throckmorton criticising the annulment of Henry VIII's first marriage in the early 1530s; Peter and Paul Wentworth inveighing against the queen's abuse of parliamentary privilege in the 1560s and 1570s. While these are all examples of dissension in the Commons, it is worth recalling too Henry VIII's concern about the potential opposition in the Lords during the Reformation Parliament (1529–36), the imprisonment of Bishop Gardiner by successive aristocratic regimes in Edward VI's reign (partly because he represented a serious parliamentary threat), the opposition of catholic bishops and peers to

the Edwardian Reformation, Lord Paget's conduct in April–May 1554, and the stubborn resistance of Marian bishops to the Elizabethan Settlement in 1559 (see Chs 4–6).

Yet in both houses these were exceptions to the normal co-operation which existed in Tudor assemblies. If Parliaments had been the regular occasion for conflict and opposition, would monarchs have continued to call them despite the frequent need for additional revenue? In 1629 Charles I provided the answer when he resolved to dispense with Parliaments for the time being and instead resorted to non-parliamentary levies in order to balance income and expenditure. The decision, however, was the outcome of a deadlock between the king and the governing class which had caused business to grind to a halt. Until the 1620s criticism, dispute and opposition were just aberrations from the norm. Tudor monarchs learned to live with them as part of the give-and-take of the parliamentary process. In any case, when disagreement and dissension occurred they were more often not the consequence of 'matters of great moment' (such as royal policies or national issues) but rather of contentious local, sectional or economic Bills. Most of the conflict and lobbying was between competing interests within the governing class and not between the Crown and that class. There were no signs of escalating political tension. Nor is there any substantial evidence that the roots of Stuart conflict can be traced back to the Tudor Parliaments.

This revisionist version of sixteenth-century parliamentary history is the reverse of the old, established *orthodoxy*. Formulated by A. F. Pollard, elaborated and brought to completion by J. E. Neale, reinforced by Wallace Notestein, Conyers Read and others, and influencing an entire generation of Tudor scholars, the orthodox interpretation has held sway for much of this century. Indeed, until the mid-1960s it enjoyed a remarkable and general acceptance. As late as 1960 G. R. Elton bestowed upon it his *imprimatur*.[2] What then are the essentials of this persuasive orthodoxy? They can be described briefly, but the important initial point to remember is that they all reinforce a kind of subordination, prologue-like, to the coming climax of the mid-seventeenth century. The Tudor century is not to be studied in its own right, but as a mere introduction to the political convulsions of the 1640s and 1650s. It is a period to be ransacked for the origins of the English Civil War and Revolution.

According to the orthodox historians, Parliament 'rose' in legislative and political authority under the Tudors, the crucial point of change being the 1530s. Until that decade the competence of statute and the authority of Parliament were limited. Statute could not deal with matters spiritual, nor did it encroach upon the sanctity of property in any general way. However, the 1530s changed all that. In 1532–34 the *spiritualia* as well as the *temporalia* of the papacy were transferred to the Crown. And in 1536 the dissolution of the monasteries, the suppression of the franchises and the Statute of Uses carried through a property revolution which was authorised by Acts of Parliament. Statute had proved itself to be omnicompetent – capable of dealing with any aspect of human affairs. This was not universally apparent at once, nor were the implications immediately perceived. However, the Act of Six Articles which, in 1539, set forth a corpus of orthodox catholic doctrine, the Edwardian prayer books, the Marian reaction and the Elizabethan Settlement were all enacted by parliamentary authority. Gradually they brought the point home: Parliament was sovereign and there was nothing which it could not touch.

Nor was this the sum total of change. Within Parliament there was a shift in power. During the 1530s the Commons superseded the Lords as the more important legislative chamber. It seized the initiative in business, and became more politically conscious, sensitive of its privileges, willing and able to criticise and oppose the Crown. Thereafter, in contrast, the House of Lords slithered from its former superiority towards political impotence. It lost its independence and instead compliantly assisted the Crown to achieve its parliamentary objectives and to control the more assertive Commons. Repeatedly we are told that there is little to be learned about the Elizabethan Lords. The fact that foreign ambassadors and diarists rarely had much to say about its political activities was regarded by Neale as a register of its lack of importance. Such a conclusion raises the question whether the significance of a legislative assembly should be gauged by its politicking rather than by its record of business. Nevertheless that was the common attitude of historians until the mid-1960s.

Inevitably it was a point of view which concentrated attention on the Commons. Was not the lower house the focus of opposition to the Crown during the great constitutional crisis of 1640–42? Therefore the roots of that opposition were traced back through the history of the Commons in the previous century. They manifested themselves as early as 1510 and 1523 over matters of the purse (see pp. 59–60, 61–2). In the 1530s members were critical of Henry VIII's marital schemes and schismatic policy. The house was also stubborn in its hostility to the Bills of uses and proclamations – a protracted resistance which extended over several sessions. Then, in Mary's reign, a politically-charged atmosphere spawned an organised parliamentary opposition. It was, as Neale admits, 'a flash in the pan', but it was also, according to both him and Notestein, the precursor of a persistent and troublesome opposition in the Elizabethan Commons.[3] They focused their attention exclusively on examples of its resistance to Marian policies and ignored the Lords. In particular they settled on the Parliament of 1555 as the exemplar of early organised resistance to the Crown. Naturally that resistance was Commons-based, as was demonstrated when some members challenged the Bill to restore first fruits and tenths to the papacy, and when Sir Anthony Kingston locked the doors of the House and secured a snap division which defeated an official Bill to penalise exiles.

From that point, Neale then extended the story of organised opposition through Elizabeth's reign. The dynamic was ardent, radical protestantism (i.e. puritanism) which mingled love and devotion to the queen with its desire to drive her along the road towards a godly Genevan Church and society. However, there was now a significant difference. Whereas the Marian opposition had been negative and obstructive, this was a positive, constructive force with an alternative programme of its own. So there was born Neale's 'puritan choir', a radical party which attempted to ram through Parliament in 1566/7 and 1571 a reform programme, consisting of the so-called Alphabetical Bills, the *Reformatio Legum Ecclesiasticarum* and a Bill to revise the prayer book. In the sessions between 1563 and 1571 it also pressed the queen to marry or name a successor in order to avoid the dreadful alternative of another catholic, Mary Stuart, on the throne.[4] These attempts failed, but parliamentary opposition did not die. In the 1580s there were the presbyterian campaigns to replace the Anglican prayer book with the Geneva-style directory of worship and in 1597 and 1601 there was the general clamour against the harmful monopolies granted by the queen.[5] By 1601, as many a well-rehearsed schoolboy will tell us, the House of Commons had become a power to be reckoned with, able and willing to challenge the Crown's authority. With his magisterial authority Neale set the seal of authenticity on this tradition when he wrote that 'By Elizabeth's reign, a balanced history of parliament would be almost as predominantly a history of the House of Commons as it is in early Stuart times.'[6]

Yet how valid is the picture of a lower house marching steadily onwards and upwards to the constitutional confrontation of 1640? In any case, whatever happened in the early seventeenth century, and whenever the crisis actually crystallised is not (and should not be) the particular concern of a study of Tudor Parliaments. Unfortunately the *orthodox* historians were preoccupied with what was to come and their writings were indelibly coloured by their knowledge of the future. They produced retrospective history, a search for the origins of the great political upheaval of the following century. Neale wrote that it was his specific purpose 'to banish the old illusion that early-Stuart Parliaments had few roots in the sixteenth century'.[7] That purpose coloured his thinking and dictated his argument. However, if we are to understand what Tudor Parliaments were all about, it is essential, at the very outset, to set aside that retrospective approach and assess them in their own right.

This is particularly true of the House of Lords. If Tudor Parliaments in general have been demoted to no more than a mere prologue, the fate of the upper house is even worse. It has been consigned to virtual political oblivion by a school of history which, for all practical purposes, treated Parliament as a duet of Crown and Commons, and which conceived of the institution in terms of politics, not business. To understand how this interpretation evolved, it is necessary to examine the modern historiography of Parliament in the context of modern parliamentary developments. The reform Acts of the nineteenth and early twentieth centuries, together with the constitutional crisis of Edward VII's reign, combined to produce the supremacy of a democratically elected House of Commons within the parliamentary trinity. The fact that its supremacy was short-lived, and that power has since shifted from Parliament to cabinet, does not alter the impact of these developments on parliamentary historiography during the first half of this century.

The interplay between historical and historiographical development has been underlined by G. R. Elton's recent review of the Elizabethan volumes of the History of Parliament Trust. He identified several phases in the study of Tudor Parliaments during this century. First, there was 'the story of constitutional liberty, growing steadily over the ages until conflict resolved the rivalry in the 17th century'. It was a story stuffed with 'the rise of the House of Commons, the growth of privilege, the control of the purse, the redress of grievances', and only those statutes which constituted 'landmarks of freedom' figured in this study of constitutional growth. Then in 1929 the balance shifted dramatically when Lewis Namier resolved that, in the mid-eighteenth century, party, policies and constitutional principles played little part in the reasons why men entered Parliament. 'The politics of Parliament, it came to be thought, had nothing to do with constitutionalism, liberty or even party (at least before about 1800), and everything to do with personal advancement and fortune.'[8]

Elton identified the preconceptions and misconceptions which these two fundamentally different historical approaches shared. They ignored the vast bulk of Parliament's legislative business, the Crown's role in its activities, and the performance of the House of Lords. However, he made no mention of a closer, more intimate association between them. A. F. Pollard served his apprenticeship with the *Dictionary of National Biography* during the 1890s. Biography became his forte and politics his first priority – hence his political biographies of Henry VIII and Protector Somerset and his essays on Cardinal Wolsey. As the founder of the London History school, the creator of the Institute of Historical Research, the inaugural editor of *History* and the *Bulletin* (*B.I.H.R.*), he was able to impose the stamp of his priorities on those who were to follow him. Therefore his influence was crucial to the development of parliamentary studies at London University. Neale, who followed him, faithfully observed Pollard's priorities with his biography of Queen Elizabeth. His trilogy and many articles on the Elizabethan Parliaments were political rather than institutional. Even his institutional study of *The Elizabethan House of Commons* had a heavy political and biographical emphasis: disputed elections, the composition of the house and the quality of its membership which, together, occupy almost three-quarters of the volume.[9]

The foundation of the History of Parliament Trust, inspired by Namier and administered by the Institute of Historical Research, was a logical conclusion of these developments. It was a misnomer, because it was exclusively concerned with the Commons. Even then, characteristically, it did not deal with the procedural and institutional growth of the lower house, but with its membership and elections to it. However, during the 1960s, when the Trust was slowly labouring towards a conclusion, there were signs that some historians were re-thinking their attitudes to parliamentary history. The pioneer in print was J. S. Roskell, who compared the Tudor Parliaments with their medieval predecessors and found them wanting. They met less frequently, deposed no monarch and impeached no minister or favourite. They granted tunnage and poundage for life, established no principle of 'redress before supply' and failed to appropriate taxes to specific purposes, supervise expenditure or audit accounts. Roskell formulated his arguments within the traditional framework of power politics, not parliamentary business. But when he argued that the institution lacked the capacity to challenge royal authority or oversee the executive, unless it met regularly and exercised effective financial controls, he rendered a signal service to the more realistic appraisal of Tudor Parliaments.[10] Neither circumstance existed in the sixteenth century. Only twice did the Commons offer less money than the Crown had requested, in 1504 and 1532,[11] and at no time did it refuse a grant outright. There were no 'addled' Parliaments in Tudor England.

Nor did Parliament have regular and frequent meetings. It was a royal institution, whose function was not to obstruct the king or to limit his power, but to facilitate government with laws and taxes. Therefore the dates of summons, the duration of sessions, prorogations and dissolutions all depended on the will and needs of the monarch. Between 1485 and 1529 parliamentary meetings averaged one every three and a half years and few lasted more than seven weeks. In contrast, during the crisis years of the Reformation (1529–59) there were almost annual sittings: 27 sessions in 21 of the 30 years. Under Elizabeth, however, Parliament settled back into the pre-Reformation rhythm, averaging a meeting every three and a half years (albeit for longer sessions with a mean of 10/11 weeks). The irregularity and infrequency with which it met – and the fact that in each new Parliament about half of the knights and burgesses were raw novices, ignorant of procedure and many unacquainted with their fellow members – retarded efficiency and the growth of a corporate consciousness (especially in the Commons). It also inhibited a continuous and effective supervision of royal government (assuming of course that it wished to perform this watchdog role, and of that there is no evidence in the sixteenth century).

If Roskell's criticisms were couched in the traditional political terminology and framed in terms of the old political priorities, none the less he did question the orthodox interpretation. Those who followed him, however, shed the old priorities and began to ask new questions: about the institution (rather than the politics of its members), its functions, business, procedure and records. Some of the more pertinent questions are worth reciting here. What functions did the two houses perform? What formal authority did they wield in the fulfilment of their functions, both in absolute terms and in relation to each other and to the Crown? Was their actual political muscle greater or less than the formal authority with which they were endowed? In practical terms what kinds (and volume) of business did they engage in? How (and with what degree of efficiency) did they organise themselves to transact it? Last but not least, how did they record their activities (a major concern to historians)? These are mundane questions and intrinsically much less exciting than the heady stuff of power politics and constitutional confrontations. However, there was a growing recognition that, without satisfactory answers to them, parliamentary politics were liable to be misread or even to remain incomprehensible. There was also an increasing awareness that, as Parliament was a bicameral institution of co-equal chambers, it was essential to study the Lords as well as the Commons.

In the late 1960s and 1970s there emerged, not a revisionist school, but what may be called loosely a revisionist 'position'. Tudor revisionism is inchoate and unorganised, even if most of its advocates acknowledge G. R. Elton as its standard-bearer and most prominent spokesman. In the late 1960s and early 1970s a number of general texts presaged the change of approach;[12] local parliamentary interests were explored by Helen Miller;[13] S. E. Lehmberg probed the problems of parliamentary procedure and, in his two-volume study of the Parliaments of Henry VIII, he not only acknowledged the existence of the House of Lords, but (a novel touch here) he examined its legislative role.[14] Concurrently there appeared in print a debate on the vexed and technical question of the proxies of absent bishops and peers, in itself symptomatic of the new interest in the upper house.[15] At the same time a spate of dissertations, similarly treating of legislation (and the Lords' role therein) also came to fruition.[16]

In the 1970s and early 1980s the move to revisionism gathered momentum. There was nothing homogeneous or co-ordinated in this development, which was characterised rather by its disparate elements and differences in emphasis than by an *idée fixe* or an ideological party line. During the past twenty years historians as far apart as the United Kingdom, the USA, Canada and New Zealand have been taking a fresh look at Tudor Parliaments. In most cases the only important

common denominator in their work is the belief that a sound knowledge of an institution's authority, functions, business, membership and
procedures is a prerequisite to an understanding of its politics. It has
been not a concerted campaign but a piecemeal process, largely determined by the particular (and often technical) interests of the historians
involved: the mid-Tudor House of Lords, abortive legislation, the
enacting clause in statutes, the Lords' journals and the Parliament
rolls, official managerial techniques designed to expedite parliamentary business, and so on. At first there was no overall conception
of how we should view the history of Tudor Parliaments. Furthermore, much of the early energy was directed to destructive ends, an
assault on the priorities, interpretations and conclusions of the
orthodox tradition. A particular target was Sir John Neale's claim that
there emerged, in the more assertive Elizabethan Commons, an organised political opposition which was radical and ideologically-based.
Monographs on legislation and the managerial role of the council
(the body which advised the monarch and administered the realm),
together with a reappraisal of early Elizabethan parliamentary politics,
have thrown into serious doubt his thesis (if they have not actually
demolished it).[17]

The work of destruction was not the consequence of a conscious,
deliberate and hostile exercise in historical criticism. Instead it evolved
out of the dawning recognition that significant aspects of Tudor
Parliaments had been neglected or ignored. For example, those who
led the renewed interest in the House of Lords in the 1960s discovered
only uncharted seas, and were bereft even of stars by which to navigate.
There was virtually no existing secondary literature and there was a
complete absence of accurate, collated information about such basics
as its composition, business, and procedures. L. O. Pike's 'constitutional history' of the house was a misnomer, because it was chiefly
concerned with the evolution of peers of Parliament (bishops as well as
nobles) from the feudal *tenantes in capite* of the medieval Crown. It was
a study of the rights of membership, not of the institution.[18] The same
can be said of J. H. Round, whose primary interests were pedigree and
peerage law, and Enoch Powell and Keith Wallis, for whom too the
priority was the men who sat there – their qualifications for membership, precedence, ceremony, and heraldry – not the house in which
they sat.[19] In the interim between Round and the work of Powell and
Wallis no major scholarly works on the Lords appeared in print – just a
mere handful of brief monographs.[20] At least they had the virtue of
being institutionally orientated, because they dealt with the legal
assistants to the house, its records and bureaucracy. Yet none of them
treated of the institutional fundamentals – its functions and power, the
quality and volume of its business – and they only touched upon the
way in which it organised itself to transact that business.

This neglect was one of the most serious deficiencies of the orthodoxy. However, revisionism 'rediscovered' the Lords and, as a result, its legislative efficiency, importance (and, sometimes, superiority) have been firmly established, at least between the 1530s and 1560s.[21] Lehmberg produced the first truly bicameral study of Tudor Parliaments, and one of his most important contributions was the inclusion of the convocation of Canterbury which met concurrently with Parliament.[22] Others took up the story where he left off in 1547 and carried it through the brief reigns and shaky regimes of Edward VI and Mary to the Elizabethan Settlement. After the brief, spurious primacy of the lower house in the 1530s,[23] the legislative and political initiative returned to the Lords. There it remained until there occurred a crisis and turning-point in 1553–55, when the parliamentary reputation and performance of the house were impaired by its uncharacteristic behaviour. It was factious, fractious and guilty of irresponsible conduct. As a result it forfeited royal and public confidence (see below, pp. 107–112), and surrendered to the Commons its role as the chief initiator of Bills of national scope and 'great moment'.[24]

Thereafter the Lords never fully recovered its former position, although it did not sink into the condition of abject compliance with the Crown's wishes and parliamentary insignificance which the orthodoxy assigned to it. Whether or not this thesis stands the tests of time and further research, it stands in contrast to Neale's picture of an obstreperous Marian House of Commons.[25] Finally, a similar treatment of the early Elizabethan Parliaments (1559–63) by Norman Jones has substantially rejected Neale's explanation of the Elizabethan Settlement. His scenario writes out puritan pressure and organised opposition as the parliamentary dynamic. Instead he has restored the Lords (or at least its catholic members) as the focal point of resistance to royal policies.[26]

The role of G. R. Elton was crucial to the development of the revisionist position. Before the 1970s one might have been excused for reading him as an advocate of the orthodox approach. So in *The Tudor Constitution*, published in 1960, he wrote of the Commons' transformation 'from a body of local representatives, charged with communicating the locality's grievances to the king's government, into an aspiring partner in the political government of the nation'. Conciliar management 'applied more particularly to the House of Commons, if only because the Lords could on the whole be expected to follow the government's lead without special management'. And, in the Elizabethan Commons, there emerged 'a novel kind of opposition – opposition on points of constitutional principle'. Elton continued,

[I]t is only in Elizabeth's reign that we can trace the growth of something very like a party. Thomas Norton's leadership of a coherent band in the 1560s is visible through the deficiencies of the evidence ... It thus appears that opposition in Parliament was possible throughout the century and encountered by all the Tudors, but that it grew into something regular, organised and persistently troublesome in the reign of Elizabeth.

He also accepted the importance which Neale attached to the activities of the Wentworth brothers, in particular Peter's audacious and impertinent speech in 1576 against the queen's abuse of the Commons' privileges. He endorsed Neale's dismissive verdict when he wrote that 'Little is known of the way in which the Lords managed their affairs.' When he added '[I]t is thought that they probably used much the same rules as the Commons, but with less formality and rigour', he seemed to imply that the lower house was more organised, efficient, and fertile in new procedures. In brief he did not seriously question the fundamentals of the orthodoxy.[27]

In 1982, however, a revised edition of *The Tudor Constitution* appeared. Elton's re-drafted commentaries on Parliament are themselves a commentary on his own shift in position to one of prominence in the revisionist process. Gone is the Elizabethan puritan opposition which 'did not exist'. In 1960 'the two sessions of 1563 and 1566 were dominated by the organised opposition of a group (the so-called 'choir'), who wanted to secure a formal settlement of the succession'. Now 'Apprehensions for the future of the Protestant Church played their part in the agitation of 1563 and 1566 when the Council encouraged both Houses to press the queen for a settlement of the succession . . .' Elton has discarded, indeed rejected, the thesis that Elizabethan opposition in the Commons was puritan, regular and organised. Instead he interprets political conflict, on the rare occasions on which it occurred, not as a confrontation between Government and 'opposition', but as a parliamentary expression of the faction-fights within court and council; he stresses the bicameral nature of Parliament, and its functional importance rather than its political role; and he rejects the traditional view that procedural innovations and the consolidation of parliamentary privileges are evidence of the 'maturing' or rise of the lower house.[28]

The cumulative effect of Elton's pronouncements is to displace the Commons from its central role in Tudor parliamentary history, as the vanguard and standard-bearer of constitutional liberties and a competitor with the crown for power in the State. Furthermore, because his revaluation of parliament has been a bicameral one, he has also assisted in the rehabilitation of the Lords:

[B]oth Houses had evidently been able long before this to conduct their affairs according to sensible rules – rules which they treated with great flexibility and in the Commons at least never reduced to order. The Lords, always more 'mature' and more businesslike, led the way . . . [T]hough the Commons on occasions . . . displayed a mild corporate resentment against the peers they mostly continued to take their cue from the Upper House.[29]

11

Such revised opinions are the end-product of a lengthy process by which Elton shook himself free from the orthodox framework of priorities and interpretation. The shift was observable as early as 1971, when he voiced the first major public criticism of historians' over-concern with parliamentary politics and the 'whiggish conviction . . . which urge[s] us to seek nothing but the "growth" of the Commons' independence and political ascendancy, in a constant struggle against the power of the Crown'. Instead he called for a fresh approach: to study Parliament's business as embodied in legislation. This treatment had two virtues, if it was handled in a judicious and balanced manner. First, it would not ignore or sweep under the carpet debate on great issues, disagreement and conflict, but it would set them in the actual, normal parliamentary context of co-operation in pursuit of fruitful sessions. How else could the later Tudor Parliaments have enacted so many Acts of such diverse range? In these circumstances conflict was unusual and continued conflict was 'a sign of genuine failure on the part of all concerned'.[30] Secondly, such an approach would subject the official institutional records – the journals of the two houses and the original Acts – to systematic scrutiny for the first time. It was a dismal commentary on the lopsided, politically-orientated study of Tudor Parliaments that, when Elton wrote in 1971, no-one had done this.[31] Yet, until procedures and business were properly evaluated, parliamentary politics were likely to be misread and their meaning distorted.

In 1974 Elton reiterated and developed this theme. Parliament's authority, new-found in the crisis years of the 1530s, lay not in its willingness and capacity to oppose the Crown, but in its omnicompetence, its ability to legislate on all aspects of human affairs. Parliaments existed not to criticise or coerce the king, but to serve him.[32] In the same year Elton elaborated on one aspect of the new approach when he identified Tudor Parliaments as one of the vital 'points of contact' between royal government and the governing class, enabling the Crown to test public opinion in the political nation on the great issues of the day. On the other side it gave nobles and bishops, knights and burgesses a chance to voice their current grievances and those of their absent fellows or electors. It gave occasion for ambitious careerists (especially the lawyers) to attract the attention of the monarch, a councillor or a courtier and, by an able and loyal performance, to launch on a successful career in royal service. Most important of all it allowed individuals, families, local and sectional interests to promote Bills through powerful patrons or their elected representatives. Much of the 'parliament-time' after the 1530s was eaten up by the enactment (or frustration) of private legislation.[33]

Elton pioneered the trail away from the politics of Parliament to its business, procedure and records.[34] In December 1978 he summed up the work of the past decade and stated the case for revisionism when he delivered the J. E. Neale Memorial Lecture at University College, London. He challenged the underlying political assumptions of the Neale–Notestein school and stressed, instead, the need to concentrate on the legislative purpose and interests of the parliamentary trinity. He rejected the thesis that the evolution of a Commons' journal was a measure of 'institutional growth', or that procedural innovations were intended to seize control of the house from the privy council and vest it in a puritan 'opposition'. He was dismissive, not only of the political significance of the brothers Wentworth as vocal puritan rebels, but also of the notion that there existed some kind of organised puritan 'party' with continuity from Parliament to Parliament. Instead he emphasised the normality of co-operation and the effectiveness of conciliar control.

Elton also insisted that it was not only the House of Commons which mattered.[35] However, the Lords' importance only became apparent as a consequence of the revisionists' concentration on business.[36] Its role as an initiator of Bills was always significant and sometimes superior to that of the lower house. It was the more orderly house and more efficient in its procedures; and if it conveys the impression that it was a political lightweight, then that is only part of the conditioning process in which orthodox historians persuasively pursued their obsession with the political 'function' of Parliament. This ignores the fact that so many Commons' 'campaigns' (especially in Elizabeth's reign) were orchestrated by the privy council in order to coerce the queen; that, apart from an aberration in 1553–55, the Lords remained the more responsible and constructive chamber; and that, quite apart from its formal, institutional authority, the peers sitting there exerted an invisible but powerful socio-political influence over many of their social inferiors and clients in the lower house (see Chs 6 and 7).[37]

The most recent exercise in revisionist writing marks another step in the modification of the traditional interpretation of Tudor Parliaments. In 1982 there appeared in print Norman Jones' study of the Elizabethan Settlement which, in 1559, reversed the papal, catholic reaction of Mary's reign and revived a national, protestant Church. Jones was faced with the task of reappraising two diametrically opposed interpretations, whose roll of advocates read like a *Who's Who* of early modern English historiography. The older tradition was, initially, the product of contemporary propaganda. The new protestant-heroine queen was bent on establishing a national protestant Church governed by queen and bishops. The Henrician supremacy, the Edwardian Reformation and the Marian reaction had been enacted by statute. Therefore the replacement of Mary's Church required parliamentary sanction too. However, it was only achieved after a stern struggle between the queen, supported by her faithful protestant Commons, and the catholic bishops and peers in the Lords. John Foxe and William Camden in the sixteenth century, Gilbert

Burnet, John Strype, J. A. Froude, R. H. Dixon and Henry Gee during the following 300 years, and F. W. Maitland and A. F. Pollard early this century: all repeated the same tale with but minor additions and modifications.

The other tradition is of more recent origin and rests chiefly on the magisterial writings of J. E. Neale, culminating in his trilogy which appeared between 1949 and 1957.[38] His version of events, causation and significance were widely accepted and became the orthodoxy for an entire generation of scholars, teachers and students. The general consensus was surprising, because Neale's interpretation embodied two startling novelties. He did not subscribe to the view that the Settlement emerged from a clash between queen and catholics. Instead it was the outcome of a tug-of-war between Elizabeth and some of her protestant subjects, who, despite their vocal affirmations of love and devotion, none the less wanted a more radical Church and religion than she was willing to concede. Secondly, in the process of re-writing the story of the Settlement, Neale switched the centre of parliamentary gravity and power from the upper house (where an influential catholic minority was entrenched) to the lower (which was dominated by busy puritans).

In his turn Jones questioned both traditions. While he found both of them too simplistic, he came down on the side of the older one. Neale's thesis depended on the presence in the Commons of a hard core of puritans (spearheaded by Marian exiles who had drunk deep in the springs of reformed religion: Geneva, Frankfurt, Strasburg). These were the men who supposedly dominated the house and led the campaign for a new and radical Church based on the best continental protestant models. However, Jones rejected Neale's claim that there existed some kind of puritan 'party' in the 1559 parliament, showing there were no more than 20/25 religious radicals or puritans out of 400 members. Moreover there were only four exiles (characterised by their intimate connection with Elizabeth or Sir William Cecil). Nor did the exiles, the other parliamentary puritans, and their sympathisers outside share a common religious position, aim and purpose. Without a puritan party or an effective puritan leadership, how could there have been a well-drilled, disciplined and effective parliamentary campaign?[39] Jones concluded that, from the very beginning, Elizabeth sought to re-impose royal government on the English Church and an order of worship based on a modified version of the 1552 prayer book. With skill, tact, and the capacity to compromise and make concessions, she achieved more or less what she wanted. Throughout she had to take into account the cupidity of some, the unbending principle of others, the threat of foreign powers and, above all, the intransigence of catholics in the upper house. The recognition that the last of these was so important restored the Lords to its rightful place in the trinity, during one of the more critical parliamentary episodes of the century.

This brings us to the present state of Tudor parliamentary studies. Revisionism began as a process of doubting, then questioning, by individual historians. It developed into a piecemeal attack on various aspects of the orthodoxy and then, as it entered a constructive phase, it evolved into a unified and coherent interpretation of its own. There always remains the possibility that, at the end, one myth will have replaced another. Therefore it is not the purpose of this volume to preach the revisionist line. Instead its object is to synthesise the tested and acceptable elements in both the orthodox and revisionist positions in an attempt to produce a more balanced and realistic history of the Tudor Parliaments.

REFERENCES AND NOTES

(*Note:* Abbreviations of titles used in the references here and elsewhere are given in square brackets following the full title.)

1. G. R. Elton, 'Tudor Government. The Points of Contact. 1. Parliament' ['Points of Contact'], *T.R.H.S.*, 5th Series, XXIV (1974), 183–200.
2. G. R. Elton, *The Tudor Constitution*, Cambridge, 1960, pp. 244–7, 253–61, 282–8, and especially 300–4.
3. J. E. Neale, *Elizabeth I and her Parliaments* [*Eliz. Parls*], 2 vols, London, 1953, 1957, I, pp. 21–6; W. Notestein, 'The Winning of the Initiative by the House of Commons' ['Winning of the Initiative'], *British Academy*, XI, London, 1926. 'There appeared in the Commons something almost like a Protestant party which yielded ground only as it was again and again outvoted.' Ibid., p. 11.
4. Neale, *Eliz. Parls*, I, pp. 85–240.
5. Ibid., II, pp. 60–83, 145–65, 216–32, 352–6, 376–93.
6. J. E. Neale, *Elizabethan House of Commons* [*E.H.C.*], London, 1949, pp. 15–16.
7. Neale, *Eliz. Parls*, I, p. 11.
8. G. R. Elton, 'Members' Memorial', *London Review of Books*, 4 (9) (May–June 1982), 14–15.
9. Neale, *E.H.C.*, pp. 21–320.
10. *The History of Parliament. The House of Commons, 1509–1558*, S. T. Bindoff (ed.), History of Parliament Trust [hereafter *H.P.T.*], 3 vols, London, 1982; ibid., 1558–1603, P. W. Hasler (ed.), 3 vols, London, 1982; J. S. Roskell, 'Perspectives in English Parliamentary History', *B.J.R.L.*, 46 (1964), 448–75. (Reprinted in E. B. Fryde and E. Miller (eds), *Historical Studies of the English Parliament*, 2 vols, Cambridge, 1970, Vol. 2, pp. 296–322.)
11. Even on one of these occasions it is not certain that this is what actually happened. The earlier episode derives only from William Roper's biography of his father-in-law, Thomas More. Written many years after More's death in 1535, the account is suspect and certainly unsubstanti-

15

ated. There is, however, certainty about events in 1532. The Commons voted less than the king wanted. Whether Henry's refusal either to accept or reject the grant was a petulant gesture, it is impossible to say. Lehmberg thought it likely 'that he was dissatisfied with the smallness of the Commons' grant and decided to bid for a larger sum at a later session', but that is only conjecture. (R. S. Sylvester and D. P. Harding (eds), *Two Early Tudor Lives*, New Haven, 1973, p. 199; S. E. Lehmberg, *The Reformation Parliament, 1529–1536 [Reformation Parliament]*, Cambridge, 1970, pp. 147–8, 158).

12. For example A. G. R. Smith, *The Government of Elizabethan England*, London, 1967; C. Russell, *The Crisis of Parliaments: English History, 1509–1660*, Oxford, 1971.

13. H. Miller, 'London and Parliament in the Reign of Henry VIII' ['London and Parliament'], *B.I.H.R.*, XXXV (1962), 128–49. This drew attention to the important parliamentary role of urban mercantile interests. Although London's legislative labours bore meagre fruit in Henry VIII's reign, the time-consuming nature of its activities in the Commons pointed up the need to examine the part played by local interests in Parliament.

14. S. E. Lehmberg, 'Early Tudor parliamentary procedure: provisos in the legislation of the Reformation Parliament', *E.H.R.*, **85** (1970), 1–11; ibid., *Reformation Parliament*; ibid., *The Later Parliaments of Henry VIII, 1536–1547 [Later Parliaments]*, Cambridge, 1977.

15. V. F. Snow, 'Proctorial Representation and conciliar management during the reign of Henry VIII' ['Proc. Rep. Henry VIII'], *H.J.*, IX (1966), 1–26; H. Miller, 'Attendance in the House of Lords during the reign of Henry VIII' ['Attendance'], *H.J.*, X, **4** (1967), 325–51; V. F. Snow, 'Proctorial Representation in the House of Lords during the reign of Edward VI' ['Proc. Rep. Ed. VI'], *J.B.S.*, VIII (May 1969), 1–27; M. A. R. Graves, 'Proctorial Representation in the House of Lords during Edward VI's Reign: A Reassessment' ['Proc. Rep. Ed. VI's Reign: A Reassessment'], *J.B.S.*, X, **2** (May 1971), 17–35; V. F. Snow, 'A Rejoinder to Mr Graves' Reassessment of Proctorial Representation' ['A Rejoinder'], *J.B.S.*, X, **2** (May 1971), 36–46.

16. For example C. G. Ericson, 'Parliament as a legislative institution in the reigns of Edward VI and Mary', London (Ph.D.), 1974; M. A. R. Graves, 'The Tudor House of Lords in the reigns of Edward VI and Mary I', Otago (Ph.D.), 1974; and J. I. Miklovich, 'Legislative procedure in the reign of Henry VIII, 1536–7', Cambridge (Ph.D.), 1975.

17. M. A. R. Graves, 'Thomas Norton, the Parliament Man: an Elizabethan M.P., 1559–1581' ['Thomas Norton'], *H.J.*, **23**, I (1980), 17–35; ibid., 'The Management of the Elizabethan House of Commons: The Council's Men-of-Business' ['Council's Men-of-Business'], *Parliamentary History*, **2** (1983), 11–38; N. Jones, *Faith by Statute. Parliament and the Settlement of Religion, 1559 [Faith by Statute]*, London, 1982.

18. L. O. Pike, *A Constitutional History of the House of Lords*, London, 1894.

19. J. H. Round, *Studies in Peerage and Family History*, London, 1901, and *Peerage and Pedigree. Studies in Peerage Law and Family History*, 2 vols, London, 1910; J. E. Powell and K. Wallis, *The House of Lords in the Middle Ages [Medieval Lords]*, London, 1968.

20. For example E. R. Adair and F. M. Greir Evans, 'Writs of Assistance from 1558 to 1700', *E.H.R.*, **36** (July 1921), 356–72; A. F. Pollard, 'The Authenticity of the Lords' Journals in the Sixteenth Century', *T.R.H.S.*, 3rd ser., **8** (1914), 17–39; 'The Clerical Organisation of Parliament', *E.H.R.*, **57** (Jan. 1942), 31–58; 'Receivers of Petitions and Clerks of Parliament', *E.H.R.*, **52** (Apr. 1942), 202–6; 'The Clerk of the Crown', *E.H.R.*, **57** (July 1942), 312–33.

21. See Lehmberg, *Reformation Parliament* and *Later Parliaments*; M. A. R. Graves, *The House of Lords in the Parliaments of Edward VI and Mary I [Mid-Tudor Lords]*, Cambridge, 1981; ibid., 'The Mid-Tudor House of Lords: Forgotten Member of the Parliamentary Trinity' ['Forgotten Member of the Trinity'], in *European History and Historians*, F. McGregor and N. Wright (eds), Adelaide, 1977, pp. 23–31; ibid., 'The House of Lords and the Politics of Opposition, Apr.–May 1554' ['Politics of Opposition'], in *W. P. Morrell: A Tribute*, G. A. Wood and P. S. O'Connor (eds), Dunedin, 1973, pp. 1–20, 253–8; Jones, *Faith by Statute*.

22. The assembly of the clergy of the southern province of Canterbury. York convocation normally met in the north shortly after the end of the parliamentary session.

23. G. R. Elton, *England under The Tudors*, London, 1955, pp. 174–5. The prominence of Lords or Commons in any particular session was determined frequently by the location of the chief minister of the day. So the duration of the Henrician Commons' supremacy (1529–36) coincides in time with the presence of Thomas Cromwell there. For the way in which the centre of parliamentary gravity swung back to the Lords when Cromwell and later William Cecil were elevated to peerages, see Chs 4 and 7.

24. The importance of Bill initiation is considered below, Ch. 2.

25. For critical reviews of this thesis, see J. Loach in *E.H.R.*, **98** (July 1983), 623–5 and C. S. L. Davies, 'Listing the lawmakers', *Times Literary Supplement*, 22 Jan. 1982, p. 172.

26. Jones, *Faith by Statute*, pp. 1–168. Cf. Neale, *Eliz. Parls*, I, pp. 33–84.

27. Elton, *Tudor Constitution* (1960), pp. 244, 255–6, 282, 302–3.

28. Ibid. (1960), pp. 302–3; ibid. (1982), pp. 235, 250, 268, 308, 310–11.

29. Ibid. (1982), p. 250.

30. G. R. Elton, 'Studying the History of Parliament', *British Studies Monitor*, ii, I (1971), 4–14; also in Elton, *Studies in Tudor and Stuart Politics and Government [Tudor and Stuart Pol.]*, 2 vols, Cambridge, 1974, Vol. II, pp. 3–18.

31. Apart from A. F. Pollard's essay on the Lords' journals. See above, n. 20.

32. 'A meeting of Parliament continued to be an occasion for doing work, for achieving ends, not simply one for parading protests or making claims.' Elton, '"The Body of the Whole Realm": Parliament and Representation in Medieval and Tudor England' ['Body of the Whole Realm'], in *Tudor and Stuart Pol.*, II, pp. 19–61.

33. Elton, 'Points of Contact', 183–200.

34. G. R. Elton, 'The Early Journals of the House of Lords' ['Early Lords' Journals'], *E.H.R.*, lxxxix (July 1974), 481–512; ibid., 'The Sessional

Printing of Statutes, 1484–1547' ['Sessional Printing of Statutes'], in *Wealth and Power in Tudor England*, E. W. Ives, R. J. Knecht, J. J. Scarisbrick (eds), London, 1978, pp. 68–86; ibid., 'The Rolls of Parliament, 1449–1547' ['Rolls of Parliament'], *H.J.*, XXII, 1 (1979), 1–29; ibid., 'Enacting clauses and legislative initiative, 1559–81' ['Enacting clauses'], *B.I.H.R.*, liii (Nov. 1980), 183–191.

35. He wrote of the role assigned to the upper house in the orthodoxy: 'The Lords stood in the wings and made their rare appearances as a body – rather like the chorus in *Iolanthe*'. G. R. Elton, 'Parliament in the Sixteenth Century: Functions and Fortunes' ['Functions and Fortunes'], *H.J.*, **22**, 2 (1979), 256.

36. Ibid., 255–78.

37. See also H. Miller, 'Lords and Commons: Relations between the two Houses of Parliament, 1509–1558' [*Lords and Commons: Relations*], *Parliamentary History*, I (1982), 13–24.

38. Jones, *Faith by Statute*, pp. 1–3; J. E. Neale, 'The Elizabethan Acts of Supremacy and Uniformity', *E.H.R.*, lxv (1950), 304–32; ibid., *Eliz. Parls*, I, pp. 33–84.

39. Jones, *Faith by Statute*, pp. 61–9.

Chapter two

THE TUDOR PARLIAMENTS: PROCEDURES, RECORDS, PERSONNEL AND PRIVILEGES

Although there now exists a sizeable and growing literature on parliamentary procedure, much of it treats procedural developments as political phenomena: evidence of the 'maturing' of the Commons and the way it seized the political initiative from the Crown.[1] Recent research, however, suggests that innovations and refinements were not intended to weaken royal control of Parliaments. New procedures were simply the means by which Parliaments carried out their chief function – legislation – and were designed only to raise the level of their productivity and efficiency.[2]

The most important evidence of what Parliament did, and how it did it, is its own records. These, like the procedures which they recorded, underwent significant changes under the Tudors. The parliament roll in chancery, once the only real record of parliamentary business, became less and less informative until it ended up as no more than a copy of the text of Acts.[3] This may have been the consequence of two related processes. In the past the activating force of Parliament and its record repository had been chancery. Its departmental head, the lord chancellor, presided over the Lords and the parliamentary clerical staff were recruited from it. From 1497, however, the clerk of the parliaments (who was Parliament's senior bureaucrat, served the Lords during the session, and wrote up the parliament roll at its end) ceased to transmit the final copies of new Acts to chancery. Instead they remained in his possession and formed the nucleus of an embryonic parliament office.

Secondly, the evolution of journals for each house rendered the parliament roll redundant as a record of business. The Lords' journal probably evolved during the fifteenth century, although only a few fragments survive before 1510.[4] As the upper house was the nucleus of the medieval Parliaments, it is not surprising that it was the first to keep a regular record of its business. Even so it began as the clerk's personal journal, compiled to assist him in his duties. This explains its austere terms of reference: opening and closing ceremonies, licensed absences

19

and proxies, joint conferences, the commitment of Bills and their readings. Debate was not recorded because it did not help the clerk to fulfil his responsibilities. His prime concern was to know the stages which Bills had reached, to whom Bills had been committed, and who had been authorised to stay away (partly because he received fees for registering their proxies). The Tudor clerks of the parliaments were already heirs to an old tradition of parliamentary recording. However, they continued to improve and enlarge their record, especially John Taylor, who began the daily attendance register in 1515.[5] During the Reformation Parliament the clerk's journal became an official record. This was confirmed in 1597, when Lord Burghley moved the Lords to appoint a committee to supervise its contents.[6]

The Commons was a relative newcomer and therefore a laggard, no less in its records than in its procedures. The first journal, in 1547, confined itself strictly to Bill-proceedings, licences of absence and privilege cases. During his tenure as clerk (1548–66) John Seymour inserted details about opening and closing ceremonies and, more important, committee chairmen to whom Bills should be given. His successor, Fulk Onslow, recorded the membership of committees, as well as the conveners, and he took separate notes of debates too. However, the evolution of the Commons' journal after 1547 is not a sign of institutional growth. To some extent it is a distortion, caused by the survival of some materials and not of others. Seymour's journals were 'scribbled books' whereas Onslow's were fair copies. It is also, as Elton points out, the consequence of the different habits of different clerks and the fact that Onslow was supplying Elizabeth's parliamentary manager William Cecil (now in the Lords) with information on the Commons' proceedings.[7]

The assembling of a new Parliament was the last link in a chain reaction. When king and council decided to call one, the lord chancellor instructed his clerks to devise a 'pawn'. This was the blueprint for activating a parliament. It recorded the date of assembly, listed the bishops (or their deputies)[8] and peers to whom writs of summons should be sent, named the legal assistants who were to be called to advise the Lords, and included an instruction to sheriffs to ensure that elections were held within their jurisdictions.[9] Writs were drafted and dispatched, using the pawn as a master list. Usually at least six weeks were necessary for elections to be held and the returns sent to chancery, before Parliament met. The opening formalities were elaborate and decorous,[10] but they could also affect the outcome of the session. The lord chancellor opened proceedings with an address to the two houses. It combined a eulogy on the virtues of the monarch and his/her government, a survey of the current political situation and a declaration, couched in general terms, on the reasons for calling a Parliament. On his skill might depend Parliament's response to royal needs, especially if they involved taxation. Secondly, the Commons elected its speaker, who protested his unworthiness and had to be led reluctantly to his chair by two privy councillors. Behind this ritual was the reality: that the speaker was, in practice, always the Crown's nominee.[11] His role in determining the order of business was crucial if official Bills were to have priority over private ones.

The meeting-places of the two houses tell us something about the history of Parliament. The Lords, as its historic nucleus, continued to occupy the parliament chamber in Westminster Palace. In contrast the Commons was accommodated outside the palace, normally in the chapter house of nearby Westminster Abbey. However, during Edward VI's reign (probably in 1549/50) it acquired a new and permanent home in Saint Stephen's Chapel. This lay within the palace precincts and the physical shift in some sense symbolised, belatedly, the arrival of the Commons as a co-equal member of a bicameral Parliament.

Their seating arrangements were equally revealing. The physical structure of the Lords derived from earlier parliamentary history, with the throne (symbolising the royal presence) at the upper end and, at the lower, the bar of the house. The Commons could not proceed beyond this point at the opening and closing ceremonies, a reminder that, until a short time before, it had not been regarded as part of Parliament proper. In the centre of the chamber sat the king's professional council who had always been an integral part of Parliament. The seat of the speaker – the lord chancellor – and below him his clerks were further reminders of Parliament's origins and growth, in this case its intimate association with chancery. As for the members, the lords spiritual occupied benches running the length of the chamber on the right-hand side of the throne. When the abbots disappeared, the benches were reduced to one. Opposite and facing them were the lords temporal, with an 'overflow' bench at the far end, in front of the bar and facing the throne. The physical separateness of the two orders and their 'confrontational' position across the chamber (reminiscent of Government and 'opposition' benches today) may have contributed to the friction between them and to the anti-clericalism of the lords temporal.

A few ephemeral changes occurred in the Lords' seating arrangements. The Act of 1539 'for placing of the lords in parliament' gave Thomas Cromwell pre-eminent place as the vicegerent (deputy in spirituals) of the supreme head, ruled on the position which officers of State were to occupy and admitted, if necessary, the presence of the king's secretaries to advise 'of such letters or things passed in council'. However, Cromwell was executed in 1540; the officers of State were already members of the house or (if not) sat on the woolsacks as advisers; and the secretaries usually sat in the Commons – not a sign of its growth but of the fact that the Lords was already well served with legal and administrative expertise. Another change was equally short-lived, when a commission in 1547 gave Protector Somerset a special seat 'next on the right hand of our seat royal'.[12] Within two years he had been unseated.

There was not the same concern with order and precedence in the Commons. It emulated the Lords, with the speaker's chair at one end, before him the clerk's table and at the other end a bar, where suitors and their counsel might plead their cause for or against a private Bill. However, there was one fundamental difference. Benches, placed on either side of the house and behind the speaker's chair, were not allocated but 'everyone sitteth as he cometh, no difference being there held of any degree'. However, there were significant exceptions. The privy councillors sat around the speaker's chair, where they could whisper instructions on the ordering of business. On their right hand sat the members of London and York. Perhaps this was appropriate for the first and second cities in the realm. But it also became important under Elizabeth, when London's members and Burghley's clients, such as Thomas Norton and William Fleetwood, worked with the council to push through its business.[13]

Although the life-tenures of most bishops and peers gave them a considerable experience of Parliaments, it remains true that the two houses were composed of amateur legislators. Fortunately they were served by professional bureaucrats who were frequently recruited from the lord chancellor's own department, chancery, though less so as the century progressed and the parliament office established its independence. The clerk of the parliaments (in the Lords), the underclerk (in the Commons) and their assistants performed a variety of services. They held Bills in their custody, read the text of each one aloud at the first reading, transmitted them to committees appointed to scrutinise them, and (at a price) transcribed copies for interested members. They wrote out amendments, engrossed paper Bills on to parchment, endorsed them once they had passed the house and transmitted them to the other. They scribbled reminders of committee chairmen who held Bills and those to whom others should be passed. Moreover, after 1547 the clerks of both houses were keeping journals. The role of the Lords' clerk, however, was more important. He organised the evolving parliament office. At the end of the session he intoned the royal assent, or veto, to each Bill passed by the two houses. Finally he supervised the enrolment of statutes on the parliament roll and arranged with the king's printer for their publication. He was, after all, the clerk of the parliaments.[14]

The Lords continued to enjoy the professional skills of men whose predecessors had once been members of the Crown's permanent council of advisers: the judges, serjeants-at-law, its attorney and solicitor, and the master of the rolls. They had long since lost the right to speak in debate or vote on Bills; in other words they had ceased to be co-equal with the bishops and peers. However, this altered rather than diminished their importance. They resolved legal disputes arising from private Bills and handed down advice on matters of law, especially whether Bills before the house adversely touched the king's prerogative or proved harmful to the commonwealth. In addition they drafted official Bills, scrutinised measures which had been put into the Lords first or had come up from the Commons, and sat on committees with bishops and peers to amend them. Sometimes these committees consisted solely of legal assistants. At other times a Bill might be referred to a single assistant to amend it or simply to engross it on parchment. Finally, they acted as intermediaries between the two houses, carrying down completed Bills, messages and requests for joint conferences. A scrutiny of the early Henrician and late Elizabethan Lords' journals, together with recent research on the Parliaments of 1547–58, reveals that, throughout the century, the legal assistants remained an essential ingredient in the Lords' record of legislative productivity and efficiency.[15]

However, professional assistance, bureaucratic or legal, was of little use unless the membership of the two houses was organised to transact the legislation before it, in the time available to it (especially under Elizabeth, who preferred short sessions). Familiar and tested methods of conducting business were essential. The starting-point of such legislative procedures was the devising of Bills. Who drafted them and placed them in Parliament? Authorship raises a number of related problems, partly because the contemporary classification of Acts into public and private was not determined by the criteria of scope and content. Public Acts were not necessarily of general scope, while those designated private were not always local, sectional and individual. The acid test was whether fees had to be paid to the clerks during the passage of a Bill.[16] If so, it was private. Even if this contemporary and technical distinction is set aside and a classification determined by scope and content is adopted, it does not necessarily identify the provenance of Bills. Not all 'public' measures, concerned with the general interest, were official in origin, nor were local or particular Bills always sponsored by private members.

Parliaments were called for money and/or urgent legislation, but the council also took the opportunity to devise other Bills for the commonweal. Cromwell frequently scribbled reminders to himself to this effect; in 1552 Edward VI referred to 'certain devices delivered to my learned Council to pen' and in 1553, 1554 and 1558/9 at least, council committees performed the same task. Cromwell often used his personal secretariat to draw Bills, while the Elizabethan council sometimes employed expert draftsmen such as the lawyer Thomas Norton. Nevertheless except in times of crisis, such as the 1530s, 1553–54, 1559 and 1571/2, the council's legislative programme was a modest one and hardly warrants the description. It tended to act in an *ad hoc* fashion, typical of Tudor government in general. It might prompt one of the houses to devise a measure, as Henry VIII did with the Six Articles Act in 1539 and Sir Walter Mildmay with the anti-recusancy law in 1581. Alternatively the Commons or Lords might respond to a member's motion and, with the council's blessing, authorise a committee to draw a Bill.[17] Also, great ministers were petitioned by private interests and individuals to promote their legislative proposals. If they did so, they threw a kind of official mantle over them. Thus there was a grey area between identifiable government measures and those of unmistakeably private origins.

It was customary for certain classes of Bill to be entered into one particular house first or to originate there. Thus lay taxation was always initiated in the Commons, but the clerical subsidies voted by the Canterbury convocation were invariably confirmed by the Lords first. Most estate Bills began in the lower house, whereas the great majority of attainders, restitutions of an attainted traitor's heirs, grace Bills (bearing the *sign manual* – the monarch's signature and therefore assent – when they entered Parliament) and royal pardons commenced in the upper chamber. These apart, Bills might be entered into either house. The placement of official measures was determined by two considerations: where the chief minister sat and the likely sympathy of each house to those measures. So the shift of Cromwell from the Commons to the Lords was accompanied by a re-direction of official Bills. Similarly in the 1530s the government preferred to face the opposition of the lords spiritual after the Commons had passed its Bills. However, genuinely 'private' (that is local and individual) Bills, as well as unofficial measures of a general nature, concerning the economy, social order and other matters were different. It was natural that most of them should be promoted in the lower house by the elected representatives of local interests and economic lobbies.[18] Of course occasionally it might be sound tactics to put them into the Lords first. London would do so in order to give them a certain momentum when they ran up against the resistance of rival urban interests in the Commons. Likewise in 1563 Geoffrey Tothill, burgess for Exeter, placed one of its Bills in the Lords and another in the Commons because 'if we should have put both in at one place then peradventure the house would not be best contented with two bills for our private City'.[19] Nevertheless the overwhelming majority of private Bills commenced in the lower house.

Wherever a Bill was placed, it went through a recognised procedure of scrutiny, debate, revision (if necessary) and approval. Gradually, in the course of the sixteenth century, both houses settled on a uniform three-reading procedure. Earlier inconsistencies and flexibility faded away, to be replaced by a more rigid observance of what came to be regarded as the only acceptable legislative procedure. Although it became hallowed, even sanctified, by time, it was no more than the most sensible, practical and effective way of enacting statute law. In the absence of a printed text, the literal first reading informed members of the contents of a Bill, the second allowed discussion of its contents, and the third ensured its textual precision and clarity.

Slowly both houses moved towards three readings as the norm. Almost half (46 per cent) of the twenty-six Bills which passed the Lords in 1510 were read more or less than three times. In 1547 the proportion had dropped to 40 per cent, in 1558 to 32 per cent and in 1597 to only 20 per cent. The same drift to uniformity is unmistakeable in the Commons. The Bills which deviated from the norm averaged between 30 and 40 per cent between 1547 and 1558 and had fallen to 21 per cent by 1581. Moreover many of the deviants were grace Acts, clerical subsidies, pardons, attainders and restitutions, whose passage was often a formality, with no more than a single reading. Experienced parliamentarians, such as Sir Thomas Smith and John Hooker, certainly wrote about the three-reading procedure as if it was the norm and the parliamentary clerks, imbued with a preference for bureaucratic tidiness, showed an increasing respect for it. If a Bill passed on two readings they would be recorded as the first and third. In the case of four readings the last one might be designated another 'third' or simply left unnumbered.[20] The houses thought along the same lines. On several occasions, when a measure had two second readings it was resolved that the latter was 'to stand for no reading'. The widespread belief that there should be procedural uniformity hastened the day when it became a fact.

This growing attachment to the three-reading procedure is understandable, because it proved to be the most workable, effective way of making statute. Although the two houses did not slavishly imitate each other and, despite the fact that the process was not static but continued to evolve, we can identify its chief characteristics. Bills were kept by the clerks until the lord chancellor or speaker, who ordered business in their respective houses, called for them to be read aloud. This was the literal first reading, designed to inform members of the contents of a Bill. Earlier in the century it was not unknown for a Bill to be debated, committed for amendment, rejected, or even passed at this stage.[21] In 1510 6 of the 48 Bills before the Lords were thus committed, compared with 1 out of 59 in 1601.[22] As late as 1581, however, the speaker had to ask members not to discuss Bills at the first reading. Nevertheless the convention that this stage was merely informative eventually triumphed. An Elizabethan member could write that a Bill's contents were 'disliked of many . . . but not effectually argued unto of any man, for that it was the first reading'. However, it was tempting to speak at once, while the text was fresh in the memory. After all, one Elizabethan subsidy Bill took two hours to read aloud while in 1581, for example, the Commons listened to the text of ninety-two Bills.

The second reading was the crucial stage, when the substance of a Bill was discussed. By mid-century the lower house, which was large, growing and encumbered with many novices, had to impose strict rules of debate. According to Sir Thomas Smith in 1565, members had to avoid 'reviling or nipping words', address the speaker and speak only once a day to each particular Bill. His idealised picture, that 'in the disputing is a marvellous good order used', should not be taken too seriously. Members would hum, hawk and spit during an unpopular speech. Arthur Hall, himself a victim, observed that some of them behaved as 'they durst not do in an Ale-house, for fear of a knock with a pot'. An Elizabethan speaker lamented the 'great confused noise and sound of senseless words', while another, in 1601, scolded behaviour 'more fit for a grammar school than a Court of Parliament'.[23]

Despite the freedom to voice dissent, genuine free speech did not exist. Members could be reprimanded, even punished, for speaking without respect or restraint on matters touching the Crown. In the 1530s they watched Cromwell and took their cue from him. Sir George Throckmorton avoided Parliament on official advice after criticising Henry VIII's intended divorce. Thomas Broke, member for Calais, was interrogated by a panel of bishops after speaking against the Six Articles in 1539, William Strickland was excluded (by the council) for his religious proposals in 1571 and Peter Wentworth was hailed to the Tower (by the Commons) in 1576 for irreverent speech against the queen. Members were constrained by both the rules of the house and the watchful eyes of monarch and council.

In one respect the Lords enjoyed greater freedom. It was a small body, initiating fewer Bills, and therefore its debates were probably more informal and under less pressure of time. So 'he that will, riseth up and speaketh with or against it; and so one after another as long as they shall think good'.[24] However, bishops and peers, no less than knights and burgesses, needed to be cautious when they touched the royal interest. Stephen Gardiner might reminisce that there was 'free speech without danger' in the Lords, but Henry VIII's occasional presence at crucial debates (a practice not followed by later Tudors) must have inhibited discussion. Lord Paget was disgraced because of his parliamentary behaviour in 1554. Elizabeth banished several leading nobles from court because they supported the parliamentary succession campaign in 1566/7. Gardiner's words do not ring as true as those of Richard Robinson, who wrote in the 1590s, that both houses 'have also freedom of speech . . . so it be with observing decorum of dutiful obedience to the Prince'.[25] In practice this could be an intimidating restraint on discussion.

At the end of the second reading a Bill might be rejected, but this became increasingly uncommon. If no amendments were necessary it would be 'engrossed'. With the exception of grace bills, which came into Parliament on parchment and signed by the king, Bills were written on paper. If emendation was not required after the second reading the Bill was copied on to parchment (i.e. engrossed). Usually, however, a committee was appointed to revise it, add provisos (additional clauses) or even draft a new Bill. The choice of committees in the Commons was a noisy and random business, with members shouting names and the clerk noting those he could hear in the hubbub. In contrast the Lords was more discriminating. There was a growing tendency to apportion committee membership between the senior peers, bishops and barons, and anyone who had spoken against the substance of a Bill could not be chosen because 'he that would totally destroy will not amend'.[26] Also, many nominated members had relevant expertise or local knowledge.

Committees to revise Bills were infrequent in the earlier sixteenth century. In 1510 the Lords initiated over half the 20 Acts and handled 48 Bills, but only 6 were passed to committees for amendment – in every case by legal assistants. In 1515 perhaps twenty were committed but once again to the same experts, ranging from the king's attorney alone to panels of judges and serjeants-at-law. Only once did bishops or peers sit alongside them.[27] Gradually the house became less dependent on the professionals, though never able to dispense completely with their assistance. So in Henry VIII's later Parliaments most of the committed Bills went to them. In any case the move towards regular commitment was a slow process. In 1540 only 11 of the 80 Acts were so treated in the Lords and in the two succeeding reigns the rate of commitment fluctuated between 20 per cent and 60 per cent.[28] Inexorably, however, procedures became more uniform, especially under the influence of Burghley's neat and tidy mind. By 1597 commitment of Bills had become commonplace.

Moreover the bishops and peers were becoming more confident of their own ability to do this work themselves. In 1572 lords temporal sat on every committee, the lords spiritual on two-thirds and on every one they constituted a majority. A few Bills were still committed to legal assistants in 1597, but only for scrutiny of points of law. The rest were assigned to bishops and peers. One or two of the legal assistants were named as well, but they were no longer co-equal committee members. They were instructed 'to attend their lordships', presumably to offer advice when required.[29] The bishops and peers had completed their apprenticeship in Bill revision which, at the same time, had become routine in the legislative process.

The first reference to a Commons' Bill committee (in 1529) was probably not a novelty – in the 1530s a member could refer to a Bill which had been 'committed *as the manner is*'.[30] However, the practice had not been regularised. According to Neale the mid-Tudor Commons was 'a rather easy-going assembly' in which only a minority of Bills were committed. But his claim that 'by the latter part of Elizabeth's reign the roles of the two Houses had been reversed' is unjustified. In 1581 several measures were committed after the first reading and 30 per cent not at all. Although, twenty years later, Bill

committees were still not essential, irregularities were being eliminated and commitment after the second reading was becoming the
norm.[31]

Occasionally precise and detailed work of committees is recorded in
surviving sheets of notes with their recommended changes: 'in line 16
put out the following words . . . and insert these . . .' and so on. In 1571
John Hooker gave a rare glimpse of their thoroughness. He described
how legal counsel argued the case of two conflicting parties over a Bill
concerning Bristol, before they were sent outside while the Commons'
committee deliberated and reached a conclusion.[32] However, they
were beset with problems. Many members did not attend and committee chairmen had to ask the house for more time or replacements.
Lawyers were notorious absentees, preferring to deal with their clients'
causes in the central law courts next door. Committees which were
well-attended could be equally ineffective. William Fleetwood wrote
of one in 1584, when at least sixty turned up: 'Twenty at once did
speak' and so 'we sat talking and did nothing until night', when the
exhausted chairman ended proceedings.[33] Nevertheless committees
proliferated in both houses, not only to revise but also to draft Bills. *Ad
hoc* committees dealt with cases of privilege and other unusual
occasions as they arose. In the 1570s pressure of business encouraged
the Commons to appoint standing committees, which scrutinised and
sometimes amalgamated Bills on popular subjects such as cloth manufacture. The Elizabethan Commons, always in search of time-saving
devices, also developed the 'general' committee which in time evolved
into the committee of the whole house. The speaker, an official
nominee, was replaced by a chairman and the formal rules of debate
were discarded. It was not, as Notestein argued, an 'opposition' device
to wrest the political initiative from the government. It was just
another way to get through as much business as possible.[34] Like most
other procedural developments, these changes in committee practice
were the work of the time-conscious privy council.

When a committee had completed its task of revision, it reported
back to the house through its chairman or a designated spokesman. If
the house approved the recommended changes, it promptly gave them
two readings. This brought them into line with the Bill, which was then
ordered to be engrossed. The house then proceeded to the third
reading which was increasingly (but not invariably) confined to the
wording, not the substance, of the Bill. Finally it was put to the vote.
Once again the small upper house was also the more efficient one. Its
clerk conscientiously recorded the number and names of dissenters.
Indeed it became the right of members to have their disapproval
entered in the journal: for example, on 8 occasions in 1542–45, 51 in
the Edwardian Parliaments, and 39 in the Marian. The fact that dissenters could be identified illustrates the way in which the Lords precisely
tallied the votes for and against a Bill. Its members voted one by one,

orally and individually, from the most junior baron, via the bishops, to the highest-ranking peer of most ancient lineage. Sir Thomas Smith confirmed this in the 1560s when he wrote that they 'give their assent and dissent each man severally and by himself . . . saying only content or not content. As the more number doeth agree, so it is agreed on or dashed.' If this was inconclusive two chosen members, one for and one against the Bill, would go from bench to bench, poll the house and tot up the votes.[35]

This practice was unmistakably superior to that of the Commons, as the jurist Edmund Plowden pointed out in the mid-sixteenth century:

> [T]he Majority of Voices in the Upper House may be easily known, because they are demanded severally, and the Clerk of the House reckons them; but in the lower House . . . the Assent is tried by the Voices sounding all at one Time.[36]

In other words the Commons voted by acclamation and the group which achieved the highest decibel level was liable to win. This was patently unsatisfactory and gradually there evolved the 'division'. If the acclamation was challenged, the Commons would divide and appoint tellers to count the two sides. The earliest recorded divisions were in 1523, 1532 (when Henry VIII attended) and 1534. Although the house also resorted to them in 1542 and 1545, they were rare before 1559 – only 7 under Edward VI and Mary. As in so many other ways, change occurred more rapidly in the Elizabethan Commons. The sessional incidence of 3/4 divisions between 1559 and 1581 rose to 7 in 1589 and 1593, 13 in 1597 and 17 in 1601.[37] The division procedure replaced the crude practice of acclamation and enabled the lower house to approximate to the Lords' more precise vote-counting technique.

Bills which failed in either house could not be re-introduced in the same session. However, those which passed one chamber were duly endorsed by the clerk and despatched to the other. If the Lords was the house of origin he wrote at the bottom *Soit baille aux communs* ('Let it be sent to the commons') where, on completion of its passage, the underclerk noted *A ceste bille les communes sont assentuz* ('to this Bill the commons have assented'). When the lower house was the initiator the legends were reversed (*Soit baille aux seigneurs*, etc.). Whichever way the legislative traffic travelled, from upper to lower house or vice versa, Bills were delivered with due ceremony and solemn ritual.

The second chamber to receive a Bill put it through more or less the same process of scrutiny, especially as the two houses conformed more and more closely to a standardised three-reading procedure. However, there were important modifications. The Bill arrived on parchment. Its substance and wording had already undergone scrutiny and revision and so, frequently, Bills passed through the second house more rapidly. However, it was certainly not unknown for a measure to be amended, redrafted as a new Bill, or rejected. Sometimes there was a lengthy interplay between Lords and Commons about amendments proposed by the second chamber, although more often than not such episodes illustrated a joint co-operative endeavour to get things right, rather than conflict and confrontation.

At the end of the session those Bills which had passed both houses awaited the royal assent. By then the monarch, with the advice of the council, had decided on their fate. Public Bills became Acts with the formula *Le roy [la royne] le veult* and private ones received the royal response *Soit fait comme il est desire*. The response of a grateful monarch to a subsidy Bill was more ornate: *Le roy remercie ses loyaulx subjects, accepte leur benevolence, et ainsi le veult.* Not that all Bills received the royal assent – it was not unknown for Henry VIII to veto them with the misleading standard formula *Le roy s'avisera* [The king will consider it]. Elizabeth was more cavalier, rejecting nine in 1584/5 and twelve in 1597. In 1571 she personally explained to the assembled houses why certain Bills had failed and, in the following year, she advised that the veto formula was meant literally with respect to the great Bill against Mary Stuart. Of course Elizabeth did not reconsider it. However, her concern to inform (or beguile) Parliament testifies to the Crown's concern to pursue the politics of co-operation, rather than confrontation.[38]

The most important Tudor procedural development was the movement towards standardisation. This is not evidence that the two houses, especially the Commons, politically 'matured'. Although private members might exploit procedures for specific political ends, they were concerned essentially with business efficiency, not political manipulation. Frequent Parliaments between 1529 and 1559 and the growing volume of public and especially private legislation compelled councillors to search for answers to current parliamentary problems. Official business had to be pushed through; time had to be allowed for the governing class to fulfil some of its parliamentary expectations; and the quality of legislation had to be maintained. The task was made no easier by the preference of Mary, and more particularly Elizabeth, for short sessions.

However, the duration of daily sittings was expandable. Traditionally both houses sat only in the mornings (and not on Sundays), although even before the 1530s it was not unknown for emergencies and a heavy workload to dictate otherwise: in December 1529 one sitting lasted late into the night. We know little about the Commons' habits before its first journal in 1547, but in Henry VIII's reign the Lords normally sat between 9 a.m. and twelve or one o'clock. However, late in the session, when time was short and business pressing, the upper house might meet at 7 or 8 a.m. and even in the afternoons. In the following reigns the pattern was repeated: at first a decorous and civilised start at nine (occasionally even ten) in the morning and then, as the session wore on, the need to assemble at an earlier hour. A long-term trend is evident. In 1549/50 the Lords sat before 9 a.m. for only 20 per cent of the session; in 1552 it was 37 per cent, in 1554 50 per cent and in 1571 64 per cent. Afternoons became more common: only occasionally before 1558 then more frequently, albeit with fluctuations, under Elizabeth. Committees sat before, during, and after the morning session. So in 1593 the earl of Essex was 'every forenoon, between seven and eight, in the Higher Parliament House, and in the afternoons upon committees, for the better penning and amendment of matter in bills of importance'.[39]

The Lords had less time at its disposal, because occasionally it did not sit on Fridays (when the bishops attended convocation) or on Wednesdays (when noble and episcopal councillors sat as judges in star chamber). However, the Commons was under much greater pressure. It had to cope with the formidable volume of private and other unofficial legislation which flowed in after the 1530s and, in consequence, a leisurely manner of doing things had to give way to a more businesslike one. Its normal hours – from eight to eleven a.m. – were gradually extended. Some sittings commenced at seven o'clock, with Bill committees assembling even earlier, and stretched to midday or beyond. They lapped over into the afternoons, rarely at first but frequently in Elizabeth's reign. In 1571 the practice was regularised when, on the motion of one of Burghley's clients, the house agreed to sit from three to five p.m., three days a week, for the first reading of private Bills. Shortly afterwards this became a daily practice and extended to second readings as well, in order to ease the pressure on morning sittings and allow more time for official business and other important public Bills. The experiment was repeated in 1572 and 1576, but then it inexplicably faded away, only to be revived by a councillor in 1601.[40]

The pressure of unofficial legislation was a matter of continuing concern to councillors and the unwieldy, inefficient, Bill-clogged Commons was their chief problem. Perhaps they heeded the sage advice of an experienced Elizabethan member who identified 'the number of private bills', especially those of London, and 'matters of long argument' as the most serious threats to official business. His solution was to get time-consuming activities off the floor of the house and into committees.[41] The council did what it could. Burghley's men-of-business were innovative in time-saving procedures, such as the specialist committees for cloth and timber, while the Lords chivvied the Commons along with urgent messages and advices to order their Bills into priority.[42]

Harmonious bicameral relations were crucial to the success of Tudor Parliaments. The Lords usually held the initiative as the older, more prestigious chamber and as the assembly of the social élite. It used these natural advantages to good effect in its dealings with the

Commons: not only messages but also deputations and especially joint conferences. Either house could call for a conference, whereupon each would appoint some of their number to meet together for discussion. This enabled them to resolve potential or actual disagreements over particular Bills, thereby avoiding confrontation and preventing the frustration of desirable laws. However, it was an irregular practice until 1571, when the Commons resolved that, in future, it would seek conference whenever Bills from the Lords were 'needful to be considered of, added unto or altered'.[43]

Having made this decision, some members had second thoughts. In an hierarchic, status-conscious society like Elizabethan England, a group of knights and townsmen, even when reinforced by some privy councillors, was at a distinct disadvantage when confronted with Burghley, Leicester, Archbishop Whitgift and other great bishops and peers. At such conferences their lordships remained seated while the Commons' members stood before them. In 1581 one of the lower house pondered whether 'there is no one thing that hath so shaken the true liberty of the house as often conferences . . . by terrifying of men's opinions'.[44] He explained that the lords did not terrify members, but that they, obsequious towards their social superiors and knowing that nothing in the Commons was secret, conformed to their opinions. The lower house took the wise precaution of resolving that its committees, in conference with the Lords, could not bind it to anything without its approval. Despite these misgivings, the joint conference was used frequently thereafter to accelerate business and raise productivity.

The lords' social prestige remained an intimidating force for most burgesses and even many gentlemen. Moreover collectively, as a house, their lordships could stand on their dignity. So too could the Commons. However, as Elton has pointed out, the Tudor 'Lords came to treat the Commons with the same courtesy that they had hitherto expected from the Lower House'.[45] This was the consequence of the emergence of a bicameral Parliament in which the two houses enjoyed equal authority, not of some novel rise to political power on the part of the Commons. On certain occasions, however, the Lords was perfectly capable of applying effective pressure on the other house. This was not only because of its social superiority but also because many members of the Commons believed that the Lords was really the voice of royal authority. As we shall see, the latter was less than the whole truth because the Lords was prepared, when necessary, to take an independent stand.

On the other hand, the upper house was a responsible body which usually acted in concert with the Crown. This was most obvious in the matter of taxation. The Commons alone could initiate lay taxes, but the realities were quite different from the procedural formalities. Indeed, it looks as if privy councillors often took the lead and the house followed. A member of the Elizabethan Commons advised the council that, when the session began, it should have 'the Subsidy books ready written both in paper [the initial draft] and parchment [the final form]'. This was no novelty. In both Henry VIII's and Elizabeth's reigns subsidy preambles were drafted by prominent councillors. In 1581 a privy councillor, Sir Walter Mildmay, and Burghley's client, Thomas Norton, dominated the Commons' subsidy committee. Norton drafted the 'articles and heads' of the Bill and possibly its final text.[46] The Lords too lent its support. On one occasion (1593) its pressure led the Commons to increase its initial offer to the queen. In 1532 and November 1558 the lord chancellor led a delegation of peers to the Commons to plead the Crown's need for 'some reasonable aid'. In January 1558 the upper house intruded itself even further into the taxing process. A joint conference appointed three sub-committees which devised the terms of the tax and presented them to both Commons and Lords.

Subsidies apart, however, the legislative roles of the two houses were determined by the evolving three-reading procedure of Parliament. The key here was the initiating process – whichever house initiated a Bill usually (not invariably) became the chief formative influence on its final form. It performed the chief labour of revision and refinement and it engrossed it. In most cases the other house approved it, sometimes amended it, and only infrequently re-drafted it. That this was not a process fraught with disagreements, deadlocks and failures is due to the fact that both houses were moving towards the same uniform three-reading procedure. Procedural uniformity was in turn the product of a natural, bicameral interaction and cross-fertilisation. Pre-Tudor Parliaments must have worked out a basic set of rules for the enactment of statute.[47] The older house, with its corpus of legal assistants, had probably taken the lead. However, once the Commons had emerged from its role as petitioner to that of co-equal member of a legislative body, it needed to refine its techniques. When it did so, it probably took the Lords' procedures as its model. At the same time it had much to offer. Its lawyer members probably assisted its procedural development. So did the growing and much greater volume of business with which it had to deal. New peers and legal assistants with Commons' experience took with them their knowledge of its evolving procedures. The reverse process occurred when secretaries, the Crown's legal counsel and serjeants-at-law, who had sat on the woolsacks, were elected to the Commons. So the two houses advanced on parallel lines towards the fully-rounded three-reading procedure.

The capacity of Parliament to perform its functions properly depended not only on known and effective procedures but also on the privileges of members and the rights ('liberties') of the two houses. Members needed the reassurance that they could attend without restraint or the fear of arrest and that, once there, they could discuss the measures before them. If no such formal guarantees were provided by the Crown in the early Tudor Parliaments, Sir Thomas More, as speaker, certainly requested free speech in 1523. However, it was a freedom limited to 'every thing incident among us' – in other words matters placed before them and not anything which exercised their minds and passions. Moreover, it excluded 'licentious' talk, especially against the monarch. Despite similar petitions by successive speakers and the Crown's allowance thereof, no monarch would tolerate uninhibited free speech. Elizabeth successfully resisted the attempts by Paul and Peter Wentworth (in 1566, 1576 and 1587) to establish that as a right. Generally she made a distinction between matters of State, on which no-one could speak without explicit royal consent, and commonweal issues, on which no such controls were imposed. Under the Tudors the principle of free speech was established, but its range and extent depended on the monarch. Although it was open to challenge, Elizabeth successfully maintained its limited definition.

Freedom from arrest was equally essential to the effectiveness of Parliaments. This privilege did not apply to felonies, but it protected members from arrest consequent upon civil actions, in particular debt. Its umbrella extended to cover servants, on the grounds that their attendance was necessary to ensure the effective parliamentary service of their masters. However, until 1542 an imprisoned knight or burgess could be released only by the lord chancellor's authority. Then, in that year, George Ferrers was arrested for debt and imprisoned in the City. The Commons acted on its own authority to secure his release and by this precedent it established a claim that its serjeant-at-arms' mace was sufficient warrant both to liberate its members and to arrest and punish those who offended it. Henry VIII lent the massive weight of his authority in support of the Commons. Later privilege cases, such as that of Arthur Hall, burgess for Grantham (1576 and 1581), reinforced both this particular privilege and the Commons' right to discipline outsiders and members.[48] The Lords was no less sensitive about such matters, as Henry Lord Cromwell's case reveals. He had been 'attached' (arrested) for contempt by the court of chancery. In 1572 he appealed to the Lords which resolved that, as there were no precedents for the attachment of a peer 'having place and voice in parliament', chancery's action was invalid.

Freedom from arrest was frequently abused, in particular because a member who was freed by privilege could not be seized again. The government was aware that some were wriggling free from creditors by this means, while others secured election to enjoy the flesh-pots of London without fear of arrest.[49] Although the Commons censured Arthur Hall for a gross abuse of the privilege in 1576, it was generally over-indulgent towards its members. The Lords, in contrast, was more circumspect and responsible. Its decision in Cromwell's favour was qualified by the proviso that if, in similar cases in the future, it could be shown that a 'lord of the parliament' ought to be arrested, then such action should be taken. Furthermore in 1581 the house narrowed the definition of servants eligible to seek privilege. This was fortunate because, as Elton points out, the peers had so many clients and other men serving them in various capacities.[50]

The Crown's role was crucial in the development of parliamentary privilege. It was willing to allow members a special position over and against the rights of other subjects, and supported those liberties which enabled the two houses to do their job properly. The Bill of 1515, which empowered the Commons' speaker to license and thereby to control and even prevent the early departure of members, received the royal assent. The Crown did not protest when Thomas Copley in 1558 and Peter Wentworth in 1576 were detained for offensive talk in the house – though that is hardly surprising because their speeches were directed against the monarch. Elizabeth also left the Commons to its own devices when it expelled and imprisoned Arthur Hall in 1581. Freedom of speech was a more sensitive issue and, as we have seen, it was never an unqualified privilege, especially under Elizabeth. Finally there was a grey, undefined area – when a member was arrested at the behest of the Crown. The drift of parliamentary thinking on this matter was well-demonstrated by the Commons' furore when William Strickland was sequestered by the council in 1571 for introducing a Bill to reform the prayer book. Thereafter Elizabeth trod more warily and arrested members during a Parliament only for acts committed before it met. However, even as late as 1593 an attachment was justified on the grounds that the Crown had taken the action.[51]

Nevertheless, parliamentary privileges underwent important developments under the Tudors. First, these were formalised by the Commons' speaker's formal petition for them at the opening ceremonies – the first recorded request for freedom of speech, made by Thomas More in 1523, is the best-known example. Over many years and in many Parliaments the Crown repeatedly acceded to such petitions as acts of royal grace. Time and repetition, however, can transform a genuine grant into a mere formality and there is no doubt that Elizabethans, in particular the Wentworth brothers, regarded such privileges as parliamentary rights. On the other hand parliamentary privilege rarely became a political issue. Although, when it did so, it was usually in the Commons, this was because members of the Lords had other ways and other avenues (such as the royal court) to influence, oppose or attempt to alter royal policies. For most knights and burgesses this was the only available public platform on which to air their views. In the same way the Commons' speaker regularly petitioned for access to the monarch and council. The lord chancellor did not need to do so because he was himself prominent in government and in constant touch with the centre of power. In any case privilege was usually no more than one of the prerequisites of the effective accomplishment of Parliament's business.

Once that business was accomplished and the closing ceremonies were over, members made their way home. They were probably unaware of the flurry of bureaucratic activity which they left behind: the Acts were recorded on the parliament roll and the original Acts were filed away for safe-keeping by the clerk of the parliaments, after they (or copies of them) had been sent to the king's printer for rapid publication and circulation throughout the realm.[52] This process of disseminating new statutes was essential to a Parliament's success. Its Acts were a response to the needs of the government, the governing class and society at large. However, the efficacy of new laws depended not only on the care and skill with which they were drafted, revised, and refined but on their enforcement. The first step was to inform royal officials in the countryside, especially the justices of the peace and the county courts, of their contents. At that point new statutes passed beyond the control of the legislators and into the realm, where their effectiveness would be fully tested by local officials under local conditions.

REFERENCES AND NOTES

1. For example Notestein, 'Winning of the Initiative'; Snow, 'Proc. Rep. Henry VIII', 1–26; ibid., 'Proc. Rep. Ed. VI', 1–27; Neale, *Eliz. Parls*, 2 vols, passim.
2. Elton, 'Functions and Fortunes', 267–9; ibid., *Tudor Constitution* (1982), pp. 249–50.
3. Elton, 'Rolls of Parliament', 1–29; Lehmberg, *Later Parliaments*, pp. 247–9.
4. Elton, 'Early Lords' Journals', 482–7.
5. Ibid., 490–1.
6. *Journals of the House of Lords* [hereafter *L.J.*], London, 1846, II, 195.
7. Elton, 'Functions and Fortunes', 262–7.
8. They could not sit in the Lords but, in the absence of a bishop or during an episcopal vacancy, they organised the election of lower clergy to the convocation of Canterbury.
9. Sheriffs conducted county elections and sent precepts to enfranchised boroughs to do the same.
10. Neale, *E.H.C.*, Ch. XVIII; Powell and Wallis, *Medieval Lords*, pp. 543–4, 547–50, 555–7; Lehmberg, *Reformation Parliament*, pp. 76–80; ibid., *Later Parliaments*, pp. 251–2. From 1571 the opening ceremonies included administration of the oath of supremacy to all members.
11. Neale, *E.H.C.*, pp. 354–7.
12. Graves, *Mid-Tudor Lords*, p. 149.
13. Neale, *E.H.C.*, pp. 364–5; M. A. R. Graves, 'Thomas Norton', 18–19, **23**, 28–35.

14. Graves, *Mid-Tudor Lords*, pp. 120–3; Neale, *E.H.C.*, Ch. XVII.
15. For example Graves, *Mid-Tudor Lords*, pp. 125–40, 155–6; *L.J.*, I, 18–42; ibid., II, 227–59; Lehmberg, *Reformation Parliament*, p. 247.
16. Neale, *E.H.C.*, pp. 335–41, 343–4.
17. For example the Act for the maintenance of the navy (1563) which originated in a motion by one of Elizabeth's admirals, William Winter. Neale, *Eliz. Parls*, I, p. 114.
18. There are many examples of such Bills in *H.P.T.*, 1509–58, passim; ibid., 1558–1603, passim.
19. *Historical Manuscripts Commission*, Records of the City of Exeter, 73 (1916), 51.
20. For example Lehmberg, *Later Parliaments*, p. 258; Graves, *Mid-Tudor Lords*, pp. 150–1.
21. Lehmberg, *Later Parliaments*, pp. 257–8.
22. Calculated from Lords' journals. *L.J.*, I, 3–9; ibid., II, 229–58.
23. Neale, *E.H.C.*, pp. 370–1, 404–7; idem, *Eliz. Parls*, II, p. 384.
24. Sir Thomas Smith, *De Republica Anglorum*, ed. L. Alston, Cambridge, 1906, p. 53.
25. Richard Robinson, 'A briefe collection of the queenes majesties most high and most honourable courtes of recordes', ed. R. L. Rickard, *Camden Miscellany*, XX, 3rd ser., lxxxiii (1953), p. 10.
26. Graves, *Mid-Tudor Lords*, pp. 160–2.
27. Calculated from Lords' journals, *L.J.*, I, 3–9.
28. Lehmberg, *Later Parliaments*, pp. 258–60; Graves, *Mid-Tudor Lords*, pp. 160–1.
29. *L.J.*, I, 194–223.
30. Lehmberg, *Reformation Parliament*, p. 240; ibid., *Later Parliaments*, p. 260.
31. Neale, *E.H.C.*, pp. 371–5.
32. Hooker's Journal, in T. E. Hartley (ed.), *Proceedings in the Parliaments of Elizabeth I*, Vol. I, 1558–81, Leicester, 1981, p. 247. Both houses, especially the Commons, resorted to quasi-judicial proceedings of this kind and not just in committees. Promoters and opponents of a Bill would be summoned to the bar of the house, where they would present their respective cases through their lawyers and with documentary evidence if necessary.
33. British Library [B.L.], Lansdowne MS. 41, fo. 45.
34. Neale, *E.H.C.*, pp. 377–9; Notestein, 'Winning of the Initiative', pp. 23, 32, 36–8; Elton, 'Functions and Fortunes', 269.
35. Lehmberg, *Later Parliaments*, p. 261; Graves, *Mid-Tudor Lords*, pp. 163–6. Most Bills passed without recorded dissents.
36. *The Commentaries or Reports of Edmund Plowden*, 2 pts, London, 1761, I, p. 126.
37. Lehmberg, *Later Parliaments*, pp. 222, 261; Elton, *Tudor Constitution* (1982), pp. 252–3; Neale, *E.H.C.*, p. 399.
38. Lehmberg, *Later Parliaments*, pp. 267–8; Neale, *E.H.C.*, pp. 426–7.
39. Neale, *Eliz. Parls*, II, p. 295.
40. Graves, 'Thomas Norton', 24–5; Neale, *E.H.C.*, pp. 367–8, 379–80.
41. B.L., Harleian MS, 253, fos. 32–6.
42. Graves, 'Thomas Norton', 25.

43. *C.J.*, I, 87.
44. B.L., Harleian MS, fos. 32–6.
45. B.L., Harleian MS, 253, fos. 32–6; Elton, *Tudor Constitution* (1982), p. 235.
46. Graves, 'Thomas Norton', 31–2; B.L., Harleian MS, 253, fos. 32–6.
47. Elton, 'Functions and Fortunes', 268.
48. Neale, *Eliz. Parls*, I, pp. 333–45, 407–10; Elton, *Tudor Constitution* (1982), pp. 261–2; Lehmberg, *Later Parliaments*, pp. 165–71; *H.P.T.*, 1509–1558, II, 130–1.
49. Elton, *Tudor Constitution* (1982), pp. 262, 303.
50. Ibid., p. 262.
51. Ibid., pp. 262–3.
52. Elton, 'Sessional Printing of Statutes', pp. 68–86.

Chapter three

THE PRE-REFORMATION PARLIAMENTS, 1485–1529

PARLIAMENT IN 1485

The Parliament which Henry Tudor, first king of a new dynasty, summoned in 1485 already had a long history. It had travelled far from the unicameral institution which, in the early fourteenth century, had had no clearly defined functions, procedures, records or membership. It had shed its earlier judicial character and by Henry VII's reign it was first and foremost a taxing, legislative and consultative assembly. The king could not make, amend and repeal laws or (with the dubious exceptions of the benevolence and forced loan)[1] impose taxes on the laity without the consent of Parliament. Moreover it was normally politic (and sometimes essential) to use Parliament as a sounding board for public opinion on royal policies and actions. In other words it had become a 'political' assembly. However, despite parliamentary opposition to such kings as Edward II, Edward III, Richard II, and Henry VI, we should not read 'political' in simple terms of conflict and a competition for power in the State. It is better to heed the measured words of those who preached the parliamentary sermons in the fifteenth century: that Parliament met to 'hold colloquy and treaty concerning the government of the realm' or to put it more succinctly, as Bishop Russell did in 1483, it was 'the place of worldly policy'.[2]

Between their inception and the accession of the first Tudor, Parliaments had undergone also a fundamental change in their institutional structure. They had begun as meetings of the king, his professional counsel and his great council of lay and ecclesiastical magnates. Sometimes, but not always, they were afforced – and even then not for entire sessions – by representatives of the English shires (knights) and of some boroughs (burgesses). However, significant changes occurred in Edward III's reign. Representatives of the lower clergy withdrew to convocations (ecclesiastical assemblies) of Canterbury and York.

More important, the knights and burgesses formed a separate chamber that later became known as the House of Commons. This left the king's professional counsel, together with the nobles, bishops, abbots and priors (though not all of them) in possession of the parliament house – the progenitor of the House of Lords.[3] By 1400 two houses existed, but the 'lower' and newer one remained in an anomalous, indeed contradictory, position. Although a real Parliament demanded its presence, it remained formally outside the institution proper – a fact commemorated in fossilised form today, when MPs, including the prime minister, are not permitted beyond the bar of the House of Lords at the opening ceremonies of Parliament. In practical terms the Commons petitioned for legislative action, but did not assent to it. During the fifteenth century, however, political circumstances and precedents which acquired the force of constitutional convention altered the position. By 1485 the Commons was fast approaching an equivalence of constitutional authority with the Lords. The process was completed in a sequence of solemn judicial decisions such as that in 1489, when the judges were unanimous that an Act only had validity if the Commons as well as the Lords and king had assented to it. At the same time the Lords had been transformed from the nucleus of Parliament into just one of its two houses.

This should not be misread as an early phase in a whiggish and evolutionary interpretation of parliamentary history, a step on the long road to the ultimate political ascendancy of the Commons. It was an institutional development which created, out of a primitive unicameral Parliament, a trinity of king, Lords, and Commons. For most of the time and on most matters – except what seemed to be unwarranted financial demands or lack of 'good governance' – the lower house remained docile, reluctant to take the political initiative. Moreover, though medieval Parliaments had been exploited by a baronial opposition to royal policies or by noble claimants to the Crown, the king and not the 'house of lords' remained the motivating force. Parliament was still a royal institution, designed to assist the king in the business of government. He summoned, prorogued, and dissolved it. He ensured that a sufficiency of councillors was elected to provide an official 'front-bench' in the Commons and that a competent royal servant was elected to be its speaker. He also exercised considerable discretionary authority in the issue of writs to the Lords. The king could exclude peers, not only on the specific grounds of minority, lunacy, poverty, or service abroad but also, more generally, because nobility was not yet recognised as synonymous with 'peerage of parliament' – the right to be summoned to the upper house. It was not until the 1530s that a peer, ordered to stay at his post during the parliament time, could be advised that 'I send you the writ because it is the order that every nobleman should have his writ of summons of a parliament'.[4] Like other strong kings among his predecessors, Henry VII retained the whip-hand over an institution which had been evolved to co-operate with him in the cause of stable government and not to obstruct or limit him.

As for the two houses, their parliamentary roles had already been cast. The Commons had long since acquired the sole right to initiate lay taxation. Nevertheless the Lords enjoyed inestimable advantages. It continued to be the more prestigious and politically independent assembly. As the legatee of the earlier, medieval Parliaments, it enjoyed the assistance of the Crown's professional counsel (judges, attorney and solicitor, king's serjeants, and master of the rolls) the inherited experience and records of the parliamentary secretariat (headed by the 'clerk of the parliaments') and well-tried procedures applied with flexibility. Above all the Lords' formal institutional authority was bolstered by the 'invisible' social influence of its members, who comprised the élites in Church, State, and society. In brief, the first Tudor presided over parliamentary meetings in which king, Lords and Commons ranked in that order, both in prestige and practical importance.

PARLIAMENT: THE POLITICAL CONTEXT, 1485–1529

Between Henry VII's accession and Cardinal Wolsey's fall in 1529 eleven Parliaments met – not more than one every four years. None of them lasted long, averaging only 10/11 weeks apiece and totalling no more than 110/120 weeks during the 44 years.[5] The longest (1512–14) sat for just over 20 weeks (and spread over three sessions) while, at the other end of the spectrum, the Parliament of 1510 was dissolved after a mere 34 days. This hardly suggests the creation (or continuation) of a strong and vital parliamentary tradition – and to some extent such a conclusion would be the right one.[6]

The pre-Reformation Parliaments of early Tudor England have common characteristics which endow the parliamentary history of this period with some kind of unity. This may be surprising, because seven of them sat in the reign of Henry VII, while four of them met under the very different regimen of his son. The two kings were not only men of strikingly dissimilar personality, they also represented fundamentally different traditions of kingship. Henry VII emerged from the chaos of the fifteenth-century dynastic wars. His concerns were urgent, immediate and primarily dynastic: to secure his tenure of the throne and that of his descendants. The prerequisites were pacification of the realm, the restoration of law and order, and financial self-sufficiency. All necessitated the king's constant attention to the grinding routine and minutiae of administration. In contrast his son was the self-confident heir of the union of the two conflicting houses of Lancaster and York. Henry VII was obsessed with 'good governance', laboured to achieve financial solvency and, to that end, his foreign policy (with the occasional exception) was isolationist and pacific, whereas Henry VIII was expansive, extravagant and imperialistic, and the chivalric, military and courtly elements of his kingship derived from the dukes of Burgundy. The father preferred a thorough (sometimes extortionate) exploitation of his hereditary revenues, while the son looked to Parliament to finance his continental wars.

However, any simple arithmetical analysis of the frequency and duration of Parliaments must take into account not only these contrasting styles of kingship but also the changing political circumstances in which the two kings operated. When it does so, a different parliamentary picture emerges. In the first tentative decade of the reign, when Henry VII was grasping his way towards consolidation of his power, he called five Parliaments (1485, 1487, 1489–90, 1491–92, and 1495), but in the last fourteen years he summoned only two (1497 and 1504). Indeed, on the second of these occasions he publicly advised that 'for the ease of his subjects, without great, necessary, and urgent causes' he would not call another Parliament for a long time.[7] He was as good as his word. Five years later he was dead, without another summoned. Subjects who knew that another Parliament meant another tax might well applaud; but the paucity of Parliaments coincided with the years in which Henry VII intensified his campaign to enforce statutes penal and recover his fiscal rights as feudal overlord. Some of his practices, in individual cases, were blatantly extortionate, as his agent, Edmund Dudley, later admitted. So the political pot slowly simmered with resentment. When his son succeeded him, it boiled over.

Henry VIII's early years were characterised by a brief parliamentary 'revival': in two ways – frequent sessions and in the Commons' spirited criticism – and for two inter-related reasons. In 1510 the governing class finally rebelled against his father's financial policies. The new king paraded his reforming aspirations and gave Parliament its head, permitting legislation against the financial abuses of his father's government, punishing his chief agents and generally reversing his financial policies. However, Henry VIII's motives were not altruistic. He was bent on military adventures in Europe for which he needed money. As a *quid pro quo* for the surrender of his father's profitable financial practices he sought – and received – parliamentary taxes: the traditional grant of tunnage and poundage for life in 1510, fifteenths and tenths in 1511/12 and the introduction of an income tax, the subsidy, in 1513/15. The voracious needs of Henry's war chest and the failure of the new subsidy to realise the anticipated sum resulted in a spate of parliamentary sessions, six between 1510 and 1515. The last of these was marked by an anti-clerical outburst in the lower house, although this was not a Crown–Parliament confrontation but an attack on clerical privilege, in which the king and his faithful Commons were on the same side (see pp. 60–61).

However, this occurred during Thomas Wolsey's rise to a position of unequalled supremacy in Church and State. Temperamentally he was an autocrat and he must have retained sensitive memories of the clerical humiliation of 1515. Consequently there was only one Parliament (1523) during his long ascendancy, and that was forced upon him by the financial necessities of an expensive foreign policy. The uproar which met his demands for more money can only have confirmed his distaste for Parliaments. No more were called until he fell from power six years later. Therefore it is necessary to see the pre-Reformation Parliaments in their proper perspective. They remained important occasions in the vital continuing relationship between the king and his governing class – a collaborative exercise in taxation and legislation and a sounding-board to test the acceptability of his policies. So it was a clear warning to the king when, in 1523, a member of Parliament bluntly told him that his acquisition of Therouanne, a meagre return for so much treasure and blood, had cost the Crown and the kingdom 'more than twenty such ungracious dogholes could be worth'. Part of Parliament's worth lay in the frankness of its speech and the cautionary notes which it could sound.

Nevertheless early Tudor Parliaments were examples of an institution which had only occasional value to the Crown and which, moreover, was notably acquiescent when it met. Apart from the early flurries of Henry VII and Henry VIII these were lean years, especially between 1497–1509 and 1515–29. This poverty of Parliaments contrasts dramatically with previous centuries when, for example, Edward III had called forty-eight in a reign lasting half a century. Parliaments had continued to meet, more or less annually, until, and during, the Wars of the Roses. However, under strong Yorkist kingship the incidence fell and continued to do so under the early Tudors. Parliament could not be a vital constitutional force unless it met frequently and regularly. There were other symptoms of 'decline' or at least signs of acquiescence: no Tudor ministers were impeached; there were no attempts to appoint the king's councillors, no refusals of requests for money and no instances of appropriation of supply.[8] On the other hand, Parliaments proved themselves incapable of providing the king with enough of what he needed most – money. Edward IV (in 1472–75) and Henry VII (in 1489) had secured parliamentary grants for foreign wars, but they had been hedged in with humiliating conditions and, in any case, they did not yield what they should have done (because of such practices as under-assessment and the misappropriation of funds by the collectors). Local resistance and, in 1497, a Cornish tax revolt further diminished the volume of coin which trickled into the treasury as a consequence of parliamentary grants. Wolsey's innovation, the subsidy (income tax), fared no better because it required two supplementary votes by Parliament in 1514–15 to make up the amount *originally* anticipated in 1513/14. Parliament was failing to deliver the goods to a needy monarchy.

THE RECORDS OF EARLY TUDOR PARLIAMENTS

Where did Parliament stand at this moment in its history? It is a question difficult to answer because of the poverty of official sources. As it was a place of business, and its business was legislation (which included grants of money), the detritus of its activity consists of evidence of its law-making activities. In the late Tudor period these included the records of business (the journals of the two houses), some paper drafts of Bills, the original Acts (clean copies on parchment on which the two houses and the king had recorded their assents), the parliament roll (on to which the clerk of the parliaments transcribed the text of public Acts) and the king's printer's edition of statutes, published after each Parliament. However, not so much survives from an earlier age. The paper Bills were, in any case, consumed in the great parliamentary fire of 1834. Some have survived, scattered about the official and personal papers of those great Parliament men, Thomas Cromwell and William Cecil – but few before then. The Commons' journal did not come into existence until 1547 and the Lords' business record survives, in more or less continuous form, only from 1510, although vestigial evidence dating from 1449, 1453 and 1461 indicates a much older record, befitting the chamber which had a much longer institutional history as the parliament house.[9] The original Acts survive only from 1497 (and then not for 1523 and 1529). The series of medieval statute rolls, which recorded the text of Acts, ceased probably in 1468 and certainly before Richard III's reign. This loss may seem more apparent than real. The statute roll was rendered superfluous because its place was gradually usurped by the parliament roll which, from 1484 on, began a new life in the hands of the clerk of the parliaments (although this process was not completed until after 1529). It was then that he began the practice of enrolling on it the Acts passed by Parliament. However, at the same time, the parliament roll became less and less a record of parliamentary proceedings.[10] As for the printed editions of statutes, commencing in 1484 and officially authorised from 1510 onwards, they simply add to the available textual sources of legislation and reveal nothing about the parliamentary activity which produced them. Evidence of the early Tudor Parliaments is lean fare indeed.

MEMBERSHIP

The early Tudor House of Lords, which consisted of two orders – the lords spiritual and the lords temporal – was not the equivalent of the first two estates of many continental assemblies. The lower clergy was no longer represented. Nor indeed did the bishops, abbots and priors represent the Church. They sat in the Lords as tenants-in-chief of the Crown. This received judicial confirmation in 1515 when the judges declared that the king could hold a Parliament 'without the spiritual lords, who had no place there except by reason of their temporal possessions'. For the same reason the nobles took their seats there, but also as natural counsellors of the king. Unlike, say, the first (ecclesiastical) and second (noble) estates in the French estates-general, they were not elected by the generality of clergy and nobility to represent them. They were called to Parliament individually, not as the chosen spokesmen of sectional interests but by virtue of their relationship with the king. The lords spiritual and temporal did not, as in most continental assemblies, convene in separate chambers, as the voices and guardians of jealous and competing estates – and if the theory of estates still flickered with life into the sixteenth century, the judges' decision of 1515 must have inflicted a mortal blow. Instead the peers, bishops and abbots sat together in one house, as legatees of the king's great council. They did not represent anyone – classes or communities – except, in the wider parliamentary context and together with the Commons, the community of the realm.

Membership of the upper house was not fixed but was determined by the Crown. However, its size and composition became more predictable as time, custom, and the growing identification of peerage (nobility) with 'lordship of parliament' narrowed the king's freedom to choose who should (or should not) be summoned. The two archbishops (Canterbury and York) and, with the exception of Sodor and Man, all the bishops (nineteen) were regularly called, although episcopal vacancies and absences abroad might vary this number.[11] However, writs continued to be sent to the keeper of spiritualities of the see during a vacancy and to the bishop's vicar-general if he was overseas. The number of parliamentary abbots and priors (the regular clergy) remained at about twenty-seven throughout the period. Altogether the lords spiritual totalled a steady maximum of about forty-eight. In contrast the lords temporal were fewer, but increasing. In Henry VII's first parliament they numbered only 34 and never rose above 43/45 in any of his parliaments.[12] In 1510 36 were summoned and in 1529 44. Two obvious but significant characteristics of the early Tudor Lords are demonstrated by these bald figures: that it was a small assembly[13] – at the most about ninety – and that it had, on paper at least, a majority of lords spiritual.

However, these bald figures conceal more than they reveal about contemporary political realities, in particular the Crown's power to influence or manipulate the size and composition of the Lords. Long before 1485 the bishops' right of membership had been firmly established, as the regularity with which they were all individually summoned hardened into custom. The same cannot be said of the regulars. Abbots and priors had never acquired a prescriptive right to sit in the Lords by virtue of office or as great feudatories. The early Tudor parliamentary representatives of the regular clergy consisted of less than 10 per cent of all abbots (a mere twenty-five and all but two of them from the Benedictine order) and only two priors. Although the total had settled at twenty-seven around the end of the fourteenth century, and remained fixed both in number and composition during most of the early Tudor Parliaments, Henry VIII was to demonstrate that the Crown still exercised the freedom to add to that list, by calling up Tewkesbury and Tavistock.[14]

The freedom to decide who should receive writs and who should not was greatest in the case of the peerage. The late medieval nobility was neither old nor fixed in its composition. It was a rural landed plutocracy, most of whose members had been recently ennobled, and its *nouveau* quality was maintained by a constant and rapid process of attrition (due to natural causes rather than death in battle or on the scaffold). Only a few families like the FitzAlans and de Veres could point proudly to ancient noble pedigree; therefore thinning ranks had to be reinforced by a steady flow of new recruits. Antique titles were often re-activated and bestowed upon them but, while those old earldoms and baronies had often figured in the history of the Lords, obviously their new holders could not point to a long record of regular summons to the house. This turnover of noble families must have assisted the king in maintaining his right to call up only those whom he wanted. The simple fact is that, both before and during the early Tudor period, a personal summons to an individual did not endow him with a prescriptive right – the situation was a much more fluid one. It was the Crown's undoubted right to deny writs for recognised disabilities, such as minority, royal service, absence overseas, mental illness and poverty. However, some hereditary peers were not called to successive Parliaments, even when they were eligible, and other men attended apparently without receiving writs – perhaps only a verbal summons.

While Henry VII recognised that some nobles had some kind of presumptive right to sit in the Lords, he was also ready to exclude them if they displeased him.[15] With the exception of Giles Daubeney 'it is open to doubt whether he thought in terms of creating additions to an hereditary peerage by issuing a few personal summonses'.[16] In brief Henry VII ensured that he retained the initiative in the issue of writs. His son, however, seems to have displayed a greater recognition of the parliamentary 'rights' of hereditary peers: so Lord Clinton was summoned in 1515 although his father and grandfather had not been, and Lord Burgh was called in 1529 (albeit as a new peer) despite the fact that his father (the second baron) had not received writs between 1496 and 1523. As a consequence, Henry VIII hastened the process whereby 'lordship of parliament' became synonymous with peerage. In other words, the right to be summoned to the House of Lords was becoming the distinguishing mark of noble status. This did not deprive the king of all initiative. He continued to deny writs on the grounds of minority and absence overseas. Like his father, he excluded Burgh because of his insanity and, after 1523, the earl of Kent received no summons because of his poverty. So Henry VIII was still prepared to suspend the parliamentary rights of individual peers when he considered that the circumstances warranted it. Nevertheless his freedom of action was narrowing as nobles came to regard writs of summons as a prescriptive right.

Finally there were the 'men of law' who had originally attended as part of the king's professional council and who continued to be summoned when Parliament evolved into two houses. It has been said that, as a result of this process, the lords spiritual and temporal were reduced to one chamber of a bicameral institution. This is to misread the nature of the change. It would be truer to say that the knights and burgesses seceded to form a separate and new house which only gradually came to be accepted as part of Parliament proper. The bishops, nobles, and men of law remained in possession of the parliament house. At its lower end there was a bar beyond which, at the opening and closing ceremonies, the Commons could not proceed. At the upper end was the throne, symbolising the presence of the king, the other party to the original parliamentary process, even though he had ceased to attend its business sessions.

One important alteration had occurred in the power structure of the upper house since the emergence of a bicameral Parliament. On the surface little had changed. The men of law continued to be summoned: most of the judges of king's bench and common pleas (and, though there is no evidence that barons of the exchequer were called to Henry VII's Parliaments, the chief baron was certainly there in 1512, 1515 and 1523), as well as some of the king's serjeants-at-law, and the king's attorney and solicitor. The numbers fluctuated, but as many as nine/twelve sat in Henry VII's House of Lords.[17] Nothing changed when his son succeeded him. In 1510 an observer noted that 'The master of the rolls and chief judges, with other judges, clerks and officers, kept their room on their sacks as accustomed'. Thirteen years later a herald's drawing depicted the woolsacks occupied by two chief justices, eight judges, and four serjeants-at-law. The Lords' journals confirm that the judicial presence was not confined to the opening ceremonies. In 1515 at least five judges, the attorney and solicitor and several serjeants were recorded as actively assisting the house in its legislative business.[18] This is hardly surprising, because they were members of the king's professional council and an essential part of the original nucleus of parliament. Furthermore, Parliament was still 'the high court' and it was appropriate for the judicial element to be present.

However, the role of the legal assistants had changed. They were no longer members co-equal with the bishops and nobles and they had lost the right to speak in debates or vote. Instead they were summoned to Tudor Parliaments on writs of assistance, in order to counsel the Lords (when asked) and to provide a professional stiffening to a chamber of amateur legislators. Much of their help was of a practical kind. In February–April 1515, for example, they introduced, amended, revised and redrafted Bills, and wrote fair copies of them on parchment. Usually these tasks were assigned to a single assistant. A Bill might be passed for 'reformation' to a committee, which was sometimes composed of lords spiritual and temporal but more commonly consisted solely of legal assistants. So the house assigned the Bill concerning the king's debts to the judges, serjeants, attorney and solicitor, and another to the chief justices and serjeants, who were required also to consider whether a third was in the interest of the commonweal. Most active of all the assistants, as he was to remain throughout the century, was the attorney-general. The clerk's journal conveys an omnipresent impression of an officer much in demand as, in 1515, John Ernely reformed a dozen Bills, redrafted, introduced and engrossed others and even carried measures, bearing the Lords' assent, down to the other house.[19]

It was less a case of the power of the professional counsel being diminished than of its being transformed into something silent in debate, while remaining formidable in legislative skills. Others received no writs but attended none the less and their presence was crucial: the lord chancellor, who was responsible for activating a Parliament and presided over the Lords, the master of the rolls and the masters of chancery – the Lords would not have been the same efficient chamber without them. However, the silent role imposed on the men of law (rather than any novel power of the lower house) did encourage some of them (though not the judges) to seek election to the Commons, where their freedom to speak and the prestige of their office could render greater service to the Crown. Sir William Nottingham, the king's attorney, did so as early as 1453.[20]

In contrast to the Lords, the other house was large (296 members) and, in some sense, it was representative. The question remains, whom did it represent? Statutes of 1429 and 1445 limited the shire franchise to resident landowners with an annual income of 40s. derived from freehold land, and restricted borough elections to 'citizens and burgesses'.[21] However, in practice the borough franchise varied enormously (but was usually propertied), the residential qualification was freely flouted (increasingly, as the 'carpet-bagging' gentry invaded the boroughs, especially from the early fifteenth century onwards)[22] and, behind the scene, influential peers promoted clients and pulled electoral strings. Several points emerge clearly from the pre-Tudor and early Tudor electoral history of the Commons. First, in so far as it was representative it did not represent individuals by some kind of democratic head-count. It represented organic communities – shires and boroughs – and it mattered less how members were chosen than how effectively they promoted the interests of their communities. Secondly, the residential qualification was commonly ignored, because the smaller and poorer boroughs were only too willing to elect gentlemen who would serve without wages. Thirdly there was the secret, but sometimes overt, hand of aristocratic patrons intruding their gentlemen-clients into boroughs and playing a more delicate hand in the gentry-dominated shire elections. More important was the 'borough-hunting' of officials – 'members of the royal affinity in the wider sense'.[23] We should not regard the House of Lords as some kind of fossil, divorced from the mainstream of society, but as the assembly of a social élite whose fortunes were interwoven with those of the gentry elected to the other house. The two houses did not express the different and even competing interests of two separate social groups but rather the common concerns and priorities of one 'political nation', in which the peerage and greater gentry were the dominant force.

ATTENDANCE

While only those who were summoned to the Lords could attend, debate and vote, there was no guarantee that they would turn up and perform their parliamentary duties. Indeed, absenteeism was the bane of the medieval and early Tudor Parliaments – some even had to be adjourned for lack of members. In 1454, when the Lords could muster a presence of only forty-five out of 105 who had been summoned, fines were imposed on absentees. Twenty years later the lord chancellor had to threaten members of both houses with punishment if they failed to appear; and in 1515 the Lords once again fined absentees, while an Act of the previous session was designed to deal with the same problem in the Commons.[24] Clearly the problem did not abate during the early Tudor Parliaments. However, our knowledge of attendance and absenteeism in the upper house is largely circumstantial, at least until the survival of a Lords' journal. Even then, it was not until 1515 that the clerk inserted an attendance register in his daily record. As the journal for 1523 is not extant, precise information is available only for the two sessions of 1515. During the first session (February–April) fourteen (or 15%) of the lords spiritual and temporal attended regularly (three-quarters or more of the daily sittings); another thirty-five (38%) put in an appearance; and forty-three (47%) did not turn up at all.[25] In November–December the figures improved (18%, 41% and 41%) but still remained unimpressive,[26] and they confirm that the old problem of endemic absenteeism continued. So too do the daily attendance figures when, in the first session, numbers rose above 40 only once, and fell as low as 19, 18, 7, 4 and 2.

An analysis of the 1515 sessions reveals other significant characteristics of the early Tudor attendance record:

1. The abbots and priors had a lamentable record, with only half their number attending at all, and few frequently.

2. Those who regularly appeared and must have borne the brunt of business were a mere handful. In February–April 1515 they numbered only fourteen and included such predictable figures as those bishops who were also important royal officials, like Wolsey (York), Richard Fitzjames (London) and Richard Fox (Winchester) and heads of great noble families such as the Howards (Norfolk and Surrey), Stanleys (Derby) and Staffords (Wiltshire).

3. On paper the lords spiritual had a majority (50–42) and (despite J. S. Roskell's insistence that the house was effectively secularised before the Reformation because of the regulars' poor record, they maintained it in practice. So, in February–April 1515, the peers outnumbered the lords spiritual on only eleven of the thirty-nine days on which attendance was recorded. Moreover in the next session three-quarters of the bishops turned up and more abbots and priors attended regularly. Helen Miller argues that they did so in order to defend the liberties of the Church against the anti-clerical backlash unleashed by Hunne's case (see below, pp. 60–61).[27] This should be a warning not to indulge in simplistic and sweeping generalisations about parliamentary developments. Long-term trends may be discernible from hindsight, but each parliamentary session was different, the product of particular circumstances. In so far as there was a process of change, it was not smooth and certainly not inexorable.

Bearing this in mind, it cannot be assumed that, in the early Tudor Parliaments for which no attendance register has survived, the Lords' record slavishly followed that of 1515. In any case the Crown made due allowance for the absence of members who were in royal service, abroad, or wished to stay away because of sickness, great age, or for other personal reasons. So there had evolved a system of licensed absenteeism which was becoming an endorsement of both the right and duty of lords spiritual and temporal to attend. The would-be absentee applied to the king, his lord chancellor or some other great minister for permission not to come. Both the application and the permission (or refusal) might be verbal or written. The procedure served several purposes: it confirmed the member's right to attend (especially as peerage became increasingly identified with 'lordship of parliament');

it enabled the king to determine whether he needed the services of particular bishops, abbots and nobles. Perhaps too he could use it to exclude critics, opponents and those out of favour, though there is no evidence that this technique was used before the 1530s.

Out of the licensing procedure there evolved the practice of *proctorial representation*. This practice had its origins in the medieval convocations – the Canterbury and York assemblies of the Church in England – and long before the early sixteenth century it had been adopted in the House of Lords.[28] When an applicant's request for a licence was granted, it was on condition that he named a proctor or proctors to exercise his voice in his absence. This has been misread by one recent historian who assumed that the proctor was empowered to wield a proxy vote on behalf of the absentee, whenever the Lords 'divided' (i.e. voted on a Bill before it). In this way the king's councillors could and did accumulate proxy votes, add them to their own, and thereby constitute a formidable, even decisive, voting block in the house. However, with one exception – in 1581 when there was a 'tied' vote and proxies were called for – there is no evidence that proctors exercised absentees' votes in a Tudor parliament. Proctorial representation served two purposes. It confirmed and kept alive the absentee's right to sit in the Lords and it bound him to all decisions taken by the house, and indeed by Parliament, in his absence.[29] One thing licences and proxies did not do was to solve the problem of endemic absenteeism; it seems likely that the same problem afflicted the Commons.

LEGISLATION

Despite contemporary descriptions of the medieval Parliaments as 'the high court', their judicial activities (such as impeachment), and their curial appearance, they did not merely declare what the law was; rather they made law, they legislated.[30] In a parliamentary sermon of 1442, the lord chancellor spoke of 'prudent ordaining, for which cause parliaments . . . are chiefly summoned and held', and he stressed their duty 'to establish new laws'.[31] The early Tudor Parliaments were primarily legislative assemblies with a long and robust history of lawmaking behind them.

However, they met in a new political climate engendered by the strong kingship of the Yorkists and Henry VII. It was a climate inimical to the growth or continued health of Parliaments and there is a consensus of opinion among a number of historians that the institution stagnated. According to S. B. Chrimes 'little or nothing of much significance occurred' during Henry VII's reign and, in particular, 'few legislative measures enacted were of any great importance'. J. R. Lander went further and posited an actual decline in its legislative and taxative significance. While the Crown used the occasion of a Parliament to pass new laws, they were not sufficiently numerous or important to warrant calling it frequently. The penny-pinching attitude of the Commons towards royal requests for taxation strengthened the disinclination. Indeed, the most serious opposition to Henry VII concerned money when, in 1504, he sought the customary feudal aids for the knighting of his eldest son (already knighted and dead) and the marriage of his eldest daughter (already married). These could only be collected after a searching enquiry into the feudal obligations of all landowners, which may well have been Henry's real motive, part of his campaign to discover and enforce prerogative rights. The Commons must have read his intentions, however. It was only after much friction and lengthy discussion that it offered him an aid of £40,000, to be assessed and collected in the same way as parliamentary taxes. His decision to accept only £30,000 was probably an attempt to mollify an angry Commons and restore harmonious relations.[32]

An isolationist and therefore inexpensive foreign policy and a more thorough exploitation of hereditary revenues seemed a better alternative. It dispensed with the tedious burden of frequent assemblies and, so far as the governing class was concerned, it protected the purses of the rich.[33] The rigorous enforcement of feudal dues and statutes penal, together with the imposition of recognisance bonds, was, in the short term, more lucrative for the Crown than cap-in-hand requests to niggardly Parliaments. Thus the combination of new, strong, conservative government and financially unresponsive assemblies led to a decline in both frequency and duration.

This kind of approach embodies a degree of truth, but it is unbalanced and one-sided. Even before the 'revolution' of the 1530s, Parliament was not just an occasion for the king to extract money and laws. It was, as always, a 'coming-together' of Crown and governing class and each had its expectations. Chrimes might dismiss the legislative record of Henry VII's Parliaments because few of the 192 Acts of his reign were of major importance to the Crown. Yet their intrinsic significance should not be denied. Over twenty Acts restored attainted persons or (more usually) their heirs. The lawyers' hands were writ large in legal reforms concerning murder, abduction, bail, fraud and counterfeit, writs of error, perjury (two Acts) and jurors' untrue verdicts. Landowners' deer, pheasants and partridges were protected. Acts ranged geographically from Calais (three) and the Isle of Wight to Berwick and Carlisle. Manufacturers and merchants, supplying small domestic markets, were shielded by protectionist measures against imports of foreign bowstaves, silk, lace, ribbons, and wine conveyed in 'forrayne bottomes'. London always loomed large, with two Acts concerning its mayor and others on its exports and the affairs of its 'broiderers', butchers, drapers, upholsterers and the merchant adventurers. So did England's staple industry, cloth: the deceitful making of fustians, worsted shearers (two), and woollen cloth (three) were all subjects of statute. Every aspect of England's economy was grist to the parliamentary mill: cordwainers, tanners and itinerant pewterers, hats and caps, weights and measures (three), the sale of salmon, servants' wages and the 'frye of Fyshe' in Norfolk and Suffolk. Penal laws were directed against vagabonds and usurers (two apiece). The export of bullion and horses was prohibited. A xenophobic touch was expressed in measures expelling Scots and levying duties and taxes on resident foreign merchants. Nor did the great men go away empty-handed: Berkeley, Devon, Oxford, Surrey and Viscount Welles all obtained beneficial Acts.

The catalogue and range of Acts are seemingly endless. It will not do to measure Parliament's efficacy or success solely in terms of the king's needs or the fulfilment thereof. All parties to the parliamentary process had much to gain and the picture which emerges is one of a vigorous institution. On the other hand, Henry VII did not surrender the legislative initiative, even if he was not, as Francis Bacon claimed, 'the best law-giver to this nation'. [34] It is impossible to identify the origin of most Acts. Conversely, however, it cannot be assumed that all Acts cast in a petitionary form were devised by private interests. [35] In 1504 almost one-third of the statutes (12 out of 40) were framed in this way and at least six of them had been introduced with royal approval. Moreover, some of the Acts cited above were royal, not sectional or local, in origin. They were statutes penal, designed to regulate trade and industry, punish offenders with fines, and so swell the king's income. The clerk's description of Acts (there were no official titles) often disguised their real purpose and content. So a statute of 1504, which petitioned 'against unlawful ordinances by Bodies Incorporate', actually deprived the City of London of control over its livery companies. The general impression is that, while Henry VII needed few new laws, he kept a firm controlling hand and usually got what he wanted. He was even prepared to tamper with Acts by making additions to them after they had passed the two houses – on one occasion two years after Parliament had been dissolved. [36]

A new king, Henry VIII, brought a new season. Parliaments met frequently – six times in seven years – and they were often in critical mood, about the late king's financial practices (1510), repeated demands for war revenue, and clerical privilege (1515). Yet their legislative value to the Crown was very limited. Six sessions produced only 121 statutes, over thirty of which were restitutions or other measures benefiting individuals. Apart from the occasional statute, such as that empowering the speaker of the Commons to license (or refuse to license) the early departure of members from Parliament (yet another attempt to combat endemic absenteeism), and apart from a handful of Acts concerned with military and naval matters or personally beneficial to the king and members of his family, only the grants of taxation were matters 'of great moment' to Henry. It was, perhaps, his need of money and the Commons' power of the purse which kept Parliament alive. After all, though it had no formal right to participate in policy making, Parliament could have a decisive impact on foreign policy if it did not provide sufficient funds for war. Nevertheless the omens were not propitious for its future. As Wolsey rose to power the parliamentary lights dimmed. His authoritarian instincts were reinforced by his humiliating memories of the anti-clerical outburst of 1515. Only one Parliament (1523) met during his period of ascendancy (c. 1515–29) and that was forced upon him by the cost of his (or Henry's) militant diplomacy. The experience did nothing to confirm king or minister in their love of Parliaments. Henry was bluntly informed of the Commons' unwillingness to finance the acquisition of useless scraps of territory in France; and when Wolsey visited the lower house to plead the Crown's financial needs, he was rebuffed. Although this Parliament passed thirty-five Acts, sixteen concerned individuals, most of the remainder dealt with local and sectional interests, and the grant of taxation was much smaller than the cardinal had hoped for. No more were summoned until his fall in 1529. In the longer-term context of the Tudors' first forty-four years, the Parliaments of 1510–15 and 1523 were aberrations from the norm.

What place did each of the houses occupy in the larger tapestry of early Tudor parliamentary history? It might be argued that the Lords' legislative role declined. The king not only exercised a superior power over the two houses, but Henry VIII may have continued the independent, even cavalier, practice of his father: nearly ninety provisos to Acts between 1510 and 1523 bear only the sign manual, and no evidence that either Lords or Commons had passed them.[37] Meanwhile the Commons was taking the last short steps to parity with the upper house. This is illustrated by minor procedural changes which, while insignificant in themselves, were indicative of bigger things afoot. In 1497 the clerk of the parliaments wrote *Missa a dominis* but not a formula of assent on Bills sent to the Commons. However, in the next Parliament (1504) a new clerk, Richard Hatton, added the formula of assent, a practice continued by his successor John Taylor (1510–23). What it signified is that, although many Bills were couched in the old petitionary form, the Commons was no longer a mere supplicant, petitioning the king to provide a remedy by consultation with the Lords. Both houses now recorded their assents as equal partners in a bicameral legislative process. It was a mark of courtesy by the Lords towards its new partner, as well as an acknowledgement of that fact. In the longer term the evolution of journals, which replaced the parliament roll as the record of business, lent a kind of bureaucratic endorsement to the emergence of a bicameral Parliament.[38]

Despite the Crown's superiority and the Commons' novel parity, it would be rash to assume that, as a consequence, the early Tudor Lords' legislative role not only changed but also diminished. In the absence of original Acts and Lords' journals for much of the period, and the lack of a Commons' record throughout, it is impossible to make adequate comparison either with its own medieval performance or with the early Tudor lower house. Nevertheless, for a variety of reasons it was less prominent. First, there was a considerable volume of private and other unofficial legislation, and enough can be gleaned to show that individuals, lobbies and communities were using their elected representatives to promote their interests. In 1510, for example, two-thirds of all Acts commenced in the Commons and included sumptuary legislation, common law reforms, trade with Denmark, and the inevitable statutes on the cloth industry. Abortive Bills covered a broad spectrum of economic activity and local interests: weavers, artificers, physicians, a merchant dispute and the renovation of Dover pier, foreign hats and, of course, wool and cloth. The lower house was the natural forum in which the aggrieved and ambitious, the victims and beneficiaries of economic conditions, and the concerned governors of local communities could all make their voices heard and use their knights and burgesses to serve their advantage. Many were busy on behalf of friends, kin, or constituents. Sir Andrew Windsor obtained Acts and provisos for his family. The Cinque Ports' members secured free annual fairs for Sandwich and, in 1515, exemption from the subsidy, while John Hales promoted Bills for Canterbury.

London had the most active lobby. Sir Robert Sheffield was instructed to oppose the grant of tunnage and poundage to the new king in 1510, part of a campaign mounted by the merchant adventurers. London's members retreated in face of an unsympathetic council and Parliament, but they fought all the way, proposing deferred tax-payments, no increases in tax-rates and finally reduced penalties for tax-evaders. London had little success in Henry's Parliaments, but it was not for want of trying. It drafted its own legislative programmes, in 1515 its members promoted five Bills, and in 1523 John Hewster petitioned the king on the merchant adventurers' behalf. In the same session William Shelley promoted a Bill on the subject of London's dispute with Henry over appointments to certain city offices. Members hunted out support for Bills, with Thomas Neville being asked to secure the support of his father, Lord Bergavenny.[39] The evidence is patchy, very little being known about Henry VII's Parliaments, but there is no doubt that local communities and economic pressure groups lobbied members and sponsored Bills in the Commons through their elected representatives. Revisionist studies have emphasised the importance – and formidable volume – of private Bills in the later sixteenth century. It is clear, however, that even before the 1530s, which gave Parliament a new prominence, the Commons was providing legislative solutions to the needs of the local and sectional interests within the governing class.

Secondly, the Parliaments of 1510–15 and 1523 were called to fuel the Crown's military and diplomatic adventures. Since their prime purpose was to vote money, the Commons, which alone could initiate revenue grants and determine the maximum sum, held the parliamentary spotlight – even though peers paid the subsidy too. Thus when Parliament objected to the government's financial demands in 1523, it was bound to lead to a confrontation between Wolsey and the Commons.

Finally, it was the lower house which, in 1510, took the lead in the reaction against Henry VII's financial practices and in 1512–15 against clerical abuses. Nevertheless, and despite these important instances of the Commons' initiative, it would be wrong to reduce the Lords to a cypher. Its early Tudor record was one of solid, skilful, and conscientious legislative activity. Many Bills were placed there, including some which might have been more appropriately promoted in the other house: on artificers, labourers, weights and measures (1497), vagabondage and silk imports (1504), Staines bridge (1510), leather imports (1514), sumptuary regulations, boatmen's wages and wool exports (1515). Thomas More put several London Bills into the Lords. In all, just over 40 per cent of the Acts commenced there. Not that there was any consistent pattern – much depended on the particular circumstances in which Parliaments were called. The Lords' share of successful Bills could fluctuate rapidly from 19 per cent (in 4 Henry VIII) to 68 per cent (5 Henry VIII), while the proportion beginning in the Commons ranged from 32 per cent (5 Henry VIII) to 91 per cent in November 1515. As we have seen, all Parliaments were, in a sense, unique and it behoves us to be cautious about extrapolating from the particular to the general. There was no progressive decline in the Lords' role as an initiator of Bills or Acts during this period; and there was only a barely discernible shift in favour of the Commons, even when it stole the political limelight in Henry VIII's early Parliaments.

The Lords' legislative performance must be judged without reference to high politics. It retained the benefits which accrued to it as the legatee of the medieval parliaments and as the much older house. Not only did it enjoy the services of the legal assistants and parliamentary bureaucracy. It had had more time to evolve the most practical and efficient way of transmuting the rough ore of Bills into the polished and finished product. The early Lords' journals reveal that the three-reading procedure already existed in essentials. While the Commons attained legislative parity in this period, the upper chamber remained an efficient, experienced old hand in the business of law-making. The more dramatic political activities of the other house between 1510 and 1523 should not obscure this fact.

RELATIONS BETWEEN THE CROWN, LORDS AND COMMONS

Not only the theory but also the practice of early Tudor Parliaments bore vestigial traces of an earlier concept. The continental notion of 'estates' was not yet dead, even though the bicameral organisation of Parliament bore little relation to it (see p. 45).[40] Some men talked and wrote of Parliaments which consisted of three estates – the lords spiritual, lords temporal, and Commons – but did not include the Crown. To monarchs, theorists and politicians, the king stood above the court of Parliament; he was not part of it.[41] This was reflected in the enacting formula of Tudor statutes, as we can read in one form thus: a prayer addressed to the king that 'he, *by the advice* of the Lords spiritual and temporal and his Commons in this present parliament assembled . . . enact . . . that . . .' The other runs, 'it is enacted by the King . . . with the advice and assent of the Lords and Commons . . . and by the authority of the same', or, more briefly, 'be it enacted by authority of this present Parliament that. . . .'. The first form implies a separateness: the king receiving advice from his Parliament and acting on it. He remained the lawmaker. In contrast the longer version of the second form clearly suggests a collaborative legislative exercise between three partners, albeit with the king as the senior one. Finally, the short form absorbs the individual parties – king, Lords and Commons – into the one institution, Parliament. It is significant, therefore, that in 1485 the first formula, with its emphasis on the monarch's separate, extra-parliamentary role, was used in most Acts, but that the second formula was adopted in the most important statute of all, that declaring the new king's title. However, the enacting clause in that measure refers to the assent of the Lords only, 'at the Request of the Commons' – as if members of the lower house were still petitioners and not full participants in the making of law. Elton stresses that 'the formula had not become standardised' and that 'enacting clauses could still vary almost freakishly'.[42] Nevertheless bureaucratic forms usually reflect real changes, even if they sometimes pass through a confusing transitional period before they catch up. In Henry VII's reign parliamentary developments had outstripped the forms and phraseology employed by the clerks.

By 1523 they were catching up. Sixteen laws were made by the king 'with the assent' of the two houses. More significantly, nine were enacted by the simple formula of king, Lords and Commons, and four just 'by the authority of this present parliament'. Only six Acts did not conform to the growing standardisation and the general drift is unmistakable. Even before the Reformation, bureaucratic practice was adapting its language to parliamentary developments. The Commons had become a co-equal house in a bicameral institution. It was now an integral part of Parliament and, even more important, so was the king. It only required the crisis of the 1530s to transform this trinity into a mixed sovereign which could deal, without restraint, in all aspects of human affairs.

As we have seen, the Lords was not a 'victim' of this development. Its composition gave it considerable influence, both in the 'inferior' house and in the counsels of the king. It was a case of changing role rather than of declining importance. The Lords had its legal assistants and clerks. It had fewer organisational problems simply because of its size and collective experience – when it had less than one-third of the Commons' membership and when, barring capital offences or royal displeasure, its occupants could anticipate tenure for life. Moreover (the point has already been made) peers in the Lords and gentry in the lower house were not the spokesmen of rival and competing estates, but members of one homogeneous socio-economic group – and the bishops and abbots must be included, despite the divisive force of anti-clericalism. As nobles comprised the social élite, so they constituted the natural leadership in society. It would have been unnatural for that leadership not to find expression in Parliaments: noble (and to a lesser extent episcopal) influence in elections, peers' kin, followers and servants sitting in the Commons and so on.

Unfortunately there is no substantial evidence of this, because even the prolonged labours of the *History of Parliament Trust* have identified only one-fifth of the knights and burgesses in the Parliaments of 1510–23. Even in that small sampling, however, there are signs of electoral patronage exercised by the great men of the land, not only Henry and Wolsey but Suffolk, Oxford, the Courtenays in the west country, and Lords Bergavenny, FitzWalter, Marney and Monteagle.[43] For Henry VII's Parliaments we are more fortunate. Nearly two-thirds of the Commons' members are known, and there is ample evidence both of the electioneering activities of the dukes of Buckingham and Norfolk and other peers, and of the presence of their clients in Parliament. The residential qualification was being ignored in many boroughs, which were accepting carpet-bagging gentry, sponsored (and even sometimes nominated) by great nobles and, less frequently, bishops such as Ely and Winchester.

There is, however, no evidence and no reason to suppose that such patronage had a political motive. Aristocratic patrons did not engineer the election of clients in order to pursue their public and private quarrels in Parliament. The ability to seat their followers in the Commons simply reinforced their status and prestige, a parliamentary expression of the patron–client relationship which characterised Tudor society at its upper levels. On the other hand, the parliamentary patronage of peers and bishops did have two important consequences: it strengthened the connection and likelihood of co-operation between the two houses; it also reinforced the Lords' authority within the bicameral relationship.[44]

It should be pointed out that the lords spiritual and temporal were summoned also to the great councils, another consultative organ available to the king. Little is known about them and their frequency was declining, but their importance should not be ignored. They discussed major policy matters 'which might transcend in importance most of the matters, largely routine and legalistic in character, which came before the lords and commons in the parliaments'.[45] At least five met in Henry VII's reign, of which three actually authorised financial levies before Parliaments met to give their assent. Even though, unlike Parliament, the great council was a dying institution, it does underwrite the collective importance of the lords spiritual and temporal in the counsels of the king.

Was Parliament dying too? The last great council was called in 1496. After 1497, only one Parliament met during the last twelve years of the reign. Chrimes is dismissive, because 'No change in the relations between the king's government and any part of parliament occurred.'[46] Yet this may be the simple consequence of our ignorance, because virtually nothing is known about parliamentary politics under Henry VII. In contrast the veil has been lifted on events in 1510. It was the first Parliament of Henry VIII, who came to power on a 'reform ticket'. He gave the signal for reform when he arrested Empson and Dudley, his father's financial agents, and the lower house followed the royal lead when Parliament met. There was no Crown–Commons confrontation, but there was some hard bargaining on some aspects of the proposed legislation designed to prevent a repetition of Henry VII's punitive financial policies. The main impulse came from the Commons, but the Lords did not take a back seat, while the Crown was also deeply involved. So the Act protecting landowners whose titles had been threatened by untrue inquisitions (1 Henry VIII, c. 12) began with a preamble of complaint which, we might assume, had been drafted in the lower house. In fact it did not originate in either house.[47] In contrast, the Act strictly limiting the time during which prosecutions under statutes penal were permitted (1 Henry VIII, c. 4) did start in the Commons. However, it ran into stiff resistance in the Lords. A compromise was eventually reached in which the Commons was the loser, agreeing to an extended limit of three years. There was also a three-cornered contest between king, Lords and Commons over the duration of the Act: was it to endure 'to the next parliament' or 'for ever'? Henry, who preferred the finite period, won (though in 1515 it was made permanent). Elton rightly concludes that there is ample evidence of rigour and 'busyness' on the part of both houses, as Bills went to and fro in redrafted or amended form. Disagreements there were but no confrontations. Business was conducted, for the most part, in a co-operative spirit, with the Lords keeping an eye on the prerogatives of the Crown and the rights of its subjects.[48]

The frequent Parliaments of the next few years were called for money, but that of 1515 also erupted into a major political crisis. As in 1510 this was no simple king–Parliament confrontation. It was both an expression of anti-clericalism and a conflict between the secular and ecclesiastical courts, behind which lay the competing claims of the royal prerogative and papal authority. On each issue, the king tended to side with the laity. The result was a clash between convocation and Parliament and, within the latter, between the lords spiritual and the rest. The origins of the crisis can be traced back to the Hunne case. Richard Hunne, a London merchant (and possibly a heretic), clashed with the clergy over the payment of fees for spiritual services. He brought an action in the king's court, was arrested on charges of heresy, and a few days later was found strung up from a beam in the bishop of London's prison. The Church pronounced a verdict of suicide, but it smacked of murder. Unfortunately for the clergy, Parliament met at that moment.

The Hunne case now merged with a separate but related cause. In 1512 Parliament had passed an Act limiting benefit of clergy to men in holy orders. 'Benefit' enabled clerics accused of capital crimes to be tried in an ecclesiastical, not a common law, court. Naturally there was abuse of this loophole in the law and many who were only technically in orders escaped punishment. In the common law courts, those who could read a verse of the first psalm – the 'neck verse' – were transferred to the Church courts where their punishment (if convicted) was nominal. The Act of 1512 was designed to restrict this privilege to the priesthood, but it was only to endure until the next Parliament. By the time it met, in 1515, the issue of benefit of clergy had become linked to the Hunne case. Bishop Fitzjames of London elevated the issue to one of principle, when he decided to protect the clergy implicated in Hunne's death by an appeal to clerical immunity from prosecution in the king's courts. He named the abbot of Winchcombe to preach at London's most popular pulpit, Paul's Cross, on the text 'Touch not mine anointed' on the day before Parliament met. He also rallied the bishops and regulars to the Lords, where they blocked the re-enactment of the statute of 1512. A joint conference of peers, knights, and burgesses petitioned the king to resolve the dispute and he responded with a popular Tudor device: a disputation, in the royal presence, between canon lawyers representing the two sides. In the short term the clerical lobby won. The disputation was inconclusive, a Commons' attack on Winchcombe was ineffective and the renewal of the 1512 Act, after passing the lower house, stuck in the Lords.

When Parliament was recalled late in the same year, there was fuel enough to light new fires. A Franciscan friar, Henry Standish, had led the anti-clerical lobby in the disputation organised by the king. He became the target of hard-line ecclesiastics and, in October, they accused him of heresy before convocation. Standish was saved by the bell – the following month Parliament re-assembled. When the lords spiritual blocked another Commons' Bill to renew the 1512 Act, it looked as if the circumstances of the previous session were to be repeated, especially when the king arranged a disputation to consider the charges against Standish. This time, however, it took place in the presence of members of both houses and the common law judges. When Henry sought a judicial opinion, the judges pronounced Standish's opponents guilty of the dreaded offence of praemunire. This was a deadly weapon because it was so vague: any encroachment on the king's 'regality' (whatever that meant) was punishable by perpetual imprisonment and the loss of goods. Clerical opposition collapsed and, before a joint meeting of the two houses, Wolsey knelt and begged the king's pardon. This humiliation probably explains why only one Parliament was called during the next fourteen years. The larger problem of ecclesiastical jurisdiction and immunities went unresolved; but when John Taylor concluded his journal with the observation that 'in this parliament and convocation, perilous discords arose between the religious and secular power, over the liberties of the Church', he touched on the political essence of this assembly: a parliamentary conflict between laity and clergy and an upper house split into warring factions of lords temporal and spiritual.[49]

This was not to be the cause of disturbance in the next Parliament. In 1523 it was the hoary issue of money: aid for England's involvement in Europe. In theory this should not have involved the upper house because grants of taxation were initiated by the Commons. The Lords could diminish or reject but not increase the amount. However, it was not uncommon for it to send a deputation down to persuade, pressure, and cajole the other house into action. On 20 February 1512 the lord chancellor first advised the Lords that Parliament had been called to finance defence against threats from the Scots and French, and then headed an impressive body of members to the Commons, in order to deliver the same message. A similar stimulus was applied to the lower house in February 1515.[50] This was an accepted procedure, but in 1523 Lord Chancellor Wolsey had a rough ride. On 29 April he explained the current diplomatic situation to the Commons, pointed out the obvious – that successful war and defence were impossible without money – and sought a generous grant. The house considered his demands excessive and appointed a number of members to meet him, plead the kingdom's poverty, and beg him to move the king 'to be content with a more easier sum'. According to Edward Halle (admittedly a savage critic of Wolsey and possibly a member of this Parliament),[51] the cardinal replied 'that he would rather have his tongue plucked out of his head with a pair of pinsons, than to move the king to take any less sum'. Eventually the lower house grudgingly voted an inadequate tax, at which Wolsey was 'sore discontent'. In a last desperate throw he tried to involve the Lords, claiming that they had already 'granted iiiis of the pound'. It was not true 'for in deed, they had granted nothing but hearkened all upon the Commons'. If this was so, the upper house displayed a delicate sense of constitutional propriety. Commons and cardinal were left to battle out the central issue in this most disturbed of early Tudor Parliaments.[52]

This was, to all appearances, a head-on collision between the chancellor and the Commons. The Lords seems to have taken no part after Wolsey's initial approach to the lower house. But did Norfolk, Suffolk, Northumberland, Dacre, and other critics and opponents of Wolsey, with clients in the lower house, have any hand in the confrontation of 1523? Later examples of inter-cameral collaboration suggest that this was possible. Whatever way we explain the 1523 Parliament, it is hardly surprising that, after his personal humiliation in 1515, Wolsey advised the calling of only one during his ascendancy. However, when the cardinal fell, the king immediately turned to Parliament and, in late 1529, the writs for a new assembly were despatched.

REFERENCES AND NOTES

1. 'Dubious' in two senses. Their legality was questionable – indeed, benevolences had been declared illegal by a statute of Richard III, although they were still occasionally levied. Technically they were gifts and loans, not taxes, even though in practice they amounted to much the same thing. See J. R. Lander, *Government and Community, England 1450–1509*, Cambridge, Mass., 1980, p. 99; Elton, *Tudor Constitution* (1982), p. 44.
2. Lander, *Government and Community*, p. 62.
3. The Edwardian changes divorced England from continental parliamentary practice. There the assemblies comprised a three or four-tier structure, based upon the organisation of society into estates, those who prayed, those who fought and those who laboured – in other words the clergy, nobility and 'third estate'. Edward III's reign created a bicameral Parliament, not an assembly of estates.
4. J. G. Nichols (ed.), 'The Chronicle of Calais', *Camden Soc.*, XXXI (1846), p. 166.
5. Elton, *Tudor Constitution* (1960), p. 228 and no. 3 and ibid. (1982), p. 233; S. B. Chrimes, *Henry VII*, London, 1972, p. 13 and n. 2; R. L. Storey, *The Reign of Henry VII*, London, 1968, p. 118.
6. Especially if we bear in mind how misleading is the formal estimate of a session's duration. For example, the Parliament of 1510 met on 21 January and was dismissed on 23 February, thus lasting almost five weeks. However, during that time there are no recorded afternoon sessions in the Lords; and when Sundays (4), convocation days (5), three

days devoted to the opening ceremonies, the Feast of the Purification and a two-day adjournment are deducted, the House of Lords met to transact business on only nineteen mornings (*L.J.*, I, 3–9).

7. A. Luders *et al.* (eds), *The Statutes of the Realm [Stats. Realm]*, 11 vols, London, 1810–28, II, 669.
8. Roskell, 'Perspectives in English Parliamentary History', 448–75.
9. Elton, 'Early Lords' Journals', 482–90.
10. M. F. Bond, 'Acts of Parliament', *Archives*, III, **20** (1958), 218; Elton, 'Sessional Printing of Statutes', pp. 73, 80.
11. It fell as low as seventeen under Henry VII. S. B. Chrimes, *Henry VII*, p. 140; Miller, 'Attendance', 325; J. S. Brewer, J. Gairdner and R. H. Brodie (eds), *Letters and Papers, Foreign and Domestic, of the Reign of Henry VIII*, 21 vols, London, 1862–1910, Vol. 2, Pt. 1, pp. 351–4.
12. Lander, *Government and Community*, p. 54; Chrimes, *Henry VII*, p. 140.
13. For example 75 in 1485, 88 in 1489 and 1495 and 85 in 1510. Miller, 'Attendance', 336 n. 71; J. C. Wedgwood and A. D. Holt, *History of Parliament, 1439–1509 [Hist. Parl.]*, 2 vols, London, 1936–8, II, lxiv.
14. Ibid., lv–lvi; Powell and Wallis, *Medieval Lords*, p. 553.
15. For example, in 1485 seven Yorkist peers and three bishops were not summoned. Wedgwood and Holt, *Hist. Parl.*, II, lxv.
16. Chrimes, *Henry VII*, pp. 137–41.
17. *L.J.*, I, 10–11, 18–19; Wedgwood and Holt, *Hist. Parl.*, II, lix, lxiv.
18. Powell and Wallis, *Medieval Lords*, pp. 544, 557; *L.J.*, I, 23–42.
19. Ibid.
20. Wedgwood and Holt, *Hist. Parl.*, II, cxxxvi.
21. Lander, *Government and Community*, pp. 55–7.
22. Ibid., pp. 55–60.
23. Ibid., pp. 60–61; Lander, *Crown and Nobility, 1450–1509*, London, 1976, pp. 27–8 and n. 151; Elton, 'Body of the Whole Realm', 46–7; also see Ch. 3, pp. 58–9.
24. J. S. Roskell, 'The Problem of the Attendance of the Lords in Medieval Parliaments', *B.I.H.R.*, XXIX (1956), 172, 189–92, 196–7; Miller, 'Attendance', 338.
25. *L.J.*, I, 20–42.
26. Miller, 'Attendance', 336–7.
27. Ibid., 338.
28. V. F. Snow, 'The Evolution of Proctorial Representation in Medieval England', *American Journal of Legal History*, **7** (1963), 319–39.
29. See Snow, 'Proc. Rep. Henry VIII', 1–26; Miller, 'Attendance', 345–50; Snow, 'Proc. Rep. Ed. VI', 1–27; Graves, 'Proc. Rep. Ed. VI's Reign: A Reassessment', 17–35; Snow, 'A Rejoinder', 36–46.
30. Elton, *Tudor Constitution* (1982), p. 234.
31. B. Wilkinson, *Constitutional History of England in the Fifteenth Century, 1399–1485*, London, 1964, p. 296.
32. Chrimes, *Henry VII*, pp. 135–6, 177–83; Lander, *Government and Community*, p. 63.
33. Lander, *Crown and Nobility*, p. 72.
34. Chrimes, *Henry VII*, pp. 183–4.
35. Elton, 'Enacting clauses', 183.

36. Elton, 'Body of the Whole Realm', pp. 56–7.
37. Calculated from House of Lords Record Office [H.L.R.O.] Original Acts; Elton, 'Body of the Whole Realm', pp. 53–4.
38. Ibid.
39. *H.P.T.*, 1509–58, passim.
40. Elton, 'Body of the Whole Realm', pp. 32–3.
41. Ibid., pp. 32–5.
42. Luders *et al.*, *Stats. Realm*, II, 499; Elton, 'Body of the Whole Realm', pp. 29–30.
43. *H.P.T.*, 1509–58, passim.
44. Wedgwood and Holt, *Hist. Parl.*, I, xxxiii–iv, xxxviii–ix. Peers were willing to lobby the lower house in order to secure the passage of their Bills (for example, in 1485). N. Pronay and J. Taylor (eds), *Parliamentary Texts of the Later Middle Ages*, Oxford, 1980, p. 186.
45. Chrimes, *Henry VII*, p. 141.
46. Ibid., p. 135.
47. G. R. Elton, 'Henry VII: A Restatement', *H.J.*, IV, no. 1 (1961), 9.
48. Ibid., 24–6; J. P. Cooper, 'Henry VII's Last Years Reconsidered', *H.J.*, II, no. 2 (1959), 125.
49. See G. R. Elton, *Reform and Reformation*, London, 1977, pp. 50–8.
50. *L.J.*, I, 12–13, 21.
51. *H.P.T.*, 1509–58, II, 279–80.
52. E. Halle, *The Union of the Two Noble Families of Lancaster and York*, 1550, Scolar Press, 1970, ff. CIX(V)–CX(V).

Chapter four

THE REFORMATION PARLIAMENTS I, 1529–1553

In the summer of 1529 Henry VIII's humiliation was complete. His French ally made peace with the Habsburgs without consulting him and the pope recalled his matrimonial case to Rome for a final decision. In frustration and anger he dismissed Wolsey who had failed him and he turned to Parliament instead for a solution. In so doing he set in train a sequence of events which ushered in a political revolution in the Church, the State and Church–State relations. Unwittingly he also inaugurated a divisive religious reformation which, in time, was to thwart his ideal of religious unity within the framework of a national catholic Church. In 1532–34 he secured the annulment of his first marriage, married Anne Boleyn and, in the process, broke with Rome, established a national catholic Church and became its supreme head. In 1547 that title was inherited by his son Edward, along with the crown. However, in the course of Edward's short six-year reign, those who governed in his name, Somerset (1547–49) and Northumberland (1549–53), carried through a protestant reformation. It was a period of kaleidoscopic fortunes in which the rewards were high, the politics often brutal, and failure frequently meant death. It was also a time of social unrest, rebellions, economic dislocation, soaring inflation and foreign wars. There were, however, two threads of continuity: that Henry became – and his son remained – supreme head, and that Parliament was the invariable instrument of change in matters of Church government and doctrine.

The resort to Parliament was natural, indeed inevitable. Without the support of the governing class royal policies could not succeed and that support was best expressed through Parliament. So this period was ushered in by the Reformation Parliament, which recognised royal supremacy over the Church. It ended, in 1553, with the duke of Northumberland's desperate, unavailing attempts (first) to find a parliamentary way and then the use of force to prevent its destruction. Religion was all-encompassing and the new religious order, whereby the king replaced the pope as the spiritual father of the Church, determined doctrine and the order of worship, corrected abuses, imposed discipline and rooted out heresy, probably affected the lives of his subjects more than any social, economic, or political change.

Not that Parliaments in this period were always called to settle religion. In the normal course of events they met to grant taxes and make new laws. Times of crisis, however, also prompted the Crown to seek 'advice' which, translated into practical terms, meant an attempt to secure governing-class support for its policies. So in 1529 Henry called Parliament. Yet he had formulated no plan of campaign. The lord chancellor, Thomas More, was vague when he addressed the assembled houses, referring only to the need to update old laws and combat 'divers new enormities'.[1] By the latter he probably meant new heresies, but the Commons chose to interpret the phrase as abuses committed by the clergy and acted accordingly. In the second session (1531) the government once again failed to give a lead. Indeed, the imperial ambassador observed that 'they do not know their own minds about the measures to be proposed therein'.[2] The same was true in 1532, although the rising star, Thomas Cromwell, was beginning to translate into reality a possible solution to Henry's marital dilemma. When Parliament was recalled for its fourth session, in 1533, accident, Cromwellian design, and the sexual drives of king and consort merged together to provide the answer. In August 1532 Archbishop Warham of Canterbury, a supporter of Henry's first wife Catherine, died. The king nominated as his successor the loyal and amenable Thomas Cranmer. Armed with this knowledge Cromwell and the new lord chancellor, Thomas Audley, drafted a Bill which would prevent appeals from English ecclesiastical courts to Rome and leave the decision on Henry's annulment to the archbishop. This, in turn, encouraged the king's intended second wife, Anne Boleyn, to succumb to his ardent overtures and by January 1533 it was known that she was pregnant. Urgency now combined with opportunity. Therefore the next session of Parliament was called to transform the Cromwellian Bill into law.

When the same Parliament met yet again, in 1534, Cromwell was in control. It had to respond to a defined government programme which included Bills for the succession, completion of the break with Rome, security measures, consolidation of the political revolution, and a request for money. The Crown had resumed its natural leadership and firm guidance of Parliament. So long as Cromwell remained first in the king's counsels, that situation continued. Perhaps there was a lapse in 1536, when the Parliament was intended to deal specifically with the fall of Anne Boleyn and its consequences. The general impression is one of lack of official initiative. In 1539, however, all was order and organisation. War with France threatened and the country had to be put into a state of military readiness. The surrender of the great monasteries was under way and needed retrospective parliamentary sanction. The executions of the last three years called for the requisite statutes of confirmation. The private business of the governing class had accumulated and needed to be transacted. Cromwell seemed to oversee all, and he had in hand his own programme of social reform. Yet one matter – the settlement of religion – took him by surprise. The conservatives' victory in 1539, embodied in the Act of Six Articles, demonstrated the king's swing back to an orthodox line and exposed the vulnerability of Cromwell's reforming position. However, he was, to all appearances, in control as the new session of 1540 approached. Indeed, in April he was honoured by the king with the earldom of Essex. His programme was an ambitious one: a tax for the Crown, religious unity, a series of ambitious socio-economic reforms and the dissolution of the order of St. John of Jerusalem. However, it proved to be his swansong, because, in mid-session, he was arrested and condemned by act of attainder.

The later Henrician Parliaments had no Cromwell. The pace of reform slackened and Henry reverted to the war policies of his youth. So the Parliaments of 1542–47 were called for money, although they also dealt with succession and religion. At the same time, after Cromwell, there was a decline in managerial preparations, especially as faction conflict tore the council apart. For a while Henry smiled graciously on the conservative Norfolk–Gardiner faction but, in his last years, he transferred his favours to the 'reforming' Seymour–Parr–Herbert group. The climax came in January 1547, when Parliament dutifully confirmed the attainder of the earl of Surrey and condemned to death his father, Norfolk. Hours before the duke was due to die, Henry died instead, leaving his young son and the future in the hands of the reformers.

Edward VI lent the authority of his crown to the actions of government and he adorned the opening and closing ceremonies of Parliament. However, it was the duke of Somerset (1547–49) and his ducal rival Northumberland (1549–53) who really governed. It was they, each an *alter rex* in his own way, who decided when a Parliament should be called, what to put before it, and how best to manage it. There were two over-riding reasons for summoning it five times in less than seven years. One was money. The combined effect of Henry VIII's war debts, the military adventures of Somerset in Scotland, inflation (exacerbated by debasement) and a generous distribution of Crown lands among the ruling aristocratic clique impoverished the Crown, depleted its capital and drove it further into debt. Recourse to Parliament was Somerset's only answer: in 1547 it dissolved the chantries and granted them to the Crown; and in 1548/9 it agreed to an unusual (and less profitable) levy on sheep, wool and cloth.

The other motive was religious reformation. In 1547 this was modest enough. The Act of Six Articles and the old heresy laws were repealed, but this was part of a general statute repealing the many new capital offences, treasonable or felonious, devised in the 1530s – nor was it simply or solely an official measure.[3] However, another Act, directing that both wine and bread should be administered to the laity as well as the clergy, was an encouragement to reformers to press for further change. Royal proclamations could not stem the tide of public debate and iconoclasm unleashed by the new freedom.

The State needed some new order of worship with appropriate penalties for non-observance. In 1548/9 Parliament attempted to provide that with the first Act of Uniformity. It authorised a prayer book and decreed penalties for non-observance. Unlike the Henrician statutes on religion, which merely supported the royal supremacy with punishments for non-observance, the new prayer book was enacted 'by authority of Parliament': the Edwardian Reformation was statutory, not royal. Parliament met again in 1549/50, in the shadow of Warwick's (Northumberland's) coup and the fall of the protectorate. It was, in a sense, a Parliament forced upon Somerset's successor, but the opportunity was taken to enact further Reformation measures, in particular the suppression of Latin primers and images, and a new form of ordination for the clergy, especially for the consecration of bishops.

Parliament did not meet again for two years, but when it did Northumberland was posing as the patron of radical protestantism. Therefore the centrepiece of the official programme was the enactment of a second book of common prayer. It was a step towards radical continental protestantism and, unlike its predecessor of 1549, was unacceptable to catholics. However, there was one common denominator: they were both embodied in Acts of Uniformity and imposed by parliamentary authority, with statutory penalties for non-observance.

After four sessions the first Edwardian Parliament was dissolved. Late in 1552 it was decided that another should be called. A degree of mystery surrounds it. Of course the government needed money, partly because the burden of Somerset's mismanagement had not been cleared, but also because Northumberland had continued his practice of rewarding supporters with gifts of Crown estates. However, by the time Parliament met, Edward was in the grip of his terminal illness and there was speculation among the diplomatic corps that Northumberland would attempt to divert the succession from Mary. In fact he did not, shrinking back from the possibility of a confrontation with an unsympathetic Parliament. In the following months Edward's health deteriorated and Northumberland, desperate to save the protestant Reformation, his career, even his life, acted to muster support. His son Guilford married Lady Jane Grey, an alternative claimant to the Crown. Then Edward, the council, judges and City of London were persuaded or hectored into compliance with his scheme to place her next in the succession. As events proved, that was not enough – only parliamentary sanction would secure governing-class support and legally confirm his cause. Therefore, on 27 June, the writs for a new assembly went out and at least London elected its members. Nine days later, however, the king was dead and less than six weeks later Northumberland was beheaded.

MEMBERSHIP

There were always changes of membership between Parliaments and parliamentary sessions. Knights and burgesses chose not to stand again or they died and by-elections had to be held. New bishops were consecrated, while existing ones were 'translated' [promoted], went to their Maker or, in the topsy-turvy of Reformation politics, were deprived. Peerages became extinct for want of male heirs, sons moved into the seats vacated by their dead fathers or loitered through their minorities as royal wards. This was all part of the natural parliamentary round in which the incidence of change was, to some extent, determined by the time-span between sessions.

However, the Crown could play an important part in the process of change. In 1540–42 Henry VIII created six new bishoprics – Bristol, Chester, Gloucester, Oxford, Peterborough and Westminster – and so raised the number to twenty-seven. Conversely, under Northumberland the see of Westminster was absorbed into London, Gloucester was amalgamated with Worcester and Durham was suppressed as the ostensible preliminary to its division into two new and more manageable dioceses. Whether the existing sees were all occupied depended on the Crown's promptness in filling vacancies. Even before papal authority was extinguished in 1533/4 the king nominated new bishops who were then consecrated by the pope. It had long been customary for the Crown to leave sees vacant for extended periods and pocket their revenues, but Henry VIII's record was particularly good: on no more than seven occasions did a vacancy last for a year or more, the longest being at Coventry and Lichfield between December 1531 and April 1534. The same was true in Edward's reign, when the government needed a full bench of bishops as the doctrinal spearhead of its protestant Reformation.

The other major quantitative change was likewise the consequence of royal action. The dissolution of the larger monasteries removed the parliamentary abbots and priors and so in 1540 reduced the lords spiritual from about a half to less than one-third of the Lords. The effect was to permanently secularise the upper house. In Tudor government, however, quality always mattered more than sheer numbers. The removal of Wolsey and the elevation of Stephen Gardiner to Winchester (in 1531) and of Thomas Cranmer to Canterbury (in 1533) had a much greater impact on the Lords than the disappearance of nearly thirty regulars who, in any case, had a notoriously poor attendance record.

Changes in the Crown's religious position had a significant effect on the episcopal bench. During Cromwell's supremacy, reformers such as Cranmer, Hugh Latimer (Worcester) and Nicholas Shaxton (Salisbury) were appointed. However, when Henry reverted to a strictly orthodox catholic position with the Act of Six Articles in 1539, Latimer and Shaxton resigned and his later appointments were either staunch conservatives – George Day (Chichester), Edmund Bonner (London), and Nicholas Heath (Rochester, then Worcester) – or pliable vicars of Bray, usually ex-abbots, of whom Anthony Kitchin of Llandaff was the archetype. In Edward VI's reign, however, the conservatives were on the defensive and one by one they were deprived: Bonner by Somerset, and Day, Gardiner, Heath, Cuthbert Tunstal (Durham) and John Veysey (Exeter) under Northumberland. The motive was usually not a parliamentary one but the effect was to strip the Lords of its conservative leadership. On the other hand there is no doubt that the most dangerous of the conservatives, Stephen Gardiner, was imprisoned during the first three Edwardian sessions because of the stirs he could make in Parliament.[4]

The removal of the conservative leadership deprived the Lords of a group of accomplished Latinists, diplomats, humanists, bureaucrats, canonists and civil lawyers.[5] Their replacements, however, were not men of a meaner mould. John Hooper (Worcester) was versed in Greek and Hebrew and an energetic diocesan administrator. John Ponet (Winchester) was a linguist, classicist, mathematician and theologian, Miles Coverdale (Exeter) was responsible for one of the earliest vernacular versions of the Bible, and Nicholas Ridley was an ex-student of Cambridge, Paris and Louvain whose occupancy of London was marked by a vigorous propagation of the Gospel and a genuine concern about poverty. Change there was, but not a decline in quality.

The lords temporal did not experience the same cavalier treatment as the bishops, which is not surprising. Once the king had become supreme head of the Church in 1534, the prelates owed their allegiance to him alone and he had the authority to discipline them. Lord Chancellor Audley warned them, during a debate in the Lords, 'that the praemunire shall ever hang over your heads'.[6] Any vestige of autonomy vanished in 1547 when Edward's privy council resolved that all prelates, like other royal officials, should seek reappointment to their offices after Henry VIII's death. It followed this with a statute which empowered the king to name new bishops by his letters patent, again just like his servants in the State.[7] Indeed, that is just what the bishops had become.

The bishops of the new sees created in 1540–42 were summoned to the Lords by virtue of the offices they held. In contrast the peers were still called as the king's tenants-in-chief, his 'natural counsellors' and, in practice, because they were influential territorial magnates and members of the social élite. By the 1530s peerage had become identified with lordship of Parliament and the nobility was increasingly sensitive of its parliamentary rights. It was accepted that in certain circumstances, such as minority, poverty or lunacy, a peer could be disabled. Furthermore no one doubted that it was the duty of a royal servant to stay at his post during the parliament-time. Imprisonment was a more sensitive matter. However, it was rare for the Crown to imprison a bishop or peer in order to prevent him from attending Parliament, although Stephen Gardiner certainly was in Edward VI's reign. His protest illustrated how sensitive the lords of Parliament were about their parliamentary rights and how easily the Crown exposed itself to criticism if it infringed them:

> And being now the time of Parliament, whereof I am a member in my degree, called unto it by writ . . . it is a double calamity to be detained in prison by so intolerable wrong, and excluded from this assembly so much against right.[8]

Perhaps Gardiner's protests could be ignored because he was only a bishop, but there is no doubt that (with notable exceptions such as the earls of Devon and Hertford) (see pp. 100, 133), the Crown scrupulously respected the parliamentary rights of peers. When Viscount Lisle was ordered to remain on duty in Calais in 1536, the lord chancellor none the less wrote 'but I sent you the writ, because it is the order that every nobleman should have his writ of summons of a parliament'.[9] Noblemen were very conscious of their rights. According to one of them in 1529 'it is accustomed that our voices shall remain in the house for the advancement and furtherance of justice'.[10] He was referring to the procedure whereby licensed absentees named fellow peers as proctors to represent them; and he was saying, in effect, that proxies confirmed their right to be called, even when they had opted to stay away.

Nevertheless State action did have an important effect on the size and composition of the lords temporal. Until 1529 the changes – new creations, offset to some extent by the extinction of male lines and attainders – had been modest. Since 1509 the nobility had increased from 43 to 54. The Reformation Parliament, however, inaugurated three decades of crisis, religious change and political conflict. Loyalties polarised, doctrinal positions became more rigid and inflexible and the monarch tended to become a partisan rather than an impartial arbiter and focus of national unity. Interwoven in this tapestry were the politics of personal ambition, greed and temperamental antipathy which sometimes worked themselves out in a bloody fashion. The peers (and gentry too) were prominent in central and local government and court politics and their importance increased as the Reformation secularised politics and government. Therefore they were the likeliest beneficiaries *and* victims in a prolonged period of crisis.

This situation had a dual impact on the peerage. The government found it politic to ennoble able servants and faithful supporters. At the same time opposition peers forfeited lives and titles as a result of Henrician reprisals or Edwardian dogfights. Both processes need only be illustrated here. Henry made six barons in 1529[11] and two more (William Paulet and John Russell) a decade later, ennobled two lord chancellors (Thomas Audley in 1538 and Thomas Wriothesley in 1544), and elevated two northern loyalists (Thomas Wharton and William Eure) in 1544. Thomas Cromwell received a barony (1536) and the earldom of Essex (1540). A rising star, John Dudley, was granted the viscountcy of Lisle, his stepfather's title, as a new creation in 1542. The relatives of Henry's wives also received their share of titles, most notably Jane Seymour's brother who became Viscount Beauchamp (1536) and earl of Hertford (1537).

In the next reign Edward's aristocratic governors utilised royal patronage also in order to reward themselves and their followers. Some, including the protector's brother Thomas Seymour, were made barons; William Herbert became earl of Pembroke; several were promoted (notably Lisle to Warwick) or restored to titles which had been forfeited for treason in Henry VIII's reign; and the two men who managed the Edwardian State, Hertford and Warwick, bestowed upon themselves the dukedoms of Somerset (1547) and Northumberland (1551). However, this process of recruitment to the peerage was counterbalanced by natural wastage – and the victims of State action.[12] Despite new creations, restorations, and the issue of writs to a handful of heirs of senior peers, the combined effects of natural wastage, disabilities and executions prevented any growth in the size of the secular element in the Lords: fifty-one were summoned in 1529 but only forty-nine in 1553.[13]

The combined processes of recruitment and attrition had an important impact on the composition of the lords temporal. It has already been observed that the early Tudor peerage was less one of ancient pedigree than of recent plutocratic origin. By the 1530s, however, the survivors preened themselves as old peers, scorned the *parvenus* – Cromwell, Paget, Rich, Wriothesley and the like – and were jealous of their power. However, the process, sponsored by a State which needed their education and talents, was inexorable: by 1553 almost 60 per cent of the lords temporal consisted of new peers.

Whereas the House of Lords shrank in this period from 107 to 71, due above all to the disappearance of the abbots, the Commons continued to grow. Henry VIII added a few boroughs (including Calais), but his most notable contributions were the thirty-one seats for Wales, Monmouthshire and Cheshire consequent upon the 'shiring' of Wales and its union with England. Edward VI's governors added thirty-four members, including fourteen in Cornish boroughs – where duchy of Cornwall (i.e. royal) influence was strong.[14]

The electoral system continued to reflect the predominant interests and shifting forces in society and direct royal intervention had little effect. Privy councillors, courtiers and country gentlemen were chosen because they were great men or their clients. Small boroughs elected members in response to the request of local magnates or because they were prepared to serve without wages. Elections were simply an illustration of the way in which the hierarchical Tudor society operated. Therefore it was natural, not sinister, that the largest and/or most influential groups of members between 1529 and 1553 were courtiers and royal servants, lawyers, country gentry, and the clients and kin of peers. They were not mutually exclusive groups, because many men wore several caps. Nevertheless it is possible to detect general trends. The lower house grew as the upper diminished and by 1553 it had more than five times as many members. A large proportion of the knights and burgesses in each Parliament were new and few of them could hope to garner the experience of bishops and peers who, excepting follies and treasons, were there for life.

Finally, the invasion of the boroughs by the gentry, already under way as long ago as 1422, was gathering momentum. It was not a simple process. In Edward VI's reign, for example, the small Wiltshire boroughs returned local and 'foreign' gentlemen, royal officials, merchants from London and Bristol, lawyers, great clothiers, stewards, other servants and clients of great peers. The Commons' future was not a rosy one: it was rapidly growing larger and more disorganised; many of its members were raw novices; the residential qualifications of its members were being ignored as boroughs bartered away their freedom for a reduced wage bill; and the parliamentary beneficiaries were the peers, whose carpetbagging gentlemen-clients ousted resident burgesses and represented their towns in Parliament.

ATTENDANCE

This remained a prime managerial concern throughout the period. Indeed, the problem was exacerbated by the frequency of parliamentary sessions (twenty in twenty-four years) and their lengthy duration (averaging 9–10 weeks under Henry and just over ten weeks in Edward's reign). In 1515 the Act empowering the speaker to authorise members' departure had already indicated a need to counter increasing absenteeism when Parliament had met six times in five years and there was a growing incentive to stay away or leave Westminster early. Both the members and the constituencies who paid their wages were burdened by the frequency of sessions during the Reformation Parliament. The high cost of London lodging, inconvenience, separation from families, neglect of business, fear of contagion, the difficulty of extracting parliamentary wages from poverty-stricken or unappreciative boroughs, all fed like tributaries into one swelling mainstream of lament and complaint. Members sought Cromwell's help to secure reimbursement. Wage claims spawned legal disputes. Boroughs sought devious ways to evade their financial responsibility, compounded with members and even rewarded them for lengthy absenteeism which drastically reduced the wage-bill.[15] In 1532 the Commons' speaker, Audley, gave official voice to the mounting discontent when he implored the king 'to consider what pain, charge and cost his humble subjects of the Nether House had sustained sith the beginning of this Parliament' and unsuccessfully sought an early dissolution.[16] The problem did not go away, however. On one day in an Edwardian Parliament only 137 (out of more than 350) were present to vote on a Bill.[17] The clerk who recorded this hinted at official concern about absenteeism when he also recorded roll calls of members to discover truants and, in 1548/9, a Bill to punish unauthorised absentees.[18]

Absenteeism had been a more intractable problem in the Lords. This may be the result of fuller documentation – simply that we know more about it. In any case its past record had been unimpressive and, in the abbots' case, lamentable (see Ch. 3, pp. 49–50). The Reformation Parliament may have inaugurated an improvement in attendance, since it was in the interest of the lords spiritual to turn up in defence of the Church. On the other hand Thomas Cromwell, who was, with the possible exception of William Cecil, the peerless Tudor parliamentary manager, wanted the peers there to counter the clergy's resistance to official Bills and therefore concentrated his attention on the lords temporal. However, he had to reconcile several needs and problems: a sufficient 'presence' of lords both temporal and spiritual to transact the formidable volume of parliamentary business; the absenteeism caused by the ennui and costs of long and frequent sessions; and, if necessary, the selective exclusion of dangerous critics and opponents. Cromwell had an additional managerial weapon when dealing with the Lords. Whereas the Commons' speaker could only prevent *absenteeism* by refusing a licence *during* the session, the lord chancellor (or a favoured minister like Cromwell) could pre-empt the options of presence or absence *before* Parliament assembled. A peer might receive his writ of summons accompanied by instructions to stay away. Sometimes it was a routine directive that a trusted servant should remain at his post. In such cases the king acted lawfully because royal officials could not leave their duties without his permission.

However, the imperial ambassador charged that, in 1534, Bishop Tunstal (Durham) and three others were ordered not to attend Parliament because they opposed royal policies. As far as Tunstal was concerned, this was probably true. The other cases are more doubtful[19] but, even if the ambassador was right, 1534 was an exception. As Cromwell's parliamentary skills and experience grew, and as dissidents were eliminated or conformed, his first priority became an adequate presence. This priority became more pressing because the expense and inconvenience of frequent sessions multiplied the appeals for licences of absence, both during and after the Reformation Parliament. In addition to the regular petitions of parliamentary 'backwoodsmen' such as Lord Mordaunt (who did not attend once in thirty years), Cromwell was showered with pleas on the grounds of royal service, 'painful diseases', a cleft palate, gout and other illnesses, old age, 'corrupt creditors', poverty and 'trouble of mind'. In 1534 Lord Latimer was more forthright than most and he spoke for many others when he complained that continuous attendance since 1529 'hath been painful, costly and chargeable'. Cromwell had to resolve each request on its merits. It should be added that bishops and abbots too applied for licences,[20] but the impression remains that Cromwell's chief concern was to rally the peers to Parliament.

As his grip tightened, so did his control of the licensing system. In 1536 he advised Henry 'to grant few licences for any to be absent'.[21] Although some were still excused, the effect of Cromwell's energetic supervision was an impressive presence in the Parliaments of 1536 and 1539–40. The one apparent blemish on his record was the abbots, but they were on the way out: in 1536 pluralists and absentees reduced their number, in 1539 only nineteen were summoned and in 1540 they had all gone. Yet appearances are deceptive. Little more than half had attended in 1534, but nearly 80 per cent turned up in 1536 and 86 per cent in 1539[22] – a mark of Cromwell's managerial success. Nevertheless their traditionally poor record before 1536 and, thereafter, the declining number of eligible abbots meant that the Lords was in practice secularised before the dissolution of the greater monasteries.

Cromwell's fall resulted in a partial reversion to the Lords' poor medieval record.[23] He had no successor with the same drive and detailed attention to parliamentary management. Hence, members were freed from his discipline and scrutiny. The renewed wars with France and Scotland in the early 1540s only made things worse. Marcher peers, the captains of the French outposts and noble commanders of field forces were discharged from their parliamentary duties while many of the other members had little taste for annual Parliaments with their unprecedented demands for war revenue. Finally in January 1547, with the king's death imminent, members stayed away in droves. The daily attendance averaged only twenty-seven and almost one-third of those summoned did not even begin the journey to Westminster.

The coercive power and natural authority of the government during Edward VI's minority were significantly less than those of an adult male ruler like Henry VIII. These new conditions were reflected in the Lords' attendance record. For a variety of reasons members were freer to attend and many were more anxious to do so. First, during a minority all peers were, to some degree, participants in a 'collective' government. Secondly, as the privy council, the effective ruler, was dominated by nobles, the Lords experienced a political resurgence and, in the parliament-time, conciliar policies could best be influenced there. Thirdly, because successive Edwardian regimes engineered a religious reformation 'by authority of Parliament', it was there too that the front line of resistance occurred. The Henrician conservative bishops, led by Bonner (London), Day (Chichester), Heath (Worcester) and Tunstal appeared regularly[24] in opposition and it is clear that the council was unwilling to proscribe them. Instead their position was contested by the champions of reform, Cranmer and the Edwardian bishops such as Hooper and Ridley, who were equally assiduous in attendance. The result is that the bishops appeared more regularly than the peers. This fact, together with their much-needed theological expertise and superior education, tended to make up for their lack of numbers. It also helped to raise the Lords' attendance to a level comparable to that of the Cromwellian Parliaments.

This was achieved despite the absence of more than 20 per cent of the house from each parliamentary session. Over one-third of the absentees did not even sue out licences, which suggests that the council was unwilling or unconcerned to coerce reluctant members into attendance, but it must also provoke the question whether insecure and unstable regimes compelled at least some of them to stay away. As in the previous reign, however, the absentees were the usual mixed bunch of backwoodsmen, royal servants, the poor, ill and aged (especially the bishops who, as a group, were ten years older than the peers), and the occupants of remote sees and owners of distant estates, who were reluctant to undertake winter travel over hazardous roads. A few were disgruntled conservatives who disapproved of the religion or politics of the current regime or victims of diplomatic sickness because they had fallen from favour. Yet there is no evidence that opponents and critics of either Somerset or Northumberland were obliged to stay away. There was of course one exception, Stephen Gardiner, whom Henry VIII had regarded as too dangerous to be included in his son's council.

Gardiner apart, it was the council's concern to secure the presence of active parliament men. More characteristic were the letters sent to marcher wardens and the governor of Calais ordering them to repair to Parliament and naming deputies in their absence. Inclusion, not exclusion, was the primary objective of Tudor parliamentary management.

LEGISLATION, 1529–1553

The parliamentary history of this period lends itself to a convenient and realistic division into three phases. Each one had its own special characteristics and emphases: the schismatic and revolutionary activities of the Parliament of 1529–36; the search for religious and political order and stability and a hunt for war revenue, between 1539 and 1547; and the protestant Reformation enacted by Edward VI's Parliaments. The central unifying thread is the royal supremacy over the Church.

The Reformation Parliament was crucial to the development of the institution. Although it was called when Henry was seeking a papal annulment of his first marriage, it was not clear what role he had assigned to it, and the government gave no positive lead in the first two sessions. In 1529 the king secured only the cancellation of his debts and some laws against clerical abuses, and in 1531 he extracted a large sum of money from the clergy in return for a statutory general pardon. He was no nearer an answer to his dilemma when Thomas Cromwell entered his inner counsels in December 1531. While Cromwell did not invent the solution to Henry's problem – schism and the creation of a royal supremacy – he had the skills, imagination, and determination to translate it into reality through statute. The use of Parliament should not be regarded as a stroke of political genius, however – in a conservative, legalistic society, political realists like Henry VIII, Cromwell and Edward VI's governors were bound to do so in order to effect major changes, because there was no alternative.

Between 1532 and 1536 Henry and Cromwell (with the assistance of Lord Chancellor Audley and other councillors) secured the annulment of the king's first marriage, the settlement of the succession through the heirs of his second, and (more important) a revolution in Church, State, and Church–State relations. The politicking and legislation which achieved these ends occupied much of Parliament's time: the Act in Restraint of Annates and the Submission of the Clergy in 1532; the Act in Restraint of Appeals to Rome (1533), and in 1534 a series of Acts which severed all remaining links with the pope and transferred his powers to the king. The customary limitations on statute fell away, as statute was employed to create the structure of the new national Church and acknowledge Henry as its rightful head with supreme temporal and jurisdictional authority. It also equipped him to punish those who opposed the new order. The collaborative nature of much of this legislation, and the amount of work which it entailed, can be illustrated by the Bill designed to prevent Catherine of Aragon from frustrating the process of annulment in an English Church court by an appeal to the papal Curia. It went through a number of drafts between

September 1532 and its introduction in mid-March 1533. Cromwell was the architect, Audley and other councillors (who were members of Lords or Commons) were involved and Henry himself had a hand in it. Several bishops, abbots and other specialists in canon and civil law scrutinised it and proposed amendments, which were duly incorporated. Finally it entered the Commons and passed with only one change in the lower house and none in the upper.[25]

Catherine's supporters opposed it in the Commons, choosing as their ground the question whether statute could treat of matters spiritual and the pope's authority. They chose their ground well, because the real innovation lay less in the matter of appeals than in the far-reaching claims of the preamble. It declared that 'England is an empire' – in other words a sovereign national State, independent of all other earthly authorities, even one like the Papacy which claimed to wield spiritual power.[26] This embodied Cromwell's vision of a new form of English State, in which all subjects (clergy as well as laity) owed allegiance solely to the Crown under God. It was a State in which the king's authority was enlarged but, at the same time, one in which he, like everyone else, was subject to the rule of law, and in which the true sovereign was king-in-Parliament. Cromwell's concept of the new State was not fully realised with the pope's exclusion. The king's authority must extend everywhere and all parts of the unified kingdom must be represented in Parliament. So the semi-autonomous franchises, and the monastic orders which owed allegiance to pope as well as king, had to be suppressed; Wales and the Welsh marches (borderlands) had to be 'shired' and incorporated into the English system of land law, justice and parliamentary representation. Outlying areas such as Cheshire and Calais, though not the county palatine of Durham, were given seats in the Commons. Such changes presented Parliament with lengthy, complex pieces of legislation. The new State needed adequate funding and once again Parliament obliged, with first fruits and tenths[27] in 1534 and monastic property in 1536 and 1540. Cromwell sought statutory confirmation of his bureaucratic reorganisation of central government, too. His guiding principle was to refer all major changes for a parliamentary solution.

The Cromwellian achievement had three important consequences for Parliament:

(1) It destroyed the previous limitations on statute. In 1528 a lawyer, Christopher St German, had argued that statute 'must be consonant to the law of God'. Sir Thomas More followed the same line at his trial in 1534. He denied the validity of the royal supremacy which was 'grounded upon an act of Parliament directly repugnant to the laws of God and His Holy Church'.[28] However, More lost the argument and his head. Statute thereby proved its capacity to deal in matters spiritual. It also overrode the sanctity of property rights on a massive scale, suppressing them (in the Franchises Act 1536) and expropriat-

ing the property itself (the Acts dissolving the monasteries, 1536 and 1540). Acts of Parliament became supreme and omnicompetent law.

(2) It may be that the Crown's resort to Parliament and statute for solutions to matters great and small encouraged the governing class to follow suit. Cromwell certainly set an example with his commonweal legislation on such matters as trade, industry, the control of food prices and, above all, rural depopulation and poverty. It was devised in his office and assisted by clerks, aides and clients such as William Marshall, Richard Morison and Thomas Starkey, who produced propaganda, drafted Bills and promoted them. However, apart from writing into the statute book in 1536 the vital distinction between the 'deserving poor' and sturdy, idle vagabonds, his commonweal policy was more impressive in intent than realisation. Members of the governing class might pay lip service to Cromwellian idealism, but there was a natural reluctance to pass laws which harmed their own interests. They were much more concerned to introduce measures beneficial to their class, themselves, their kin, friends, neighbours, and the local communities and economic interests which they represented. While such a practice was not novel, the volume certainly was.[29]

The range of legislative business before Parliament is a clear indication that it served not only royal but also governing-class interests. In the first session of 1534, for example, the affairs of the pewterers, printers and worsted makers, price-fixing, enclosures, price regulation and the preservation of fowl and fish, sodomy and heresy were all considered. The need to maintain archery and relieve the distress of Midland clothiers received sympathetic responses. London had a Bill for the paving of Holborn and Southwark. Other measures concerned peers, knights, an abbot, and the unsavoury John Wolf who used his wife (also a whore) to lure foreign merchants to their deaths.[30] The subjects of statute, as well as its authority, already encompassed the entire spectrum of human affairs.

The novelty of both range and volume should not be exaggerated. A solitary Parliament between 1514 and 1529 resulted in the accumulation of a formidable backlog of governing-class business. Yet frequent sessions during the next seven years seemed unable to satisfy the demand, perhaps because so much time was spent on important government Bills. According to Lehmberg, private legislation dwindled after 1540, because, once again, there were frequent sessions and, after Cromwell's fall, there were fewer official Bills as well – in other words, any existing backlog was soon cleared. His conclusion rests on the fact that after 1540 the output of private *Acts* declined.[31] It will be seen, however, that, as the century progressed, abortive Bills, especially private and other unofficial measures, became more numerous than successful ones. Even in Henry's reign there were many failures, including ten of London's measures between 1533 and 1547.[32] During Edward's reign 166 Bills became law but 293 others did not. In the

1552 session, for example, seventy-six of the 113 Bills before Parliament failed to pass and 40–50 of them were identifiably private Bills. (Most abortive Bills have not survived and their contents have to be identified by their description in the journals.) Mary's Parliaments were short, disturbed and devoted an unusually large proportion of their time to official measures. In Elizabeth's reign, however, the spate of private and other unofficial Bills was renewed.

(3) Although the Reformation Parliament gave the institution a new prestige and authority, this should not be misread as an emerging challenge to royal power in the State. Constitutionally, of course, one cannot talk of 'king versus Parliament' in the 1530s. The Crown had become an integral part of Parliament and the important distinction now was between the limited power of *rex solus* (the king alone) and the sovereign authority of king-in-Parliament. Henry himself acknowledged both of these points when, in 1542, he informed members of the Commons

> that we at no time stand so highly in our estate royal, as in the time of parliament, wherein we as head, and you as members, are conjoined and knit together into one body politic. (See above, Ch. 3, pp. 57–58; Lehmberg, *Later Parliaments*, p. 170.)

However, the king was the senior partner, determining the timing and life of each Parliament. So long as he employed an efficient managerial team and maintained a rapport and agreement with the governing class on matters fundamental, he was the chief beneficiary of the novel authority of Parliament. Thus was Henry able to assume a royal supremacy over the Church, eliminate opponents, expropriate Church property, settle religion in 1539, arrange the order of succession, and demand annual taxation at unprecedented levels in 1542–46.

Remarkably acquiescent Parliaments repeatedly delegated legislative power to Henry. In 1532 he was granted a year during which to enforce part or all of the Act denying annates (papal taxes) at his pleasure. In this case Henry was armed with a financial weapon in his diplomatic manoeuvrings with the pope – and this was reasonable enough in an exceptional situation. However, he was also empowered to use proclamation to repeal or revive an Act concerning imported French wines[33] (1534) and to suspend or enforce the Act of Union with Wales (1536). In 1540 he was given *carte blanche* to impose penalties for non-conformity in religion, in 1543 to alter any part of the Act restricting use of the vernacular Bible, without consulting Parliament (a power specifically limited to Henry's lifetime), and two years later to dissolve chantries as and when he chose. Finally the Succession Act named his three children as his heirs but, if they died childless or failed to abide by conditions set down by Henry, he could designate other heirs by his letters patent or his will. Again and again Parliament surrendered to him the power to legislate.[34]

The developments set in motion during the Reformation Parliament were not worked out by its end. The king's related marital and succession problems frequently held the limelight until the Act of Succession, 1544. The Statute of Uses (1536) was modified by the Statute of Wills (1540) (see below, pp. 93–94). The expropriation of Church property, which had begun in 1536, continued with Acts concerning the dissolution of the larger monasteries (1539 and 1540), the order of St John of Jerusalem (1540) and the chantries (1545). The shiring of Wales and its union with England (1536) were also the subject of a number of later Henrician laws, especially that of 1543. Cromwell's bureaucratic sense of efficiency and order, the distinction (implicit in his thinking) between State expenditure and Henry's personal needs, and the dramatic increase in royal revenue spawned further legislation. He began a reorganisation of financial administration which replaced both the medieval supremacy of the exchequer and the informal Yorkist/early Tudor system centred on the king's chamber. Instead there was to be a chain of financial departments, each responsible for one source of revenue. In 1536 an Act established the court of augmentations to handle monastic property and income, and in 1540 the court of wards to administer feudal dues. Cromwellian civil servants continued the process after his death, with the courts of first fruits and tenths (1540) and surveyors of old crown lands (1542). And, like their mentor, they put them on a statutory basis.

This does not exhaust the catalogue of legislative activity. Cromwell was interested in law reform but the process seems to have gained momentum in the early 1540s, when Lord Chancellor Audley regularly presented clutches of Bills on the subject. More important politically was the king's use of Parliament in his search for a national unity which rested on religious conformity and obedience to the supreme head. The breach with Rome, the infiltration of continental heresies and Cromwell's sympathy with (if not patronage of) reformed opinions set in train a religious ferment which deeply troubled Henry. So did the threat of a catholic crusade against schismatic, 'heretical' England. His orthodox catholic response was the notorious Act of Six Articles (1539). Further measures on the diversity of opinions (1540) and the 'advancement of religion' (1543) were statutory expressions of Henry's concern about the religious fracture in society. Religion, more than anything else, emphasises the parliamentary continuity between 1529 and Henry's death.

There were novel features also in the later Henrician Parliaments. After all, they were war Parliaments and money was a paramount consideration. This contrasted with the peace of the 1530s, although even here there is a link. The King was expected to 'live of his own' in peacetime, but the Cromwellian preamble to the subsidy of 1535 justified it solely in terms of the king's 'good governance', not of the needs of war. In the early 1540s Parliament once again cancelled the king's debts and submitted to annual taxation. Henry's capacity to extract almost anything he wanted from Parliament, during and after Cromwell's ascendancy, may be the most significant characteristic of legislation between 1529 and 1547.

On the other hand there were two parties to the legislative process. One of the reasons why Parliaments were so harmonious in a period of crisis is that everyone benefited. They met frequently and, while most important council measures passed, so did many of unofficial origin. The volume of legislation was in itself a tribute to the way in which Crown and governing class collaborated in a mutual satisfaction of needs. In 1529 9 of the 26 Acts concerned trade and industry, 9 reformed the law and 3 were private. Between 1539 and 1545 over 170 public Acts (not all of which were drafted by the council) passed but so did 82 private measures. The many statutes to relieve towns, trades and occupations in distress, to 'amend' highways, pave streets, rebuild decayed boroughs, assist agriculture, protect property rights and benefit all kind, manner and degree of individuals are a register of Parliament's importance to the governing class. So was the time and care lavished on particular Bills which might affect its members. The Act to make Henry VIII heir to the earl of Northumberland (1536) had seven sheets of protective qualifications and provisos added by the lower house, while another concerning the king's bastard Richmond, in 1531, was augmented by twenty-one provisos in the Lords and another fifteen in the Commons.[35] It all smacks of collaboration between king, Lords and Commons, qualified by a scrupulous attention to the preservation of their own interests.

The fundamental difference between the Henrician and Edwardian Parliaments lies in the fact that the latter were summoned not by a formidable adult male king but by aristocratic governors in the name of a minor. Henry VIII's intention, that his son's government should rest on collective responsibility, was rapidly overturned by the duke of Somerset, who became lord protector. Somerset's policies, especially the renewed war with Scotland,[36] his patronage of a moderate protestant Reformation, his mismanagement of royal capital and income, his responses to inflation and a serious and prolonged economic crisis: all had a major impact on the nature of parliamentary business. The failure of his policies, his refusal to listen to advice and his practice of circumventing the council in the decision-making process alienated support. At the end of 1549 he was removed and, under his successor Northumberland, some of his practices were modified or reversed.[37] In other respects there was an essential continuity between the two regimes, especially in the advancement of the Reformation and the continued mismanagement and even plundering of royal capital and income. Inflation and economic crisis were also common denominators. Therefore it is not surprising that economic palliatives, money and religion were the most important and frequent subjects of official Bills and that they consumed much of Parliament's time and labours.

Government during a royal minority, however, laboured under serious disadvantages. Critics and opponents were less reluctant to challenge the legislative proposals of aristocratic regents than those of an adult king. The regents were, in turn, conscious of their vulnerability and expressed it in a number of ways. One concerned money. The 1548/9 session which met on 24 November was called for a subsidy, but there was no official proposal until 1 February. Paget told Somerset that the Commons 'thought it the first thing that should have come in parliament' and members grumbled when Christmas came and nothing had been done. The Protector's procrastination may have resulted from anxiety about the Commons' response to his request for a tax when he and other councillors were benefiting so handsomely from the king's 'generosity'. Northumberland was undoubtedly nervous, and for that very reason, when Edward VI's second Parliament was called for financial aid. When justificatory arguments for a tax were being put together for presentation to the Commons, he strongly advised that no mention should be made of the king's gifts 'in augmenting or advancing of his nobles, or of his benevolence showed to any of his good servants'.[38]

Certainly the Edwardian regimes were unstable and insecure. They were shot through with conflicts of principle (especially in religion), personal enmities and ambitions. Each internecine conflict had its legislative repercussions, with attainders and confirmations thereof for the losers and rewards for the winners. The rebellions of 1549 made Somerset's fall certain, and resulted in a number of security Acts. Yet Northumberland's position was no less vulnerable. Aristocratic regents were trapped in a dilemma: their authority was more open to challenge than that of a ruling king; on the other hand, the formal actions of a minor, even a king, might be questioned later in law. Therefore grace Bills, introduced into Parliament bearing the sign manual, were frequently endorsed by the protector, councillors and sometimes by the king's legal counsel as well.[39]

Edward's minority resulted in a decline in the Crown's legislative authority. Some of the Henrician Acts which had delegated such authority to the king (see above, p. 80) restricted that power to his lifetime, were repealed or replaced, or simply became meaningless as events overtook them. The practice was not continued under Edward and, moreover, the Henrician statute which empowered him to use his prerogative in order to repeal all legislation passed before his twenty-fourth birthday was itself repealed in 1547. The Edwardian Reformation Acts rested unambiguously on 'the authority of Parliament', doubtless because the council wanted the explicit assent of the governing class to the religious changes. Finally, the Treasons Act, the most important Act of Edward's first session (1547), demolished the structure of punitive and deterrent laws erected in the previous reign. All of the new Henrician treasons and felonies were repealed, while surviving treasons now required the evidence of two witnesses, not one. The Act of Six Articles and other laws against heresy were repealed. The Act endowing proclamations with statutory authority (1539), which had engendered much heat in the Commons, was also overturned. Once regarded as an attempt to substitute prerogative authority for statute, it was no more than an attempt to define the scope of proclamations, determine their constitutional authority (which was never intended by the framers of the Act to over-ride statute), and to ensure that they were obeyed. Its repeal was not a challenge to the prerogative but a recognition that the statutory machinery for its enforcement did not work.[40]

The great repealing Act of 1547 was not an example of the protector's liberalism. Parliament made the original Bill more liberal, yet it still retained treason by words and misprision (concealment) of treasons. Furthermore it was politically shortsighted, because it stripped a vulnerable regency of necessary deterrents and coercive weapons. This Act, indeed all the examples cited above, illustrate that while the government still provided a lead in such matters as religion, taxation and the economy, it was less in control of the legislative process.

Naturally Parliaments were none the less called to transact official business, and the council devised programmes and drafted Bills. Money was usually a prime consideration. In 1547 the chantries were dissolved in the optimistic belief that they would finance Somerset's wars. The funds raised thereby were insufficient and so, in 1548, Parliament was recalled to approve a novel indirect tax on sheep, wool and cloth (which yielded far less than the customary taxes). The next session, which met immediately after the protector's fall, repealed the tax and voted a compensatory subsidy. Although financial aid was not sought in 1552, Northumberland called Parliament for that reason a year later.

Most important of all was the enactment of a religious Reformation which produced a plethora of Bills. They were time-consuming and contentious, especially the authorisation of a prayer book in 1548/9. The first Act of Uniformity to sanction its use was preceded by a kind of curtain-raiser in the House of Lords: a public disputation between reforming and conservative bishops with knights and burgesses crowding in to watch the sport. The second prayer book, a more uncompromisingly protestant liturgy, engendered less heat in 1552. Nevertheless, in each session Reformation legislation bit deep into available time. The Bill which permitted communion in both kinds for the laity, for example, went to nine readings in the Lords.

Other official measures reacted against the public commotions of

1549 and sought to provide safeguards for the future. Most notable was the Act of 1549/50 for 'the punishment of unlawful assemblies and risings of the king's subjects', designed to prevent or punish public assemblies which might lead on to riot or rebellion. But there were others, to promote public order, protect property rights, and punish that classic Tudor villain, the vagabond. Vagabondage and the seriousness, even savagery, with which it was treated was a symptom of the economic malaise which gripped the country in the 1540s. Inflation, depression in the cloth industry, and a rising incidence of poverty and unemployment characterised the decade. Economic victims, concerned officials and enlightened observers looked around for solutions and settled for scapegoats: rack-renting landlords, enclosing farmers, parasitic middlemen who produced nothing but bought and sold for a profit, and the idle, undeserving poor. The more discerning might have heeded the wisdom of Sir Thomas Smith who recommended not punitive laws but 'to make those activities which benefited the common weal more profitable than those which harmed it'.[41] No one did. Edwardian Parliaments were deluged with Bills which were a mixture of naive idealism, a total lack of understanding of economic forces, a need to personalise economic hardship by identifying villains, and a defence of governing-class interests.

The old distinction between the official 'liberalism' of Somerset's Parliaments and the reactionary sentiments of Northumberland's no longer holds good. Recent research has convincingly demonstrated that there was no 'commonweal party' pursuing its ideals of social and economic justice in the protectorate Parliaments and that Somerset was not the 'good duke' who, according to A. F. Pollard and W. K. Jordan, patronised and encouraged it.[42] The three major commonweal Bills introduced into the Parliament of 1548/9 were devised by one man, John Hales, and while they may have enjoyed some official sympathy, none of them passed. Hales' Bills were unrealistic: one treated of depopulating enclosures for sheep-runs, a phenomenon which had already passed its peak; another attacked the traditional Tudor bogey of the middleman, and the third was an unenforceable measure to remedy the scarcity of cattle. The landed classes displayed self-interest and commonsense when they prevented their passage. Nevertheless they provoked lengthy debate and some controversy before they were aborted.[43]

If the commonweal measures were not official, government Bills were none the less numerous and occupied much of Parliament's time. However, so did genuinely private legislation, which still ran at the high level of the late Henrician Parliaments. In the 1552 session, for example, more than two-thirds of the 37 Acts and three-fifths of the 81 abortive Bills were concerned with localities, particular economic interests and individuals. Other measures were more general in scope, touching on such matters as religion and the clergy, agrarian reform, administrative abuses, crime and trade – but most of these too were put in by private members and not by the council.

The majority of unofficial Bills failed to pass because they were poorly drafted, aroused the opposition of rival interests or the Crown, or just ran out of time. But it was not for want of trying and more and more boroughs, economic interests and occupations were organising themselves to promote beneficial legislation. As in Henry's reign, London had the most organised and continuous pressure group, with increasingly sophisticated lobbying techniques.[44] If its successes were few, this was partly because it easily aroused the fear and opposition of smaller cities and towns. Nevertheless they too were organising themselves, presenting petitions, hiring agents, draftsmen and promoters and giving gratuities to parliamentary officials: Exeter sought parliamentary help to finance a new channel to the sea; in 1547 the burgesses of King's Lynn and Coventry vigorously opposed the inclusion of guild lands in the Bill to dissolve the chantries, because these financed their churches, and caused such a parliamentary stir that the council feared the whole Bill might be dashed. It took them aside and promised them that, if they 'meddled no further', the king would regrant their guild lands to them. York, Chester and many other towns were equally active.[45] The proportion of Parliament's time devoted to parochial and personal matters was considerable and growing.

The pressure of business can be illustrated in a simple quantitative way. The Edwardian Parliaments enacted 166 statutes (with a sessional average of thirty-three) but altogether they considered 473 Bills, each of which had at least a literal first 'reading'. Although their productivity level marked a significant decline from the late Henrician sessional average of forty-three Acts, they were none the less handling a formidable volume of business. Apart from the king's general pardons, mere formalities which often passed on a single reading, straightforward official Bills (such as the attainders and confirmations thereof, the clerical subsidies and 24 restorations in blood) went to three readings in each house. More complex or contentious government measures might have four, five, or even six readings. When we consider that the Edwardian Commons met on just under 300 mornings and eight afternoons, during which time it initiated 107 Acts and considered another 301 Bills (all of which had to be read aloud at the first reading) it was an impressive performance. Yet there were already ominous signs for the future. As Parliament's popularity grew after the 1530s, it became clogged with business and many of its Bills – 65 per cent in Edward's reign – failed to become law.

Within the period 1529–53 the legislative role of the two houses fluctuated dramatically, with only one constant. The Commons had a much larger and expanding membership which represented most of the political nation, whereas the Lords was small, diminishing and the members represented no-one but themselves. Consequently the lower house handled many more Bills. In Edward VI's reign it initiated 281 Bills and altogether scrutinised 408. The comparable figures for the Lords are 192 and 284. The dramatic fluctuations occurred in the initiating roles of the two chambers. It has already been observed that the initiating and proprietary house was *usually* the major formative influence on the final Bill. Therefore the house which began more successful Bills was the more productive and important one.

Of course this is a crude measure of relative significance – all Acts were not equal: some were formalities, whereas others were lengthy, technically complex and contentious. However, even when qualitative glosses are applied to such simple quantitative measurements, the results are roughly the same. During the Reformation Parliament the Commons enjoyed the Crown's confidence and superseded the Lords as the chief initiator. It began 103 of the 193 Acts, including most of the more important government measures.[46] In the later Henrician Parliaments, however, roles were reversed, when 183 Acts commenced in the Lords and only 127 in the nether house. The catalyst of change was, once again, the Crown, which now chose to place its major Bills there as well as a string of attainders and Audley's law reforms. The legislative pendulum had swung back to the Lords, where it was to remain until 1553. Almost two-thirds (64 per cent) of Edwardian Acts began there, including nearly all of the Reformation measures.[47]

Two considerations determined the relative importance of each house. One was the location of opposition and the other was the placement of the Crown's parliamentary manager. In the Reformation Parliament the lords spiritual and conservative peers were the anticipated threat to royal policies. Therefore it was political commonsense for Henry to ally with the anti-clerical lower house – a Bill was more likely to pass a hostile chamber when the other had already endorsed it. Furthermore, as Cromwell sat in the Commons, it was natural that he should have promoted there the more important official Bills, which he or his colleagues had drafted. However, on the last day of the 1536 Parliament he took his seat in the Lords. In 1539 and 1540 (until he was arrested) he was first in precedence there, as the supreme head's vicegerent. From this point on, major government Bills (except subsidies) started in the Lords.

Cromwell's removal in 1540 made no difference. Most of the important politicians, faction leaders, councillors and parliamentary managers sat in the Lords: the conservatives (Norfolk and Gardiner), the new men (Hertford and Lisle), and the ennobled lawyers and bureaucrats (Audley, Paulet and Wriothesley). So did the bishops and it was natural that, as the theological experts, they should be consulted early on Bills of religion. In any case the abbots had gone, the reformers Latimer and Shaxton had resigned, and the later Henrician appointments were orthodox catholics or simply pliant men eager to please. Conservative peers like Exeter and Montague had been eliminated. Men like Chancellor Audley and Norfolk had succeeded Cromwell as the king's parliamentary managers. Thus had the Lords become docile and obedient, even though at court some of its members were engaged in bitter faction fights. For all these reasons Henry now looked to the Lords to advance his causes. Of course each house had its own specialities: the Commons initiated lay taxation and the great majority of private Bills, whereas clerical subsidies and most attainders and restitutions commenced in the Lords. Yet there is no doubt that in 1539/40 the operative centre of Parliament shifted to the upper house.

Aristocratic Edwardian government confirmed this trend. An enlarged council, dominated by peers, their allies and clients and afforced by a few bishops, constituted a formidable front bench in the Lords. The prelates were crucial in the scrutiny and promotion of Reformation measures, while the legal assistants examined grace Bills and any measures which might touch the royal prerogative.[48] In these circumstances it was natural for the government to direct its parliamentary operations through the Lords. The conservative bishops might resist the protestant Reformation, the Commons could display flashes of independence and Edward's governors were apprehensive about asking for taxes; nevertheless Edwardian Parliaments and legislation were dominated by nobles who controlled both the council and the upper house.

THE POLITICS OF PARLIAMENT

The Reformation Parliament was a momentous event. On the Crown's initiative it carried through revolutionary changes which affected every one of the king's subjects. There was an atmosphere of crisis, tensions ran high and it is not surprising that some men criticised and even opposed the direction in which the king was moving. Sooner or later such criticism and opposition were bound to surface in Parliament, because it was the instrument of the 'Henrician Revolution'. For the first time there appeared an organised opposition group, the ramifications of which were probably greater than the evidence admits. The extra-parliamentary managers were Eustace Chapuys, the ambassador of Catherine of Aragon's nephew, Charles V, and some of her chaplains. Inside Parliament they could look to shocked conservatives like the earl of Shrewsbury and Lord Darcy, papal supporters and men of principle such as Bishop Fisher (Rochester) and Tunstal and a number of elected burgesses. They may have included members of the 'More circle' because, while Sir Thomas was as usual the equivocal, subtle and discreet lawyer, he lent support of some kind. The 'Aragonese faction', as Elton calls it, could have expected a sympathetic response from many quarters: convocation and the bishops and abbots in the Lords who were the natural defenders of ecclesiastical liberties and papal supremacy; regional conservatism, especially in the north, and court opposition to both Cromwell and the Boleyn faction. Furthermore, Catherine of Aragon was very popular whereas Anne Boleyn was not, and many regarded Mary as Henry's legitimate heir. Sir George Throckmorton, knight for Warwickshire, voiced these grievances in the Commons when he argued against the annulment and attacks on papal authority. He had secret discussions with Thomas More and Bishop Fisher and frequent meetings with other disgruntled members of the Commons at a tavern, the Queen's Head, where they discussed Parliament matters.[49]

Opposition, however, was not to be tolerated for long. An anti-clerical, anti-papal (yet still orthodox catholic) laity in both houses was essentially united with the king in pursuit of clerical abuses, the reduction of clerical privilege, the humiliation of the clergy and their submission to the king. This was achieved in 1531–32. Within the next two years the king had obtained his annulment and the total rejection of papal authority, and in 1536 the expropriation of Church property began with the dissolution of the lesser monasteries. Henry's policies, inspired by Cromwell, had been rammed through, apparently to a successful conclusion. Some, such as More and Fisher, paid for their opposition with their lives. Others got off more lightly: Bishop Gardiner of Winchester was relieved of his office of secretary and exiled in his bishopric. On one occasion Tunstal was ordered back home by the king, when he was en route to Westminster to attend Parliament,[50] while a chastened Throckmorton wrote to Cromwell as the 1534 session approached, promising to take his advice to 'stay at home and meddle little in politics'.[51]

The most important parliamentary victim of the Crown's success was the clergy. The brief resistance of the Canterbury convocation and the bishops in the Lords ended in collapse and abject surrender in 1532–33. Thereafter convocation was of little account to Parliament, while the abbots were removed from the Lords in 1539–40 and the lords spiritual were reduced to a permanent minority of bishops. Furthermore it was a divided and demoralised minority. Gradually, under the royal supremacy of Henry VIII and his son, the episcopal bench divided into three groups: reformers (whose natural leader was Thomas Cranmer); conservatives (headed by Gardiner, Bonner, Day, Heath and Tunstal until, one by one, they were deprived); and time-servers, mostly ex-abbots, such as John Chambers (Peterborough), Robert King (Oxford) and John Salcot (Salisbury). They were a beleaguered garrison, isolated by the anti-clerical temper of society, troubled by the divisive effects of new heresies and subject to the demands of a resident supreme head who was also their king. Yet they could offer no united stand in self-defence but instead fought among themselves. As the Reformation proceeded they were stripped of their pretensions, privileges, power, wealth and influence in secular government. The clergy's bureaucratic role in government rapidly diminished as a literate laity displaced them, though the new men, versed in the linguistic, legal and administrative skills which the Renaissance State required, also displaced the old-fashioned, blinkered nobles of ancient lineage. Another source of conflict was being created.

As the prestige of the clergy declined the attractions of a career in the Church shrank dramatically. Whereas many pre-Reformation bishops had noble connections, most of the new ones were of meaner social origins and status and this social separateness and inferiority probably reinforced the anti-clericalism of the lords temporal in Parliament. When the bishops were reduced to mere civil servants by the Edwardian council's requirement that they obtain letters patent of reappointment like any other official, their last shreds of autonomy vanished. Thereafter they were treated in a cavalier manner and even with contempt, as when Northumberland excoriated, abused and threatened Cranmer and his fellows in the 1553 Parliament. The theological expertise of the upper clergy was indispensable during the Reformation. They were educationally superior to any other group in Parliament; they attended regularly and busied themselves in all kinds of legislation. Nevertheless the lords spiritual became a divided and politically subordinate minority in the upper house.

The clergy was a special case, a victim of the Reformation. In the same way the Aragonese faction was an unusual phenomenon. The characteristic of the Reformation Parliament was consensus politics and it displayed a remarkable degree of agreement and co-operation in a period of acute crisis. On the other hand developments during its life fuelled the fires of new conflicts. The rise of new men aroused the hostility of old noble families. The break with Rome, together with the infiltration of continental protestantism, introduced an ideological conflict between reformers and conservatives. At first such antagonisms were muted or concealed in public and Parliament, as was illustrated in the new Parliament of 1536, which met only three weeks after Anne Boleyn's execution. Her fall was in part the consequence of a bitter faction fight at court,[52] yet the only parliamentary expressions of this conflict were the Acts which cleaned up the mess of the second royal marriage and arranged the succession through the offspring of the third.

Between the Parliaments of 1536 and 1539 fresh political lines were being drawn, not just between court factions but also between opposing religious positions. This doctrinal polarisation injected into the normal flexible, competitive Henrician politics a novel, inflexible, doctrinaire quality. Of course power politics and personal rivalries remained important: the Howards detested Cromwell and the

Seymours as *nouveaux*; Gardiner and Norfolk resented their exclusion from the king's inner counsels by Cromwell and the way he kept them from court for much of the time. Such frustrations of the power-hungry were transformed into something more deadly by ideological conflict. In 1539 they seized the opportunity of a new Parliament to score victories over Cromwell and the reformed religion which he patronised.

Henry was deeply disturbed by public unrest and commotions over religion. They were particularly menacing to a State which lacked the coercive and surveillance machinery of its modern counterpart. Therefore one of the purposes of the new Parliament was to reduce the realm to order and conformity in religion. Moreover, the occasion of a new Parliament brought Gardiner and Norfolk back to court and enabled them to seize the initiative from Cromwell. This was achieved not by an open confrontation in Parliament but by skilful manoeuvring which placed him at a disadvantage. He had promised the king the most 'tractable' Parliament he had ever had, but it certainly was not for Cromwell. [The Commons' elected speaker, Sir Nicholas Hare, was Norfolk's client.] Choosing an occasion when Cromwell was absent from Parliament, Lord Chancellor Audley introduced what turned out to be the crucial business of the session. He declared that it was the king's wish to enact a law which would end the religious fracture in society. It was natural to recommend this first to the Lords, where the theological experts sat. The house immediately responded by appointing a committee, but it seems to have taken no action and so Norfolk, who must have known that the king was vigorously asserting his natural religious conservatism, seized the initiative. He acted as Henry's spokesman and, in effect, superseded the committee. He put to the house six questions on crucial points of doctrine and a fortnight later instructed it to draw a penal law for failure to conform to this corpus of catholic dogma.

This brought the underlying religious conflict boiling to the surface, with Gardiner, Tunstal and other conservatives engaged in angry exchanges with Cranmer, Latimer and their fellow reformers. Henry played an active part in the proceedings, amending the draft of the six articles, presiding over Lords' debates on the Bill and 'confounding' the reformers with his learning. When a peer wrote that all of the lords temporal were of one opinion, what he meant was that they quickly accommodated themselves to the king's opinions.[53] Meanwhile Cromwell had been left stranded by events. Nevertheless, in Parliament his contest with the Gardiner/Norfolk faction remained decently veiled by the religious issue.

In the following year Cromwell fell a victim to Gardiner and Norfolk, but even then the veil was not torn away. He was arrested during the parliamentary session and condemned, but not by a trial which might have publicly exposed the divisions within court and council. Instead he was convicted by an Act of attainder which was a hotchpotch of derogatory comment, invention, charges of administrative initiative and other 'offences' which were less than treasonable, and accusations of heresy. The references to him as a person of 'as poor and low degree as few be within this your realm' suggest proud Norfolk's hand, while the charges of heresy may claim Gardiner's authorship. However, there is no evidence that they spoke out against him during the attainder's passage through the Lords. On the other hand both houses passed it without a hitch. So the fiction of parliamentary harmony under a benevolent king was maintained and Cromwell was condemned as a base-born miscreant who had abused Henry's generosity and trust.

Cromwell had no successor as chief minister. Instead, competing factions vied for influence and, when it became evident that Henry would not survive his son's minority, for control of government in the next reign. They also fought for a religious principle. Late Henrician faction politics are, as a consequence, complex and often confusing. The nucleus of a Tudor faction was a kinship-connection which incorporated all kinds of territorial, business, patron-client and political associations. It lacked cohesion, organisation and permanence and its membership was fluid. The division between reformer and conservative may have endowed factions with a certain ideological stiffening, but court politics, office-hunting and county rivalries were often more important. So were social incalculables like the outrage of peers of ancient pedigree, shunted aside by the brash self-confidence of new men. Any examination of late Henrician faction politics must take into account all of these considerations. After Cromwell's fall the conservative faction held sway, but in 1543/4 the initiative began to move back to the reformers and thereafter the process gathered momentum. However, behind the common religious front of the reformers were the competitive politics of such factions as the Seymour group and the Parr-Herbert interest.[54]

This complex faction competition had its parliamentary expressions, although it was still carefully concealed in the victors' statutes and couched in the language of obedient and loving subjects. Thus the attainder of Henry's fifth wife and Norfolk's niece, Catherine Howard, was a major blow to the duke's faction in 1542, while in contrast the Act which, in the following year, restricted the use of the vernacular Bible, was a triumph for the conservatives. Thereafter Henry's confidence in them faded, especially when they tried to bring down his last wife, Catherine Parr, and his archbishop, Thomas Cranmer, on charges of heresy. Gardiner was excluded from the council for his refusal to agree to a property transaction with the Crown. Finally, as Henry lay dying, Norfolk's son was executed and the duke was attainted by statute. In the king's absence it received the royal assent, in mid-session, from royal commissioners who included two of Norfolk's chief antagonists, the earl of Hertford and John Lord Russell. At the end of the reign this was the solitary hint of the frenzied faction conflict at court and even then it was clothed in the decent garb of due parliamentary process.

In the last year or two of his reign, Henry was losing control. Until then, however, he was the master politician, playing factions off against each other and retaining the initiative. He was an old and experienced king, self-confident to the point of being cavalier with his Parliaments. He attended Lords' debates, lectured deputations from the Commons, and even personally handed a Bill into the lower house. He used letters patent to authorise Catherine Howard's attainder and to give his assent to Bills in 1544 when he was kept away by 'some urgent business requiring dispatch'. Henry's parliamentary role was unique. He imposed enormous demands which sometimes strained, but never broke, the bonds of loyalty.

Much of Henry's success in the 1530s must be attributed to Cromwell, but in one matter the king was the activating force throughout and it illustrates well the nature of his relationship with the governing class in Parliament. This was a complex issue which concerned feudal dues, 'uses' (or trusts) and wills and touched the most important concerns of the governing class. Feudal 'incidents' (payments) were the financial survival of feudalism. Most of them were death duties, payable when a landowner (whose ancestors had held land from the Crown by knight service) died and his heir inherited. A rapid succession of deaths could financially cripple a family. Primogeniture – the descent of property to the eldest son or nearest relative – posed another problem for the landed class. It meant that a landowner could not provide for other relatives and servants, especially as bequests of land by will were not recognised by common law. The answer lay in the 'use', whereby a landowner surrendered legal ownership of his property to a body of trustees who administered it on his behalf and, after his death, to the use of his heir and other beneficiaries named by him – in effect a will. The 'use' had an additional advantage: the trust never died and so, as most feudal dues were death duties, they were evaded.

More and more landowners resorted to the 'use'. By 1529, however, the king's finances were in a parlous state and he was determined to increase the yield from existing sources, including feudal dues. At first he was moderate, even generous. In that year he reached an agreement with the peers in Parliament, whereby he surrendered two-thirds of his legitimate dues in return for a guarantee of the remaining third. Yet in 1532 the Commons stoutly resisted a Bill incorporating these terms. Henry warned the house that he would 'search out the extremity of the law' if opposition continued. When it did, he was as good as his word. When Lord Dacre of the South died in 1533, Henry provoked a test case to challenge the validity of uses, browbeat the judges and secured a favourable verdict.

The result was simple but devastating. Dacre's will, which his trustees would have carried out, was declared invalid. So in effect were all trusts, wills and family settlements. Armed with this judicial verdict Henry was able to push through Parliament the Statute of Uses of 1536: it denied the right to bequeath land by will; it recognised the use but declared the beneficiary (who eventually died), not the trustees, to be the legal owner; and it entitled the king to all, not one-third, of his feudal dues. This was particularly important because the dissolution of the monasteries was already under way and it was intended that all grants and sales of monastic property should be liable to feudal incidents. However, the king's victory rebounded, because the Statute of Uses was one of the causes of the Pilgrimage of Grace (1536), the most serious Tudor rebellion. Eventually Henry bowed to governing-class discontent. In 1540 the Statute of Wills declared the validity of uses, whereby property could be bequeathed by wills administered by trustees and the king's feudal rights were restricted to one-third of the lands. The whole episode is an important example of the interplay of royal and governing-class interests through Parliament and, ultimately, the need to reconcile them by some kind of compromise.[55]

Once the controlling hand of Henry VIII was removed, faction conflict at court was freed from its former constraints and became a feature of the Edwardian Parliaments. In November 1547 the conservatives' leader, Stephen Gardiner, wrote from prison:

> If it should be of any man through policy to keep me from the Parliament, it were good to be remembered whether mine absence from the upper house, with the absence of those I have used to name in the nether house, will not engender more cause of objection, if opportunity serve hereafter, than my presence with such as I should appoint were there.

Although, on another occasion, he denied that there existed 'Winchester's faction, as some term it' this is both a clear admission that it did and a threat that he would use it.[56] His continued exclusion from Parliament was political commonsense because there can be no doubt that he would have organised resistance to the Edwardian Reformation in both houses.

The other conservative bishops turned up regularly. Ten of them courageously defended the catholic position during the prayer book debate in the parliament house in December 1548, despite the harrying tactics of the earl of Warwick and the petty sniping of Sir Thomas Smith, both of whom attended this public disputation. It revealed the unbridgeable gulf between conservatives, such as Bonner, Day, Heath, Reppes (Norwich), and Tunstal, and the more outspoken reformers, Goodrich (Ely), Holbeach (Lincoln) and Ridley (Rochester). Although the former were on the defensive and out of favour, they resisted each step in the Edwardian Reformation. Six voted against the dissolution of the chantries and five against communion in both kinds for the laity (in 1547). Eight dissented when the first prayer book was passed and seven could not accept clerical marriage (1548/9). Gradually deprivations thinned their ranks and only two voted against the second prayer book in 1552. However, they did not stand alone. The earl of Derby later recalled that he, Windsor, Dacre and Stourton 'did not consent to those acts, and that the nay of them four would be seen, so long as the parliament house stood',[57] while Arundel and Southampton attempted a conservative counter-coup in 1549–50. It is difficult to believe that these ardent catholics did not use their clients in the Commons to defend a point of principle. Who, for example, inspired the lower house to obstruct the Bill attainting Tunstal for misprision in 1552, because Northumberland would not allow him and his accusers to be heard at the bar of the house?

There is evidence enough of the way in which the governing clique used both houses to further their ambitions and bring down their rivals. The protector's brother, Thomas Lord Seymour, was consumed with envy and ambition. He turned to Parliament to advance his causes and naturally he sought support in both houses. He 'had the names of all the Lords, and totted them, whom he thought he might have to his purpose, to labour them'. Several, including Dorset, Northampton, Southampton and Rutland, were canvassed for their voices. With such allies he intended to propose to the upper house that he should be made Edward's governor. He also intended to enter the Commons and there, with his 'adherents before prepared', to cause a tumult. When the council ordered his arrest during the session of 1548/9, he was charged with 'having in both the same houses laboured, stirred, and moved a number of persons to take part and join with him in such things as he would set forth and enterprise, whereby he thought to breed such an uproar and sedition as well in the said court as in the whole realm'. These were not fabricated charges. Seymour admitted that, if his ambitions were frustrated, 'I will make the blackest Parliament that ever was in England'. In the competitive, often vicious, cut-throat politics of Edwardian England even aristocratic madcaps knew that it was necessary to manipulate both houses if they were to carry out their designs.[58]

Local and personal rivalries, family conflicts and class prejudices also surfaced in Parliament and, if peers were involved, they were just as willing to employ their clients in the Commons to carry the attack to their enemies. The classic case is that of Thomas, first Lord Wharton. His ennoblement in 1544 was part of Henry VIII's policy of undermining the regional authority of the old marcher families, in particular the Cliffords, Dacres, Nevilles and Percies. Their servants and clients were seduced from their traditional allegiance by gifts of land, offices and, in Wharton's case, a barony, whereby they became the king's fee'd men. For generations Whartons had been Clifford stewards; now Thomas suddenly emerged as a rival to the earl of Cumberland and

Lord Dacre. The result was constant, sometimes violent, feuding which might be carried over into Parliament. In January 1549 Richard Musgrave introduced a Bill to abolish the office of hereditary sheriff, which Cumberland held in the county of Westmorland. Thomas Jolye, Cumberland's client, wrote to him that the author of the Bill was unquestionably Wharton. The two Yorkshire knights, 'with so many of your lordship's friends' had resisted it. Meanwhile Jolye busied himself in Cumberland's defence, securing the support of seven Commons' members to oppose it and Lord Dacre's promise to do so if it reached the Lords.[59] This episode reveals that what really mattered was the latticework of relationships between Lords and Commons and not their formal division into two separate chambers. Political bosses – Dudleys, Herberts, Howards, Seymours and bishops like Gardiner – probably engaged in similar bicameral politicking.

In Edward's reign the focal point of Parliament was the Lords, where the aristocratic governing cliques sat and most important offical Bills began. Its legal assistants could advise on points of law and the bishops could frame or refine Bills on religion. Nevertheless, Parliament was a microcosm of the political nation. It did not consist of competing estates or chambers with conflicting interests but of one homogeneous governing class, artificially separated into two houses.[60] Even during religious conflict and aristocratic tussles, the essence was a desire for co-operation, the search for compromise when disagreement occurred and a preference for consensus politics. Conflict occurred between groups within the governing class rather than between houses.

REFERENCES AND NOTES

1. Lehmberg, *Reformation Parliament*, p. 79.
2. Ibid., p. 109.
3. Elton, *Reform and Reformation*, pp. 342–3.
4. In 1551 he was deprived and so became ineligible.
5. For example, Bonner, Gardiner, Tunstal and Veysey.
6. J. A. Muller (ed.) *The Letters of Stephen Gardiner* [*Gardiner's Letters*], Cambridge, 1933, p. 424.
7. Graves, *Mid-Tudor Lords*, pp. 98–9.
8. Muller, *Gardiner's Letters*, pp. 410, 443.
9. Miller, 'Attendance', 330.
10. Ibid., p. 344.
11. Bray, Hussey, Pole (Lord Montague), Tailboys, Wentworth and Windsor.
12. Graves, *Mid-Tudor Lords*, pp. 10–11.
13. Ibid., p. 206; Lehmberg, *Reformation Parliament*, p. 37 n. 1.
14. Elton, *Tudor Constitution* (1982), p. 248.

15. Lehmberg, *Reformation Parliament*, pp. 31–5.
16. Ibid., pp. 140–41.
17. *Journals of the House of Commons* [hereafter *C.J.*], I (1547–1628), London, 1803, p. 21.
18. Ibid., 5–8, 11, 16, 18–19.
19. Miller, 'Attendance', 331–5.
20. Ibid., 330, 338–43; Lehmberg, *Reformation Parliament*, 58–60.
21. Miller, 'Attendance', 335.
22. Ibid., 337.
23. Lehmberg, *Later Parliaments*, pp. 89, 140–41, 174, 191, 218.
24. Graves, *Mid-Tudor Lords*, p. 90.
25. Elton, *Reform and Reformation*, pp. 176–8; Lehmberg, *Reformation Parliament*, pp. 166–9, 174–5.
26. Elton, *Reform and Reformation*, pp. 177–8.
27. The first year's income was paid to the Crown by a new appointee to a Church living and thereafter 10 per cent annually.
28. Elton, *Tudor Constitution* (1982), pp. 242–3; Sylvester and Harding, *Two Early Tudor Lives*, p. 248.
29. Lehmberg, *Reformation Parliament*, pp. 94–9, 158 n. 5, 230–35, 243–4, 250–53. His argument, that the volume of private legislation in 1536 was not matched by any Elizabethan session, rests upon Acts, not abortive bills which, without a Commons' journal, cannot be charted accurately.
30. Ibid., pp. 185–9.
31. Lehmberg, *Later Parliaments*, pp. 256–7.
32. Ibid., p. 256; Miller, 'London and Parliament', 145–6.
33. Lehmberg, *Reformation Parliament*, pp. 211–12.
34. Ibid., *Later Parliaments*, pp. 121, 186–8, 193–4, 221–2; Elton, *Reform and Reformation*, p. 204.
35. Lehmberg, *Reformation Parliament*, pp. 126, 244.
36. His attempt to control Scotland with fixed, permanent garrisons was ineffective and very expensive. M. L. Bush, *The Government Policy of Protector Somerset*, London, 1975, pp. 12–39; D. E. Hoak, *The King's Council in the Reign of Edward VI*, Cambridge, 1976, pp. 168–70.
37. Ibid., pp. 95–104, 142–4, 167–90, 261–2.
38. Graves, *Mid-Tudor Lords*, p. 147; P.R.O., S.P. 10/18/6.
39. Graves, *Mid-Tudor Lords*, pp. 135–7.
40. Elton, *Tudor Constitution* (1982), pp. 21–3; ibid., *Reform and Reformation*, pp. 285–6.
41. G. R. Elton, 'Reform and the "commonwealth-men" of Edward VI's reign' ['Reform and the commonwealth-men'], in P. Clark, A. G. R. Smith, N. Tyacke (eds), *The English Commonwealth, 1547–1640*, Leicester, 1979, p. 37.
42. A. F. Pollard, *England under Protector Somerset*, London, 1900; W. K. Jordan, *Edward VI: The Young King. The Protectorship of the Duke of Somerset*, London, 1968. Bush, Hoak, Elton and others have demolished Somerset's liberal image and exposed the myth of a commonwealth party.
43. Elton, 'Reform and the commonwealth-men', 35–6.
44. See Miller, 'London and Parliament', passim.

45. Graves, *Mid-Tudor Lords*, p. 182; *H.P.T.*, 1509–1558, I, 302; ibid., II, 379; ibid., III, 138, 345.
46. Lehmberg, *Later Parliaments*, p. 257.
47. Graves, *Mid-Tudor Lords*, pp. 178–9, 229.
48. For the continued importance of the legal assistants, see ibid., pp. 125–40.
49. Elton, *Reform and Reformation*, pp. 121–2; *H.P.T.*, 1509–1558, III, 452–4.
50. Miller, 'Attendance', 331–3.
51. *H.P.T.*, 1509–1558, III, 453.
52. Elton, *Reform and Reformation*, pp. 250–4.
53. Ibid., pp. 283–4, 286–8; J. J. Scarisbrick, *Henry VIII*, London, 1970, pp. 408–10.
54. Lehmberg, *Later Parliaments*, pp. 211–17; Elton, *Reform and Reformation*, p. 329; *H.P.T.*, 1509–1558, passim; Miller, 'Lords and Commons: Relations', 13–24.
55. E. W. Ives, 'The Genesis of the Statute of Uses', *E.H.R.*, lxxxii (1967), 673–97; Lehmberg, *Reformation Parliament*, pp. 133–4, 141, 235–8, 252; ibid., *Later Parliaments*, pp. 98–9; Elton, *Reform and Reformation*, pp. 147–8.
56. Muller, *Gardiner's Letters*, pp. 405, 424.
57. Graves, *Mid-Tudor Lords*, p. 89; J. Pratt (ed.), *The Acts and Monuments of John Foxe*, 8 vols, London, 1870, Vol. VII, p. 45.
58. Graves, *Mid-Tudor Lords*, pp. 88–9.
59. *H.P.T.*, 1509–1558, I, 358; ibid., II, 115, 450.
60. See Miller, 'Lords and Commons: Relations', passim.

Chapter five

THE REFORMATION PARLIAMENTS II, 1553–1558: THE YEARS OF CHANGE

In July 1553 the principle of legitimacy triumphed. Nobles and gentry flocked to Mary Tudor and the duke of Northumberland's inept attempt to divert the succession to Jane Grey collapsed. Whether or not Mary saw this as an endorsement of her catholicism as well as of Henry VIII's will, there is no doubt that she had a clearly defined programme: to restore the catholic faith and to re-unite England with Rome. Within eighteen months a combination of circumstances caused her both to enlarge and to modify that programme. By October 1553 she was emotionally committed to marriage with Philip of Spain. Protestant provocations and Sir Thomas Wyatt's rebellion replaced her initial gestures of moderation with a hard-line resolve to proceed against heretics – hence the need for heresy laws, empowering the State to burn obdurate protestants. Furthermore, at the end of 1554, she had to concede that the governing class would not countenance the restoration of secularised lands to the Church. Instead she was forced to remain content with the refoundation of a few religious houses and the return of clerical taxes – first fruits and tenths – to the papacy.

Political circumstances also dictated how Mary's programme was to be implemented. The Henrician and Edwardian alterations in Church government and religion had been enacted in statute and they could only be reversed in the same way. This fact determined the parliamentary history of the reign and, at the same time, divided it neatly into two phases. The first four Parliaments fulfilled – on parchment at least – most of the queen's ambitions. The two sessions of the 1558 assembly were of a different kind. They were war Parliaments, summoned to deal with the consequences of England's involvement in King Philip's war with France, above all the loss of Calais. However, the Parliaments of 1553–55 were not rehearsed steps in the inexorable execution of some kind of master plan. Mary's parliamentary time-table was affected and modified by a number of incalculable influences: diplomatic negotiations with the Habsburgs; governing-class responses to her policies; the impact of court faction politics; and the strength of protestant resistance. Unpredictable events, such as Wyatt's rebellion, and unforeseen obstacles, like the intransigence of the papal legate, Cardinal Pole, over the fate of secularised Church property, further complicated and delayed proceedings. As always, Tudor government proceeded in an *ad hoc* manner, dealing with crises as they arose and tempering its policies and objectives to meet the mood and opinions of the political nation.

MEMBERSHIP

Whereas the Commons continued to expand (from 377 to 400), the eligible bishops and peers fluctuated between 65 and 76 and settled at 72 in November 1558. The variations in size and composition of the lords temporal (who comprised more than two-thirds of the upper house) depended on the usual processes of attrition and recruitment, which more or less balanced themselves out in Mary's reign. While not important numerically, these changes were certainly politically significant. Nearly all of the losses were Edwardians, protestants, or critics of Mary's regime, whereas, except for Howard (ennobled when he became lord admiral) and Devon (a political miscalculation), the new creations were loyal Marians and catholics. Norfolk (released from the Tower) and the restored earl of Northumberland were powerful regional magnates with clients in the Commons. This was probably not an attempt to pack the Lords with royal creatures, but to reward loyalty, service and suffering in the catholic cause.

The queen also respected the peers' right to be summoned. Members were disabled only for the usual unexceptional reasons, such as minority, poverty, and the priorities of royal service. The delinquents implicated in Northumberland's treason – even Suffolk – were pardoned and released in time to attend part or all of Mary's first Parliament. Lord Cobham went to the Tower in February 1554 for his complicity in Wyatt's rebellion, yet he was released in time to attend her second Parliament. There was only one exception to her scrupulous observance of peers' parliamentary rights: the earl of Devon had been the figurehead of Wyatt's anti-Spanish rebellion and his presence in the Lords might spark off a xenophobic resistance to Mary's pending marriage. His imprisonment (February 1554–April 1555) and exile abroad (May 1555–September 1556) were designed specifically to exclude him from Parliament.

Mary was more cavalier in her treatment of the bishops. Although she deplored the title of supreme head of the Church, she sometimes acted as if she was one, restoring Durham and its bishop, Tunstal (months before parliamentary ratification), ending the amalgamation of Worcester and Gloucester, depriving eleven protestant bishops (for clerical marriage, heresy, or because, as Edwardian appointees, they had no right to office), automatically restoring Henrician conservatives (e.g. Bonner, Day, Gardiner, Heath, and Veysey), and filling the other vacancies with loyal catholics. All this had little to do with parliamentary management. A purge was inevitable because a catholic Church required reliable catholic bishops. Similarly the brief re-appearance of two regulars – an abbot and a prior – in 1558 expressed Mary's catholicism, not her desire to pack the Lords. On the other hand, her timing may have been influenced by parliamentary consider-ations. On 1 April, literally on the eve of her second Parliament, six new bishops were consecrated; so were two more, just a week after the commencement of her third.

ATTENDANCE

Mary came nearer to playing the 'numbers game' than any other Tudor, especially in the preparations for her second Parliament. Yet for most of the time she observed the characteristic concentration on quality, by strengthening the official leadership and selectively excising the possible foci of opposition (such as Devon). This meant concentrat-ing her attention on the Lords' membership. Her managerial prep-arations for the Commons were confined to circular letters to sheriffs (ordering the election of resident, 'wise, grave and Catholic' mem-bers),[1] the return of prominent royal servants, and indirect electoral influence through reliable supporters. She must have been of the same opinion as the imperial ambassador, Simon Renard, when he wrote that 'if the nobles are conciliated . . . there will be no need to fear the people'.[2] The key to the effective management of Parliament was a reliable House of Lords.

The Crown might respect the right of bishops and peers to receive their writs of summons, but it was another matter to ensure that they observed their duty to attend and apply themselves diligently to parliamentary business. Endemic absenteeism continued to be a plague upon both houses. The Commons' journal records divisions in which those present fluctuated between 321 and 193.[3] These figures reflected both the casual attitude of members who remained in West-minster and London and the early departure of others for home. Some obtained the speaker's licence to leave on royal service or because of sickness or 'great Business'. However, many did not and the speaker continued to respond with orders for the roll of members to be 'called'.[4] In November 1558 the house even debated the problem of absentees afflicted with illness, before resolving 'That such Burgesses as be sick, shall not take Damage by their Absence during their Sickness, for their Attendance in this House'.[5] Despite one member's proposal that they should be replaced, the house stuck to its guns. Indeed it showed every consideration to absentees. Not so the government, however, especially when such absences were believed to be a political protest against royal policies (see below p. 11).

The Lords' performance did not differ dramatically from that of the two previous reigns. As indicated in the table opposite, a majority of members put in an appearance while 'regulars', who shouldered the main burden of business, constituted a much smaller group. The house always had its parliamentary 'backwoodsmen', the aged, sick, those comfortably ensconced in distant dioceses or estates, the politically uninterested and parochially-minded. If they turned up at all they did so infrequently. The cumulative effect of sessional absenteeism and irregular attendance significantly reduced the number available to transact parliamentary business. Although the daily 'presence' rarely fell below twenty, the council must have been concerned that legislation might be hampered by a lack of members. Much depended on the labours of a dedicated minority, especially the bishops (Bonner, Bourne, Day, Gardiner, Griffith, Heath, Thirlby, Tunstal and White) and new peers – Winchester, (1st) Bedford, Montagu, North, Paget, Rich, Wharton, Williams and Willoughby. They were afforced by a handful of nobles of ancient lineage, such as Arundel, Derby and Shrewsbury. Without such men the Lords could not have functioned.

In all of these respects there was no novelty in the Marian attendance pattern. However, there was one significant difference, an overall decline in numbers. The proportion who put in an appearance fell from 82 per cent (in Edward VI's reign) to 72 per cent and the regulars diminished from 51 per cent to 34 per cent. The licensed absentees increased from fifteen to eighteen per session, those who stayed away without permission almost doubled, and the daily attendance shrank from 41 to 36. It was not a direct consequence of a royal attempt to exclude recalcitrant members. Quite the reverse. The council sought to ensure a sufficient presence. Nevertheless the inferior Marian attendance record was serious, unmistakable and symptomatic of the troubled parliamentary history of the reign.

LEGISLATION

Another symptom was the brevity of Marian sessions, averaging five weeks, compared to the nine and ten/eleven weeks in the flanking reigns. In the Parliaments of 1553–55 the queen's programme encountered stiff resistance or was endangered by selfish and disruptive

TABLE 1 – The House of Lords' attendance record in Mary I's reign.

Session	Eligible members			Average daily attendance in each session			Percentage of members who attended			Percentage of members who attended regularly*		
	Lords Spiritual	Lords Temporal	Total	Lords Spiritual	Lords Temporal	Total	Lords Spiritual	Lords Temporal	Total	Lords Spiritual	Lords Temporal	Total
1553	17	50	67	–	–	–	–	–	–	–	–	–†
1554	20	52	72	11	24	35	60	67	65	55	40	44
1554/5	21	53	74	12	25	37/38	76	81	80	52	26	34
1555	24	55	79	13	28	41	79	71	73	38	40	39
Jan–March 1558	24	52	76	16	25	41	96	81	86	46	21	29
Nov. 1558	22	52	74	9	17	26	50	56	54	36	17	23

* Those who attended 75 per cent or more of daily sittings
† There is no surviving Lords' journal (and therefore no attendance register)

103

faction politics. They were dissolved as soon as her objectives had been achieved or frustrated. It would be wrong to portray parliaments just as occasions for conflict. Mary could not have secured the enactment of her religious and marital policies in 1553–55, or the military, anti-French and financial measures of 1558, without the co-operation of the majority in both houses. Nevertheless there were signs of decline everywhere. Not only falling attendance. The number of Bills before Parliament dropped from an Edwardian average of ninety-five to forty-eight, and the number of Acts from thirty-three to fifteen (which also represented a decline in the proportion of successful Bills from 35 to 32 per cent). This was not simply because sessions were shorter, but because the official programme, embodying Mary's often contentious Hispanic-catholic objectives, consumed so much time and, in the process, squeezed out many private Bills.

TABLE 2 – The House of origin of Bills and Acts in Mary I's reign.

| | *House of origin of Bills* | | | | *House of origin of Acts* | | | |
| | *House of Lords* | | *House of Commons* | | *House of Lords* | | *House of Commons* | |
	No.	*%**	*No.*	*%*	*No.*	*%*	*No.*	*%*
1553 (1 Mary)	–	–	–	–	22	65	12	35
1554 (1 Mary)	9	18	40	82	6	40	9	60
1554/5 (1 & 2 Mary)	12	20	49	80	9	43	12	57
1555 (2 & 3 Ph. & Mary)	13	18	60	82	7	28	18	72
Jan. 1558 (4 & 5 Ph. & Mary)†	12	28	31	72	6	37.5	10	62.5

* As the Lords' journal is missing, these figures cannot be calculated.

† November 1558 has been omitted because it was an abortive session terminated by Mary's death.

There is no doubt that the Marian Parliaments were less productive. Fewer Bills were presented, more were rejected: the Lords dashed only five Bills in five Edwardian sessions, but twice as many in four, relatively short, Marian Parliaments, while the Commons rejected twelve and seventeen. This all indicates a more fractious parliamentary climate. Moreover, whilst the performance of both houses was less impressive, the Lords was the real loser. In Edward's reign it had originated fewer Bills than the Commons (192:281) but its productivity had always been higher.[6] Nor was this just because uncontentious grace Bills, restitutions, attainders and beneficial private measures (for peers, courtiers and bishops) began there, though these certainly figured. For example it was prominent, even pre-eminent, in the enactment of Edwardian Reformation legislation. However, the picture changed dramatically under Mary. The proportion of Bills originating in the Lords shrank from 41 per cent to 21 per cent and, more serious, its productivity – the proportion of Acts which started there – slumped from 64 per cent to 36 per cent.

This process can be illustrated by the Parliament of 1554/5. Summoned to authorise the pending reunion with Rome and, by implication, to settle the vexed question of secularised Church property, it was used by Mary as an opportunity to revive the laws against heresy and to protect Philip with the treason laws. The result was a miserable showing by the Lords: only half of Parliament's Bills came before it, whereas the Commons saw almost all of them; and only 1 in 5 of the Bills and 2 in 5 of the Acts began there. All but 4 of the 11 Bills which were probably of official provenance were placed in the other house first. As usual, this kind of arithmetical assessment can distort the truth and, at first glance, this may be the case in Mary's third Parliament. Apart from the revival of the old heresy laws, the core of the government's programme began in the Lords: the reunion with Rome, the treason Bill, and the reversal of Cardinal Pole's attainder for treason. In other words, the Crown still preferred to use the upper house for the initial scrutiny of its major measures, even after its misconduct in the previous April (see below, pp. 108–110).

However, the story of these major official measures does not contradict but rather confirms the depressing quantitative assessment of the Lords' performance. The restitution of Pole, who was the papal legate empowered to reconcile England to the Roman catholic Church, naturally commenced in the Lords. It was desirable that the judges who sat there should scrutinise measures which touched legal and property rights and noble title, and which might affect the Crown's prerogative and property interests.[7] Furthermore the parliamentary passage of a restitution, especially one bearing the sign manual, was usually a formality and this was no exception.

The Lords' initiating role in the other two official measures was also less significant than it might appear. When the treasons Bill was passed by the house and sent to the Commons on 6 December, it was simply the original measure which had failed in April 1554. However, the lower house threw it out and redrafted it because it was deemed to provide inadequate protection of Philip's person and political interests. Now it included arrangements to lodge power in Philip as protector of the realm and guardian of any children of the marriage, if Mary predeceased him when they were minors. It was substantially a new measure and the product of the Commons' labours.[8] Even in the case of the great reunion Bill the Lords' initiating role was only a nominal one. Although it had its first reading in the upper house, it was the product not only of a joint conference of the two houses but also of other forces – queen, king, the papal legate (who wanted to restore secularised property to the Church),[9] judges, council, landowners and their parliamentary spokesmen. The donkeywork of drafting had already been completed outside the two chambers.

When Parliament met again in 1555, the Lords' decline continued unabated, and, as the table shows, its share of initiated Bills and Acts progressively diminished. However, circumstances had changed dramatically when Mary's last Parliament met. England was at war with France and Calais had just fallen. Many of the Bills before Parliament concerned military organisation and, as the nobles were the traditional experts in war, the upper house should have played a more prominent part. The quantitative measurements recorded in the table suggest that it did. Yet six of the eight measures dealing with military organisation commenced in the Commons. So also did the four penal anti-French Bills and of course the lay subsidy. There is no doubt that the Marian Parliaments declined in quality and productivity and that there was also a shift, in authority and activity, from Lords to Commons.

At the same time the volume of legislation being put into the upper house, not only by the Crown but also by economic and local interests and private individuals, was drying up: down from 170 under Edward VI (with a sessional average of thirty-four) to fifty-three (eleven per session). In contrast the Commons remained a vigorous and popular chamber, even if its record reveals that it continued to be less efficient and productive than the Lords. So 281 Bills began in the Edwardian lower house, of which fifty-nine (21 per cent) became law. Although it was touched by the general Marian parliamentary 'decline', it still initiated 202 Bills and its productivity level actually rose to 30 per cent (sixty-one Acts). As usual it had the lion's share of petty and local, sectional and economic Bills because it was a large and representative assembly. Already the volume was so great that there simply was not enough time to scrutinise and pass (or reject) more than a small proportion. This accounts, in large measure, for its lower productivity level.

However, the Commons should not be dismissed as a mere mechanism for the enactment of unofficial Bills. Important government measures began there: the repeal of the Edwardian Reformation (1553), the heresy Bills (1554 and 1554–55), confirmation of the queen's authority (1554), and laws to punish seditious rumours and treason by words (1554–55). So too, of course, did grants of lay taxation. But the Commons' popularity and its dilemma of too many Bills and too little time do not in themselves provide a satisfactory explanation for the Lords' performance, which marked such a dramatic falling away from the years of 1539–53. The phenomenon prompts two related questions: why did it happen and, as a clue to pinpointing the answer, is there an identifiable point in the parliamentary history of the reign at which that change took place? See above Table 2, p. 104.

In 1553 the Lords, as usual, initiated rather more than half the Acts. Thereafter its share of both Bills and statutes suddenly slumped. Everything points to 1554–55 as the years of change. An examination of the politics and Parliaments of these years provides an explanation for the change itself.

THE POLITICS OF PARLIAMENT[10]

Seldom has an English monarch come to the throne with such predictable and well defined political objectives. However, this did not make Mary's intentions any less controversial or, in some quarters, objectionable. A programme which included the restoration of catholicism and papal supremacy, a desire to restore expropriated property to the Church, and the eradication of heresy (a weapon which might be used to harass owners of secularised property) was bound to cause disquiet, criticism, and even opposition. Moreover a permanent catholic restoration could only be guaranteed by a succession of monarchs of the 'right religion'. Marriage was an integral part of Marian policy, but her choice of Philip of Spain provoked all kinds of fears: England's absorption within the Habsburg colossus, involvement in future Franco-Spanish conflicts, and subjection to the Spanish brand of dogmatic catholic orthodoxy. Materialism, xenophobia and protestantism combined to ensure resistance to some of Mary's objectives. The wishes of a doting wife – to enlarge the authority of her Spanish consort, protect him with the treason laws and have him crowned – simply heightened fear and suspicion in the governing class and therefore in Parliament.

As Mary's programme could only be implemented through Parliament, the prerequisite for success was skilful parliamentary management, which could only be provided by an experienced, well-rehearsed and united team of councillors. It was Mary's misfortune (and largely her fault) that her privy council had none of these qualities. It was large and unwieldy and even the small inner ring which ran affairs lacked unity. It was divided by personal antipathies, competing ambitions and conflicts of policy, principle and ideology. These divisions polarised around two men – Stephen Gardiner, bishop of Winchester, and William, first Lord Paget. They represented two antithetical traditions and embodied most of the enmities worked out in court and Parliament. Paget owned ecclesiastical property. He was a new peer, and had been sympathetic to the Edwardian Reformation. Gardiner was an Henrician catholic bishop. He had suffered imprisonment and deprivation under Edward VI and now believed that only a papal catholic Church could prevent heresy, iconoclasm and social anarchy from engulfing the realm. Gardiner represented religious reaction and the clerical position, whereas Paget stood for secular 'politique' and anticlerical interests and prejudices. Their differences were sharpened by personal enmity. Although other politicians tended to line up behind them, the council did not, however, split along simple factional lines determined by support for Paget or Gardiner but was a veritable confusion of rivalries and a medley of voices. No Tudor monarch had a more disunited council or (except for the minor Edward) exercised less control over it.

In these circumstances the parliamentary prospects were gloomy. A united managerial team was lacking to manoeuvre Mary's programme through the two houses. Worse still, councillors abdicated their responsibility and took their faction fights into Parliament where they neglected, even sacrificed, the queen's interests in pursuit of their own. As the faction leaders and many councillors sat in the Lords it was there, rather than in the Commons, that they engaged their opponents. Their irresponsible politicking manifested itself early in Mary's first Parliament. Gardiner opposed the Spanish marriage, wanted her to marry an Englishman, and was busily promoting the suit of Edward Courtenay, the young earl of Devon. He could look to his clients and allies in the Commons for support. In the Lords peers such as the conforming Marquess of Winchester, the catholic Derby and the reforming Pembroke, who were not Gardiner's followers but agreed with him on this question, were ready to collaborate. So there emerged a loose-knit parliamentary coalition. Its attempts to lobby the queen on Courtenay's behalf collapsed, however, when she dismissed a petition from the two houses requesting her to marry an Englishman.

In council and Parliament that was the end of the matter. The coalition disintegrated and, in December, even Gardiner accepted Mary's determination to marry Philip. We might be tempted to write off the anti-Spanish campaign as a damp squib and focus our attention on the Commons. In a sense it would be right to do so. All the major conflicts occurred there: the protracted debate on the repeal of the Edwardian Reformation (when 80 of the 359 present voted against it); the lengthy proceedings on the reversal of the duke of Norfolk's attainder and, especially, the restoration of his confiscated property; and the rejection of the Bill restoring Bishop Tunstal and his lands. Nothing seemed to have changed. The Lords continued to be the chief initiating, more responsible and more productive house, and, even if it had been actively pressuring the queen to marry Courtenay, so had the Commons.

However, Gardiner was the catalyst of change. He continued to promote his own policies, which were partly the same as Mary's and partly at variance with them. They both worked to re-enact the heresy laws and restore papal supremacy, but Gardiner wanted the latter to precede the marriage. Otherwise it would look like a Spanish device and so intensify anti-papal sentiment. He also hoped to exclude Elizabeth from the succession, a proposal unacceptable to Paget. He even ignored the change in political circumstances between Mary's first two Parliaments – a change wrought by Wyatt's abortive anti-Spanish rebellion in January–February 1554. Mary and her council agreed to restrict the official programme to ratification of her marriage (which no-one would dare to oppose after Wyatt's treason) and a few other uncontentious measures. The idea was to keep the political temperature low. Gardiner, undeterred by this decision, drafted his own programme which would raise in Parliament the sensitive issues of religion, papal authority, secularised lands and succession. They were also guaranteed to raise the political temperature to fever pitch. Paget's faction was bound to resist him, including as it did protestants (or sympathisers), owners of expropriated property, and defenders of Elizabeth. When Gardiner chose (or had to choose) Parliament as the battlefield, his adversaries in the council had no option but to oppose him there.

It must have been particularly frustrating for Mary, who had made elaborate preparations to secure a tractable Parliament. Furthermore, on this occasion (and in November 1554, too) patronage was used for a specific parliamentary purpose. While this was a characteristic practice in the eighteenth century, it was a novelty in Tudor Parliaments. However, it was a normal instrument of Habsburg government, regularly utilised (for example) in the Castilian *cortes*. The imperial ambassador Renard advised Emperor Charles V on those who should be tied to the Habsburg interest with the golden cords of patronage. Gold chains, pensions and posts in Philip's household were offered to leading politicians and councillors, such as Gardiner, Paget, Arundel, Bedford, Pembroke and Howard of Effingham. Most of them were councillors who sat in the Lords and could be expected to guide Marian–Habsburg policies through Parliament. Surely, as Renard anticipated, with such influential politicians (and their numerous clients in the Commons) in the imperial pocket, parliamentary acquiescence was assured.[11]

It was not to be. Conciliar faction politics overrode all other interests when Gardiner's legislative programme encountered stiff resistance from Paget and his allies.[12] Ratification of Mary's marriage passed smoothly enough, but several of her other important measures became victims of the ensuing parliamentary conflict. The heresy Bills failed in the upper house and a Lords' committee emasculated the Bill to protect her prospective husband with the treason laws. In the white heat of their hostility to Gardiner, Paget and his faction buried some of Mary's most cherished aspirations.

After the session, guilty and frightened peers realised what they had done and in an atmosphere of mutual recrimination they frantically scrambled for royal favour. However, it was too late to mend parliamentary fences. The damage was done and most of Gardiner's (and Mary's) programme had failed. Moreover the Lords' conduct impaired its general legislative record. As we have seen, its initiating role and productivity suffered: fifteen Bills failed to complete their passage; four were rejected; dissenting votes were recorded against five others and the confirmation of Suffolk's attainder (another official Bill) stuck over a disagreement with the Commons. Mary could have taken little comfort from the performance of a house which normally displayed sober responsibility and moderation, and in which her councillors and Habsburg clients were strongly entrenched.

When Parliament reassembled (November 1554) Philip had arrived in England, the marriage had been solemnised, and Mary was reputedly pregnant. The stage was set for the last act in the parliamentary implementation of royal policy: reunion with Rome, and renewed attempts both to protect Philip with the treason laws and to empower Church and State to prosecute heresy. In addition, Mary wanted Parliament to declare her husband protector of their children and the realm, if she predeceased him.

The queen lacked confidence in the Lords after its lamentable performance in April. However, the situation had changed. Some peers, so recalcitrant six months before, now rode into Westminster in chastened mood. They were still uneasy about the Habsburg connection and their fears about secularised property had not been quieted. However, many of them now chose self-effacing absenteeism rather than confrontation. Almost a quarter of the eligible bishops and peers stayed away for the entire session. Nevertheless this was not an unusual level of absenteeism and, on the surface, business appeared to proceed normally.

The treasons Bill, however, ticked away like a parliamentary time bomb. After its passage through the Lords it was committed in the Commons, possibly at the prompting of one of Gardiner's clients. When it re-emerged it was a hybrid, combining the old Bill with the appointment of Philip as protector and guardian of his children if he outlived his wife. Although he was to be assisted by a regency council of bishops and peers, the Bill denied the latter their traditional right to choose the protector. Their rumbling discontent soon made itself heard. During the brief Christmas adjournment, Simon Renard, Mary's confidant and trusted adviser, was warned that the upper house would probably reject it, because, without consulting the peers, the Commons had drafted a Bill impinging upon their traditional privilege. However, unlike the previous April, they avoided confrontation and sought refuge in a discreet absenteeism. Before the new Bill was sent to the Lords, ten prominent peers departed, all but two without royal licence, while Bedford discreetly absented himself during its passage through the upper house.

Historians have ignored this manifestation of aristocratic resentment and concentrated their attention on the Commons – in particular on what some have interpreted as a mass secession from the lower house late in the session.[13] To describe it as a simple straightforward political protest – a walk-out – is to disregard the complexity of the situation and to ignore the 'invisible' influence of the Lords on Parliament. The Commons sometimes took a roll-call in order to discover unauthorised absentees. When this was done in early January, 106 members were absent. Although this was not an exceptionally large total, the circumstances at this particular time *were* exceptional: the 'regency' Bill was on its way through Parliament. On 14 January, when it passed the Commons, the roll was called. Was the absence of over 100 members a protest against the Bill? Or was it just another example of the endemic absenteeism which plagued the Commons? There is no doubt that the government believed their action to be politically inspired, because the absentees were indicted before king's bench.

During the court's proceedings, however, a distinction emerged gradually between political dissenters and those who might have gone home for Christmas and not returned. Parliament had sat until 24 December and then adjourned for only one day. D. M. Loades (citing Jennifer Loach) argues 'that indignation at being kept in London over Christmas and anxiety to return home were probably the true causes of [the absentees'] behaviour'.[14] Doubtless this was the determinant for some of them, yet Loades' explanation simply will not do. There were only 193 members present when the roll was called on 14 January.[15] Add to these the prosecuted absentees and the total still falls short of the membership by more than eighty. Why were no charges laid against other delinquent members? We can surmise that the government thought that it knew who were harmless absentees and who were the political dissenters.

Indeed, king's bench took action against more than sixty 'political' absentees. The goods of at least twenty-five were seized for failure to answer the charges in court. Proceedings dragged on and, before Mary died, twenty-nine were fined.[16] A large proportion of those penalised were the clients of nobles who themselves had quietly departed in late December/early January: Pembroke (11 client-absentees), Cumberland and Westmorland (2 apiece) and Arundel, Sussex and Dacre (one each). Twelve (probably more) of Bedford's clients were among the absentees. Sir Thomas Cheyne, friend of Pembroke and relative of Bedford, had nominated or chosen six. It is difficult to avoid the conclusion that Bedford and other dissatisfied peers silently voiced a protest at a Bill which they disliked by withdrawing, and persuading many of their clients to do the same.

When Mary's fourth Parliament met in 1555, political circumstances again dramatically altered. Lord Chancellor Gardiner died three weeks later. His departure lowered the political temperature in the Lords, which comported itself in a more constructive and responsible manner than in Mary's three previous Parliaments. On the other hand Gardiner had been a formidable personality, authoritarian, assiduous in attendance and attention to parliamentary business and patronage. His death left a political vacuum and led to a sudden decline in parliamentary discipline. The French and Venetian ambassadors paid tribute to the fear and respect in which he had been held[17] and his absence may explain why the Commons got out of hand in this Parliament. The queen's Bill to return first fruits and tenths to the papacy passed by only 193 votes to 126, and the measure to penalise religious exiles was actually rejected. In such circumstances the Lords might have been expected to stage a revival. However, its recent misconduct continued to haunt it. The upper house had lost both royal and public confidence and it proved difficult to lay the wanton ghosts of 1553–55. The legislative initiative had passed to the Commons.

This does not mean, either then or in the future, that the Lords faded away into the parliamentary obscurity to which Neale, Notestein and others consigned it. In November 1558, for example, an impressive delegation, headed by Lord Chancellor Heath, went down to the Commons, demanded that 'a Subsidy must be had', and swept forth in imperious manner.[18] In the first session of 1558 the Lords had not only taken the initiative but intruded itself into the taxation process. It called for a joint conference at which it informed the Commons' members that money was needed for the defence of the realm. The two houses named a joint committee which, in turn, appointed three sub-committees to examine ways and means, so 'that no way or policy shall be undevised or not thought upon'. They deliberated apart for three days before uniting to draft the terms of a subsidy Bill, which they advised the two houses to accept. The Commons' clerk described it as 'The Bill for a Subsidy . . . granted by the *Lords* and Commons'.[19] Despite its inferior Marian record, the upper house was still no cypher.

The institutional authority of the Lords continued to be augmented by the social influence of its members. This was still expressed by the peers' electoral influence and patronage, operating through their gentlemen-clients, serving as borough stewards and using the inducement that their candidates would serve without wages. Their electoral involvement remained extensive. Many members were connected to them by kinship, clientage, friendship or political alliance and in some measure owed their election to them: 105/120 (or 27–31 per cent) in October 1553, 105/130 (or 27–33 per cent) in April 1554, 100/125 (or 25–32 per cent) in 1554/5, and 110/130 (or 28–33 per cent) in 1555. In other words, between one-quarter and one-third of Commons' members owed their election, solely or partly to noble patrons, relatives or allies.[20]

In this respect Marian parliaments did not mark a break with the past. The two houses were a lattice of relationships. Noble 'electioneering' strengthened their links, lessened the possibility of conflict between them and smoothed their working relations. It also strengthened the collective prestige of the Lords in its dealings with the Commons. Moreover in times of political crisis it enabled noble politicians to exploit the Commons in order to frustrate their rivals and even royal policies. In the fractious Marian political climate the Commons was particularly vulnerable to exploitation by rival interests. Ironically, however, the greatest parliamentary manager was not a peer, but a bishop, Gardiner. His energy, ambition and high office turned 'Winchester's faction' into a parliamentary reality. He secured the return of between 17 and 26 members (including his nominees to his three episcopal boroughs) to the first four Marian Parliaments. With the support of allies, like-minded peers and co-religionists, he could depend on at least 45 to 60 clients, sympathisers and supporters in the Commons. When, in 1553, Pembroke, Cumberland, Clinton and other peers backed Gardiner's campaign against the Spanish marriage, they added 30 to 40 more members to his following there. These 'paper battalions' did not necessarily speak and vote in the required way – there were no party 'hacks' in Tudor Parliaments and they remained men of independent temper. However, more often in Marian politics they were expected to follow their patrons' lead and there is no doubt that this added to the parliamentary influence of the upper house.

REFERENCES AND NOTES

1. J. Strype, *Ecclesiastical Memorials*, 3 vols, Oxford, 1822, III, p. 245.
2. Bergenroth, G. A., Tyler, R. (eds), *Calendar of State Papers Spanish* [*Cal. S. P. Span.*], 13 vols, London, 1862–1945, XII, p. 150.
3. *C.J.*, I, 34, 41, 45–6, 49.
4. Ibid., 35, 37, 41, 47, 51.
5. Ibid., 51.
6. It initiated 107 of the 166 acts, or 64 per cent.
7. Most attainders, and confirmations thereof, commenced in the Lords for the same reason.
8. P.R.O., S.P. Mary, 11/5, fo. 1; H.L.R.O., Original Acts, 1 & 2 Ph. & Mary, no. 10.
9. For a full discussion of the knotty problem of expropriated lands, see D. M. Loades, *The Reign of Mary Tudor* [*Mary Tudor*], London, 1979, pp. 321–9.
10. For detailed studies of Marian politics and Parliaments, see Loades, *Mary Tudor*, passim; Graves, *Mid-Tudor Lords*, Ch. 8, espec. pp. 183–201; ibid., 'Politics of Opposition', pp. 1–20, 253–8; ibid., 'Forgotten Member of the Trinity', pp. 23–31; J. Loach, 'Conservatism and Consent in Parliament, 1547–59', in *The Mid-Tudor Polity, c. 1540–1560*, J. Loach and R. Tittler (eds), London, 1980, pp. 9–28.
11. *Cal. S.P. Span.*, XII, 118–19, 150, 158, 295, 297–9, 315–16.

12. The details of the Lords' conduct in this, the most disruptive of Tudor Parliaments, need not be rehearsed here. Its factious and fractious behaviour is recounted at length in Graves, *Mid-Tudor Lords*, pp. 190–5; ibid., 'Forgotten Member of the Trinity', 26–8; ibid., 'Politics of Opposition', 1–20, 253–8. See also Loades, *Mary Tudor*, pp. 83–6, 103 n. 71, 104 n. 73, 135, 168–9.

13. Graves, *Mid-Tudor Lords*, pp. 197–8. See also Loades, *Mary Tudor*, p. 272.

14. Ibid.

15. Ibid.

16. *H.P.T.*, 1509–1558, passim.

17. R. A. Vertot d'Aubeuf and C. Villaret (eds), *Ambassades de Messieurs de Noailles en Angleterre*, 5 vols, Leyden, 1763, V, 204–5; Graves, *Mid-Tudor Lords*, p. 125.

18. *C.J.*, I, 52.

19. P.R.O., S.P. 11/12/31, ff. 67–70; *C.J.*, I, 47–8.

20. *H.P.T.*, 1509–1558, passim.

Chapter six

THE EARLY ELIZABETHAN PARLIAMENTS, 1559–1566/7

Elizabeth's accession to the Throne marked a departure from the pattern of the previous thirty years, during which Parliament had assembled no less than twenty-eight times. In her reign of forty-five years it was to meet on only thirteen occasions. Although no-one knew it at the time, the Elizabethan religious settlement of 1559 marked the end of decades of kaleidoscopic politics and rapid alterations in religion. The essence of the new regime was its conservatism which combined a politically sensible search for stability with the innate conservative instincts of the queen. As she had no intention of making or allowing substantial changes to the Church created by statute in 1559, one of the most important causes of frequent Parliaments in the last thirty years had gone. Furthermore, whatever her reasons – an autocratic temper, a preference for secret politics, or a woman's defensive posture in a male-dominated world – she was not fond of Parliaments. Financial necessity and the privy council's prompting (often for other reasons, as we shall see) compelled her to call them. When she did she preferred short sessions and hustled council, Commons, and Lords on to complete official business and so make an end of it. In William Cecil she probably had the best available agent to fulfil her wishes. He was conservative, a skilful parliamentary manager and consistently loyal – even if, sometimes, he also employed Parliament to bend her opinions into accord with his.

In 1558 a Parliament could not be delayed. The nation had become deeply divided and demoralised by its experience of Habsburg government, religious persecution and the loss of Calais. Only Parliament could settle religion and so, hopefully, begin the healing process. Moreover – it was the one parliamentary constant of her reign – Elizabeth needed money. The immediate palliative was a lay subsidy, the conventional life-grant of tunnage and poundage to a new monarch, and the transfer of clerical first fruits and tenths back to her. Finally, as she remained a bastard in law, Elizabeth required legal title to the crown. All had to be achieved while England and Spain were still at war with France and protracted peace negotiations were under way. There were hopes of regaining Calais and fears of a Franco–Spanish rapprochement directed against England. Mary Stuart, married to the French dauphin, could be used as a rival claimant to Elizabeth's crown and a French army was in Scotland. It was a delicate diplomatic situation in which so much had to be achieved.

Four years later, however, Elizabeth's reason for calling a new Parliament was simple and predictable, and it was not complicated by a threatening international situation. Since 1559 her military expenses alone amounted to more than three years' income and the problem had been compounded by a costly expedition to assist the French protestants in 1562–63. However, the need for financial aid was not the whole story, even though the council (or Cecil) may have persuaded her that it was. In October 1562 Elizabeth nearly died of smallpox and the political nation glimpsed the shocking prospect of a civil war over the succession. The problem did not go away. The security and stability of England depended on the survival of an unmarried woman who had no generally acceptable heir. She must take a husband or name a suitable successor. Councillors, especially Cecil, were prepared to use Parliament to that end when it met.

Another 'problem' – religion – was also a cause of concern to councillors, bishops and indeed the majority of the governing class. The new Church was a patchwork, seemingly ramshackle affair and many issues – liturgical, doctrinal, financial and moral – remained unresolved. This had nothing to do with radical puritan programmes, which did not exist in the 1560s. It was an expression of concern by a governing class of predominantly moderate protestant complexion. The Church must put its house in order – settle unresolved issues, improve the quality of the clergy and tidy up the many loose ends and ambiguities inherent in the settlement of 1559. It had to be strong, credible and united in preparation for a possible catholic counter-attack from France and Mary Stuart, Spain and the papacy.

On all these points councillors were in harmony with their relatives, friends, political allies and co-religionists in the governing class. Thus early was the pattern set for the rest of the reign. Councillors would use Parliament not to challenge the queen's authority – they were too loyal for that – but to 'persuade' her to their point of view which, in their male-chauvinistic fashion, they felt to be in her best interests. The session of 1566/7 exemplified this. Once again the queen required financial aid and the council persuaded her to it. This was no mere cynical political exercise on the council's part; the need was genuine enough. Nevertheless councillors had bows with more than one string. When Parliament was summoned in September 1566 Cecil chaired a council meeting at which he proposed that they press Elizabeth to marry. As a political realist he divined that this had greater prospects of success than a campaign to persude her to name an heir and it became one of the chief political themes of the 1566/7 session. In his low-key way Cecil dominated the first three Elizabethan sessions and, at the same time, he is the key to an understanding of them.

MEMBERSHIP

During these years the disparity in the size of the two houses continued to grow. Whereas the Commons increased from 400 to 420, the Lords remained static at about 75–83. The bishoprics numbered 26 and the peerage declined, almost imperceptibly, from 57 to 55. The variations in eligible members from one parliamentary session to another were almost entirely the consequence of non-political processes, such as absence abroad, episcopal vacancies caused by death or translation, and the poverty or minority of peers[1] – or conversely new creations. However, one dramatic change occurred. In 1559 there were only sixteen bishops in a house of seventy-seven. This was the work of the Great Reaper, though ardent protestants rejoiced in it as the hand of God. There were also the meagre parliamentary fruits of Mary's brief monastic revival: the abbot of Westminster and the prior of St John of Jerusalem. By 1563 their brief re-appearance in the Lords was over and, except for Kitchin of Llandaff (who had survived every alteration in religion since 1545), there was almost a full complement of new protestant bishops. Even so the Lords was, and remained throughout the reign, less than one-sixth the size of the other house.

The change in its complexion was more significant. The deprivation of the Marian bishops reduced the old 'Marians' to a handful of devout peers (such as Northumberland, Westmorland, Viscount Montagu, Lumley and Vaux) and conservative loyalists like Derby and Shrewsbury. On the other side the protestant power was reinforced by new faces – Leicester, Buckhurst and Hunsdon – and the religious enthusiasm of regional viceroys such as Bedford and Huntingdon. Furthermore the early Elizabethan privy council was heavily peer-orientated and the 'offical' element in the Lords reflected this. It was an assorted mixture: Northampton the courtier, conservatives of great regional influence (Arundel, Derby and Shrewsbury), that archetypal noble civil servant Winchester, the queen's great-uncle Howard of Effingham, and those Edwardian spirits Bedford, Clinton and Pembroke. Collectively they constituted a formidable official pressure-group in the early Elizabethan Lords. If they needed prompting and support they could look to the lord keeper, Nicholas Bacon who, while not styled lord chancellor, still exercised the power and duties of that office, including 'chairmanship' of the upper house. He was more than a merely political ally of William Cecil: they had both married daughters of Sir Anthony Cooke. The omniscient Cecil, sitting near to the speaker's chair in the Commons with his lieutenants Sir Francis Knollys and Sir Walter Mildmay, could thus also marshal his parliamentary forces in the Lords through the medium of Bacon. In his quiet, tenacious and persistent way he managed all to further what he conceived as the best interest of the queen, 'good governance' and the benefit of the commonweal.

ATTENDANCE

Absenteeism was still a problem in the Commons. If anything it had become more serious because of the growing volume of business and the need for sufficient members to deal with it in short sessions. In 1559 (23 January–8 May), the longest Parliament of the reign, the eighteen members who were licensed by the speaker to depart early for their 'business' or 'great affairs' constituted only a small proportion of absentees. Attendance steadily declined as the session progressed: 219 (out of 406 members) were present on 24 February, 131 on 24 April and 114 on 1 May. There were attempts to stop the rot in mid-April, when the roll was called and a Bill was introduced 'touching Knights and Burgesses, for Attendance in the Parliament', but they had no apparent effect. On one occasion the clerk was prompted by the thin attendance to note that 'This Day Mr. Speaker, with few of this House, were here' and they read only part of one Bill before adjourning. The next session was no different. In 1563 only thirty-three applied for licences for a variety of reasons – an uncle's death, sickness, the assizes, the council of the north, and 'great affairs'; but attendance figures ranged downwards from 64 per cent to 31 per cent.

By 1566/7 the problem was just as bad, if not worse. A few, including a knight who was 'diseased with the Gout', were licensed to leave. However, many more arrived late, left early, attended irregularly or not at all. The division figures in this session suggest an attendance of between 152 and 127, or from just over to just under one-third of the members. A crucial vote over the choice of a new speaker, won by 82 to 70 early in the session, indicated that members did not race up enthusiastically to Westminster but rather drifted in as the session progressed. As it was in the Crown's interest to have enough members present to cope with the formidable volume of business, the action taken to combat this endemic absenteeism was probably officially inspired. Some licences were now issued for specified periods and with expiry dates. The roll was called seven times and on 9 November it was ordered that 'if, after the Reading of the first Bill, any of the House depart before the Rising of Mr. Speaker, without [his licence]; to pay to the poor Men's Box Four-pence' – an indication that many members were putting in only brief or nominal appearances.[2]

In the early Elizabethan Lords the problem was not of the same magnitude. If there was an exception it was the first Parliament of the reign, when thirty-seven members of the house sued out licences and named proxies. However, the Lords' attendance was not as black as this might suggest. Less than half the licensed absentees stayed away for the entire Parliament and, despite their diminished numbers, a group of catholic bishops spearheaded by Heath (York), Bonner (London), White (Winchester), Pates (Worcester), Turberville (Exeter), Baynes (Coventry and Lichfield), and Oglethorpe (Carlisle), assisted by Abbot Feckenham (Westminster), turned up, attended regularly and fought a bitter rearguard action in defence of their religion and Church. Therefore, despite the plethora of licences and some judicious episcopal absences, about sixty peers and bishops rode into Westminster to attend this most crucial of Parliaments. The regularity with which they attended, however, was another matter. The daily presence averaged only thirty-four and while the maximum was an impressive 52 (two-thirds of the membership), on three days the occupants of the Lords' benches numbered 5, 6 and 7.

It must be stressed that this was an exceptional Parliament, heralding a new political order and a new religion. The circumspect thought it better to stand on the sidelines, wait, watch and see which way to jump. When the next Parliament met (in 1563 and 1566/7) the Elizabethan Settlement, together with English support for the protestants in Scotland and France, had proclaimed the religious complexion, political drift and diplomatic priorities of the new regime. The hesitant, the timorous and the fair-weather loyalists could now come off the fence: in the first week of the 1563 session almost sixty turned up each day. Inevitably, however, the tedium of the legislative grind sapped the initial enthusiasm, good intentions turned sour and members drifted away. During the last week of the session the daily attendance had dropped to thirty-four. A similar pattern is discernible in 1566/7 when the daily presence gradually shrank from 51 to 32.

Nevertheless, as always there was a hard core of men who regularly put in an appearance and conscientiously transacted business. They sat patiently through the first readings of Bills of a technical nature, larded with legal niceties and concerned with local and personal matters which often must have seemed far removed and even irrelevant to them. They debated Bills, sat on the committees which revised or redrafted them, honed and tempered the text and voted on the finished product. In 1559, with a depleted episcopate, they numbered only 20, but in the two sessions of the next Parliament there were 32 and 24 respectively – always enough to transact the Lords' business efficiently, with the help of the legal assistants.

At the other end of the spectrum were, as usual, the backwoodsmen who made only a token appearance or did not turn up at all. Some were consistent in absenteeism: Bath and Cumberland among the earls, together with Lords Audley, Bergavenny, Ogle, Sandys, and Wharton. Despite the sessional variations, the attendance pattern did not depart from that of the previous thirty years. Like any modern trade union, university, or Parliament, it was left to a handful to shoulder the burdens and wield the power: the regional viceroys such as Huntingdon, Rutland, Shrewsbury; busy barons like Darcy of Darcy, Darcy of Chiche, Mountjoy, St John of Bletsoe, and Strange; above all the bishops, not only the catholic rearguard in 1559 but their protestant successors too. York, Durham, London and Winchester led the most potent force in Parliament and in 1566/7 the bishops accounted for almost three-fifths of those who were regular in their attendance. Even those who were unsympathetic to the regime did not efface themselves. Viscount Montagu, ardent in opposition to the Elizabethan Settlement, attended 88 per cent of sittings in the early Elizabethan Parliaments. The northern peers such as Northumberland, Westmorland, Dacre of the North and Lumley, disaffected by the erosion of their provincial authority, adhering to the 'old religion' and with a marked preference for Mary Stuart, none the less did not secede. There was no attempt to exclude the disaffected, nor did they stay away.

LEGISLATION

Elizabethan Parliaments passed a number of laws which were monumental in their intentions and which, despite the modest power of Tudor government, had a wide-reaching impact. Notable were the Statute of Artificers (1563), the recusancy law of 1581 and the Poor Law Acts of 1597 and 1601. But none were so important or central to the history of Elizabethan England as the Acts of supremacy and uniformity, which in 1559 created a new Church. To cynics it must have looked like yet another temporary arrangement which, sooner or later, would give way to something else. Nevertheless these Acts, which dealt with the government, doctrine and order of worship of the new Church, were the first priority of most of those who attended Parliament. Consequently they occupied much of its time.

It is not necessary to repeat the rival interpretations of the parliamentary progress of the two Acts which we examined in Chapter 1. Whether one accepts Sir John Neale's explanation of events or Norman Jones's interpretation, both confirm the time-consuming central place which these measures occupied in the 1559 Parliament.[3] From the introduction of the first supremacy Bill into the Commons on

9 February until both measures completed their parliamentary passage on 28/29 April, they were seldom absent from one house or the other for more than a day or two. And when they were, between 1–11 March and in early April, the flurry of activity continued in committees, council and court. The journals, correspondence and ambassadorial reports all testify to the heat which they engendered and the labour expended on them. Together the supremacy and uniformity Bills consumed much of the session and most of the passions of the two houses.

Naturally and rightly, therefore, these Acts are regarded as the centrepiece of the 1559 Parliament. Yet they were only part of a more wide-ranging official legislative package designed to settle religion, legitimise the new regime and alleviate its immediate financial problems. A lay subsidy and the life-grant of tunnage and poundage inevitably commenced in the Commons, although the Lords amended the latter and exempted Wales and Cheshire from prompt payment of the former.[4] The religious settlement brought further financial benefits to the Crown. One act, commencing in the Lords and with amendments and additions devised by both houses, restored first fruits and tenths to the queen. Another, this time beginning in the Commons but with a crop of additions from the other house, suppressed the Marian monastic houses and returned their property and profits to Elizabeth. The notorious Act empowering Elizabeth to acquire episcopal lands in return for tithes, an unpopular levy on the laity, passed the Lords but ran into trouble in the lower house and went to a division. In contrast the restitution of Elizabeth and the legitimation of her title to the crown had a smooth parliamentary passage. Each of the Bills against treasons and unlawful assemblies, placed in Lords and Commons respectively, was amended by the other house and the former required a joint conference to iron out differences. The official achievement was impressive and it emphasises the unity and common purpose of Crown and governing class. As for the two houses, it would be superfluous to quantify their roles in terms of productivity and the initiation of Acts. Everything points to the continuation of a vigorous parliamentary tradition in which both played an active, often critical, but essentially co-operative part.

However, it is understandable that attention is normally focused on the Commons. Elizabethan Parliaments were usually called for taxation, which the lower house alone could initiate. Moreover the omnicompetence and sovereignty of statute, realised in the revolution of the 1530s but dimly recognised then, now came home to roost in the relative stability of Elizabeth's long reign. Members of the governing classes had come to recognise the desirability of securing parliamentary sanction for their ambitions and of embodying them in statute, the highest form of law. Parliaments became occasions for the statutory resolution and satisfaction of all manner of local, personal, sectional, economic and legal problems and grievances. They were inundated with Bills, most of which were put into the Commons first because, as we have seen, they represented the overwhelming majority of the governing class. In 1559 82 of the 98 measures before Parliament began there. Four years later so did all but 33 of the 131 Bills considered by the Commons.

Some, but only a few, were government measures, concerned with the Crown or of general application to the kingdom. The great majority were promoted by private members. Some were general in scope, but most of them touched on the affairs of individuals, boroughs, counties and economic interests. Even in 1559, when the official programme loomed unusually large and a quarter of all Bills concerned religion, the Church and its property, just over 50 per cent were promoted by peers, gentlemen, or urban industrial and commercial lobbies. Some were intended as statutes penal, prohibiting the export of corn, horses, hides, tallow and leather, and punishing industrial malpractices such as the 'thicking' of caps and the 'deceiptful using of linen cloth with chalk'. Sometimes the parochial interests of promoters are obvious, as in the Bill prohibiting deforestation to produce charcoal for smelting – a step in London's long campaign against the ironmasters in order to preserve cheap fuel for its lower classes. Other Bills were beneficial, designed to protect nascent industries against foreign competition, or to enlarge local economic opportunities (e.g., for a fair at King's Lynn), while eight restored in blood the heirs of convicted traitors and four guaranteed secularised episcopal lands to specified peers and gentlemen.

Early Elizabethan legislation ranged broadly over the whole spectrum of human affairs: a wife's jointure, apprentices, journeymen and servants, Thames watermen and Essex clothiers, wills and common law writs, sheriffs and undersheriffs, conjuring and sodomy, rooks and red-legged crows. No corner of the realm was exempt from its attentions. Through the welter and variety of Bills, however, we can detect certain thrusts of interest which were to manifest themselves throughout the reign: for example, wine imports, the conservation of timber, leather and above all cloth and wool. Together they accounted for eighteen Bills in 1559. It was natural that most of these measures were promoted in the Commons by the representatives of local communities and economic interests (though it should be added that the majority of Bills benefiting individuals, especially restitutions in blood, were handed into the Lords first). However, the Commons' popularity was a two-edged sword because already, in 1559–67, the growing volume of unofficial Bills threatened to impede the transaction of council business. More and more time had to be devoted to literal first 'readings'. Shoddy draftsmanship necessitated the commitment of many Bills for revision, while others provoked opposition from rival interests and consumed much time in debate. In consequence the Commons' efficiency and productivity suffered: 63 per cent of all Acts in 1559 began there, but so did all but one of the 58 abortive Bills, 39 of which did not even reach the Lords.

In contrast, 15 of the 16 Bills starting in the upper house in the same Parliament became law. As business piled up in the Commons, 49 of its Bills simply failed to beat the clock, while two were 'dashed' there in the final vote, five were rejected by the Lords and one received the royal veto. Apart from its role in the enactment of the official programme, the Commons' performance was unimpressive. In 1563 it was even more so, when thirty-two of the fifty-one Acts began in the upper house (though they included a crop of restitutions which were normally introduced there). This was, by then, unusual because the Lords' role as initiator of Bills had shrunk significantly since 1553–55. Despite this (indeed partly because the pressure of business was less) it remained the more efficient chamber and registered a much higher success rate.

The legal assistants continued to make a vital contribution to this legislative achievement, as the journals of 1566/7 reveal. As always the attorney was to the fore, sitting with bishops and peers on four committees to revise Bills, joining with two judges to make another 'good, lawful, and perfect', and carrying a dozen more down to the Commons. He was not alone, however, for eight judges sat on Bill committees. Sometimes they deliberated with bishops and peers, but three measures were assigned to one or two of them and once to 'all the Justices'. Serjeants and masters of chancery were also busy in the revision of Bills and their transmission to the Commons. Furthermore, although legal assistants were silent, non-voting ancillaries, one of them became presiding officer of the house. When Lord Keeper Bacon was taken ill at the beginning of the session, the lord treasurer deputised. However, William Paulet, marquess of Winchester, was in his eighties, physically enfeebled, deaf and with a defective memory – hardly ideal qualities for the presiding officer of a chamber which lacked printed order papers and copies of Bills and in which all depended on the spoken word and the ability to memorise texts read aloud. On 25 October Winchester admitted defeat. The queen 'considering the decay of his memory and hearing, griefs accompanying hoary hairs and old age', appointed Sir Robert Catlyn, lord chief justice of common pleas, in his place. Catlyn exercised Bacon's parliamentary office until the latter returned on 9 November.[5] The episode underwrites the Lords' dependence on its legal assistants, who contributed so much to its legislative standards.

RELATIONS BETWEEN THE TWO HOUSES

It has become a commonplace to talk of Elizabethan Parliaments as a duet of queen and Commons. More important, however, is Neale's thesis that there emerged in the Commons a dynamic puritanism (radical protestantism) which pressed for a more radical religious settlement than the queen desired in 1559. Then, in 1563–67, it introduced a programme designed to improve a 'halfly-reformed' Church and campaigned to settle the succession. Money – which was important in 1559 and the very reason why Parliament was called in 1563 and 1566–67 – enhanced the Commons' importance. It alone could initiate taxation and when, in the second session, it linked supply with the succession question, it demonstrated that it could use that power as a political lever. Therefore Neale felt that his peremptory dismissal of the Lords was justified.[6] After all, it was subservient to the queen and its function 'was less to impede the Crown than to assist it in controlling the Commons'.[7]

This partial representation of Parliament ignores a number of important points. The Lords' 'misconduct' in 1553–55 was an aberration from its norm of political responsibility. Such responsibility should not be confused with political subservience: in 1559 a sizeable minority of its members was prepared to conduct prolonged resistance to royal policies as a point of principle. Moreover, as in 1533–55, Elizabethan parliamentary politicking was often an extension of court and council politics. Catholic opponents and puritan critics of the new regime, rival conciliar factions, and male councillors anxious to persuade their royal mistress to make the 'right' policy decisions; all were willing to use Parliament to their own ends. Apart from Sir William Cecil and a few other councillors, such as Knollys and Mildmay, most of the great politicians, ministers, and faction leaders sat in the Lords. With the notable exception of the catholic rearguard action in 1559, they avoided confrontation and preferred to collaborate with the Commons or use their clients there as their spokesmen and front-line troops. Even Cecil, first in Elizabeth's confidence, looked to allies and sympathetic councillors in the Lords to advance the queen's business and, if necessary, loyally coerce her into prudent courses.

Increasingly important in Elizabeth's reign was the collective social influence of the Lords. Territorial magnates – Bedford, Huntingdon, Leicester, Norfolk and Shrewsbury – were spiders spinning webs of aristocratic patronage. Many of their clients were elected to the Commons by their good offices and they were likely to be of similar political opinion and religious persuasion to their patrons. Dr Story and his allies in the Commons were acting in concert with catholic bishops and peers in 1559 when they noisily resisted religious change and caused prolonged debate on the supremacy Bill. Likewise in the campaigns to persuade Elizabeth into marriage or the choice of a successor there is evidence of collaboration, not only between the two houses but also between noble patrons and their clients in the Commons.

The peers' electoral activity continued to be extensive. In 1559

90/100 members and in 1563 130 burgesses were elected through the 'influence of a great man'. Not all 'great men' were peers, but many were. Bedford enjoyed extensive influence in three western counties, where he returned 24 and 29 members; Norfolk secured the election of 16 and 18, most of them his household servants. The rising star, Robert Dudley (ennobled in 1564), was already collecting lord lieutenancies, borough lordships and stewardships by which means he could put his clients into Parliament. In contrast, Cecil was not a great territorial magnate. In 1559 he exercised direct patronage in only three boroughs, to which he had added Westminster by 1563. His power-base was political – the queen's confidence – and his extensive electoral influence was exercised through noble allies such as Bedford.[8]

This state of affairs had a twofold significance: that the electoral influence of peers continued to reinforce the institutional authority and prestige of the upper house; and that the Commons' political 'busy-ness' was sometimes stimulated or directed by members of the upper house.

The first critical issue confronting Parliament was religion. From John Foxe to A. F. Pollard, historians explained the Elizabethan Settlement of 1559 in terms of a queen, supported by a loyal protestant Commons, overcoming a catholic party entrenched in the upper house in order to revive the royal supremacy and establish a national Church with an order of worship based on the second Edwardian prayer book of 1552. This interpretation placed the catholic bishops and peers at the centre of the drama. However, Sir John Neale saw it quite differently. The Lords was a political cypher. The catholics were only a minority and their dissenting voices were conscience votes, rather than a concerted attempt to defeat the queen's religious programme. The central feature of this Parliament was a tug-of-war between Elizabeth and a loyal but radical Commons, dominated by a vocal puritan minority. The result was a Church more radical than she would have wished. In the process of re-writing the history of the Elizabethan Settlement, Neale transferred the centre of power and political activity from Lords to Commons – symptomatic of the way in which he dismissed the upper house as politically insignificant.[9]

Recently, however, Norman Jones re-examined this Parliament. While he regarded both interpretations as too simplistic, his accorded more closely with those who wrote before Neale. There was no puritan 'party' or lobby in the Commons and the chief stumbling-block was the catholic episcopate supported by some peers, in particular Viscount Montagu. They voted consistently against each official measure on religion and in March they scored their greatest success: a Lords' committee (whose action was then endorsed by the house) deleted from the so-called supremacy Bill those parts which altered religion and the order of worship. It also left Elizabeth free to assume the title of supreme head but would not give it parliamentary sanction.[10] The

Commons was shocked but, fearful of an impending dissolution, it approved the Lords' changes. When Parliament was adjourned over Easter, this mutilated Bill awaited only the queen's assent to become law.

Thus far the differences in the two interpretations are quite clear. According to Neale, Elizabeth was conservative and especially she was concerned not to upset the delicate Anglo-Spanish peace negotiations with France (and the possible restoration of Calais). She wanted only the royal supremacy and communion in both kinds as a sop to the reformers. Having got her supremacy Bill she could have dissolved Parliament, but then she relented because, at the beginning of April, the peace treaty with France was concluded. When Parliament reassembled after Easter, the government introduced a new supremacy measure and a separate uniformity Bill. These went a long way to satisfy male prejudice and protestant aspirations: Elizabeth became supreme governor without cure of souls and a protestant Church, based on a modified version of the 1552 prayer book, was established.

In contrast Jones claimed that the queen's change of mind had nothing to do with the conclusion of peace negotiations, but was the result of the catholics' success in wrecking her religious legislation. Until the Lords drastically modified it, the supremacy Bill was substantially the same as the two Acts which eventually passed into law. It would have created a new Church with an order of worship based on the prayer book of 1552. Elizabeth needed time to rethink her tactics, weaken the catholic opposition in the Lords and make concessions to conservatives. A disputation was arranged between protestants and catholics, a popular contemporary device used in 1548 and 1553. The recalcitrance of the catholic bishops gave her justifiable cause to imprison White of Winchester and Watson of Lincoln. They were but two, but they were the stiff-necked exponents of the more extreme catholic position. As usual, quality rather than quantity mattered. Left to themselves Archbishop Heath (who believed in obedience to authority) and the rest proved to be less obstinate. The resolve of the catholic peers weakened too, and the Lords eventually accepted the two new Bills of uniformity and supremacy. In Jones' version the recalcitrant Lords, not the Commons – a willing accomplice of the queen – was the catalyst of events in 1559. His argument carries the greater weight, in particular because an analysis of the Commons' membership confirms that there was no ardent protestant reforming (i.e. 'puritan') pressure group there.[11]

Neale, however, projected the same phenomenon into the two sessions of the next Parliament (1563 and 1566/7). The parliamentary initiative and dynamic remained in the Commons where an organised puritan party, known as 'the choir', pursued its politico-religious ends. It was radically protestant and vehemently anti-catholic, devoted to Elizabeth but anxious to lead her to Geneva, pressure her to marry or name a successor, and provide the law with sharper teeth to bite the papists. The choir was no negative opposition, seeking only to frustrate royal policies. Instead it had a positive programme of its own and developed sophisticated techniques in order to fulfil its aims. The choir dominated the Commons which, in consequence, became the political focus of Parliament in 1563–67.

This aspect of Neale's thesis has also been demolished by recent revisionist studies.[12] There was no puritan choir, and the aims which he assigned to it were actually those of the council and concerned members of the governing class in both houses. Cecil and other councillors were at one with the nobility and gentry when they sought a settled succession, especially after the queen's brush with death from smallpox late in 1562. Admittedly, ardent protestants attempted to extract radical articles of faith from convocation in 1563. However, they were rebuffed when it issued, instead, a moderate corpus of thirty-nine articles. Nor did they switch their offensive to Parliament in the next session. The ABC Bills,[13] labelled A to F, were not the work of a puritan party. They were approved by Cecil and the bishops were hot in support. It was not until 1572 that a new generation of young and ardent spirits wearied of the compromises of their elders and became political activists. Even then they operated in the parishes rather than in Parliament.

All of this means that we have to jettison old assumptions. Early Elizabethan Parliaments were not political, seeking to limit or obstruct the Crown, but rather were co-operative ventures in legislation. Moreover, when political issues, such as the queen's marriage and succession, loomed large, both houses were actively engaged in the pursuit of common objectives. It would be unrealistic, however, to consider them apart from the council and the governing class as a whole: they were all members of one political family. Together, in 1563 and 1566/7, they endeavoured – and failed – to bend the will of one obstinate woman to their own.

Admittedly allies do not always remain in harmony, especially when great matters press upon them urgently. In the second of these sessions the queen prevaricated, veered, and tacked on the questions of marriage and succession and she was inflexibly hostile to the Bill which gave statutory confirmation to convocation's articles of 1562–63. There was no serious division of opinion between the two houses on any of these matters – indeed, they had mounted a joint and concerted campaign designed to lead her to the altar or at least to persuade her to nominate her heir, while the bishops had petitioned her in favour of the Bill on religion. Her obstinacy had a divisive effect – perhaps that was her intention. It became a very disturbed session in which the central issues rippled out to harm (albeit temporarily) relations between the two houses and wreck a number of their measures. Some were rejected outright and others were loaded with unacceptable amendments including the Bill to renew statutes which were due to expire at the end of this Parliament. Elizabeth won, but at a cost.

It remains possible that in the early Elizabethan Parliaments the Commons was the operative centre, though not for the reasons argued by Neale. Sir William Cecil sat there. Just as the lower house had assumed primacy when Thomas Cromwell was a member between 1529 and 1536, the same may have been true during this later period. Cecil, like Cromwell, was the parliamentary general *par excellence*. He drafted memoranda on official objectives, masterminded the government's legislative programmes, drafted bills, and promoted others which he liked. His vocal opposition to measures of which he disapproved was based on extensive homework and the careful marshalling of arguments on paper. Always he was the queen's obedient servant, concerned to transact her business. So in 1563 the Commons' clerk recorded his 'excellent declaration of the great charges defrayed by the Queen's Majesty' as a preliminary to a request for supply. He received the same praise for performing the same duty in 1566 when he wrote himself a reminder to draft the subsidy Bill before Parliament met![14] He was everywhere, on committees, drafting, debating, delivering official statements, and manipulating behind the scenes. Of course he had his rivals, especially Leicester. However, as he grew in stature, so the bishops, great nobles and their clients in the Commons, councillors such as Mildmay and Knollys, all became his parliamentary lieutenants.

Cecil walked a greasy tightrope between his duty as a royal servant and his common concern with Parliament to settle such thorny issues as marriage and succession. In 1563 it was his client, Thomas Norton, who read aloud to the Commons the petition to the queen which its committee had drafted. Three years later Cecil drew (or amended) a Commons' petition which combined its thanks for her intention to marry with a thinly veiled complaint that she had infringed their privilege of free speech. He also drafted the subsidy Bill's preamble, which incorporated the queen's promise to take a husband or name a successor. On these subjects he had no success. Nevertheless he remained the parliamentary commander-in-chief and, as long as he sat in the Commons, that would remain the operative centre of Parliament. When it met again in 1571, however, he had been raised to the upper house as Baron Burghley. It proved to be one of the turning points in the history of the Tudor Parliaments.

REFERENCES AND NOTES

1. There was the occasional exception, such as the earl of Hertford. See Ch. 7, p. 133.
2. *C.J.*, I, 53–81.
3. Neale, *Eliz. Parls*, I, 51–84; Jones, *Faith by Statute*, pp. 83–168.
4. *L.J.*, I, 549.
5. *L.J.*, I, 629–42. Catlyn performed the same function in 1571 and 1572, as did other judges later, for example Sir Edmund Anderson, Chief Justice of Common Pleas in 1586/7. *L.J.*, I, 671–4, 679, 694, 717–20, 725; ibid., II, 127–42.
6. Neale, *E.H.C.*, pp. 15–16.
7. Neale, *Eliz. Parls*, I, p. 41.
8. *H.P.T.*, 1558–1603, I, 51, 59–63, 68, 71; II, 61–3.
9. Neale, *Eliz. Parls*, I, pp. 40–1; Jones, *Faith by Statute*, pp. 1–3.
10. Ibid., pp. 99–101.
11. Neale, *Eliz. Parls*, I, pp. 33–84; Jones, *Faith by Statute*, pp. 1–168.
12. Elton, 'Functions and Fortunes', 272–3; Jones, *Faith by Statute*, pp. 169–85; Graves, 'Thomas Norton', 17–35; ibid., 'Council's Men-of-Business', 11–38.
13. Neale, *Eliz. Parls*, I, pp. 166–70.
14. *C.J.*, I, 63, 74; see below, p. 158.

Chapter seven

THE ELIZABETHAN PARLIAMENTS: THE ERA OF LORD BURGHLEY, 1571–1597

Between 1568 and 1572 there occurred the first major political crisis of the reign, provoked by Mary Stuart's flight to England and followed by the earls' rebellion in her favour (1569), the papal excommunication of Elizabeth (1570) and the Ridolfi Plot (1571), the first of many conspiracies to dethrone or assassinate her. It ended the decade in which official policy towards the English catholics had been a mixture of insistence on outward conformity and connivance at private catholic religious practice. There was a shift to persecution of the English catholic community and to an ideological cold war with catholic Europe, which gradually and fitfully rose in temperature until the outbreak of hostilities with the catholic superpower, Spain, in the mid-1580s.

The Parliaments of 1571 and 1572 were responses to the initial crisis which marked a turning point in Elizabethan politics. They were also significant in the history of Tudor Parliaments. In February 1571 William Cecil was ennobled and twice within the next sixteen months he had to stage-manage Parliament's response to the crisis. Thereafter he was to preside, without ostentation but effectively for all that, during another eight sessions before his death in 1598. He had been a member of the Commons in twelve sessions since 1542 and he had an intimate knowledge of its workings. This was to serve him well when, as Lord Burghley, he managed both houses from the Lords, which now became the operative centre of Parliament.

It was Burghley who, more than anyone else, guided England through over twenty-five years of ideological war and, finally, of military conflict. He witnessed many changes: the end of the campaign for the queen's marriage as she grew too old to bear children; the growing catholic threat in Ireland, the Low Countries, and to England itself; the shift from peace to war; and, in the 1590s, the dismantling of the High Elizabethan system under the pressures of war, economic dislocation and a new generation. Parliament always remained one of his political options in time of crisis but never, however, did he lightly recommend calling one. In 1571 Parliament was summoned to strengthen national security after the northern rebellion and bull of excommunication. In the following year it met for one reason only: to advise the queen and consider legislative action against Mary Stuart, whose activities constituted a threat to her life and throne. Speaker Bell identified her as 'a person in this land whom [many thought] no law could touch', whereas 'any person of what state, condition, or nation whatsoever [who] shall commit any felony within this realm they shall die for the same.[1] He was Burghley's lieutenant, assisting him in the relentless parliamentary pressure which might shake Elizabeth out of her reluctance to punish a fellow-queen.

As the catholic threat grew, the council resorted to Parliaments for new, harsh laws to combat it. In 1579–80 a papal expedition with Spanish reinforcements stirred up trouble in Ireland, Philip II of Spain acquired Portugal and its navy, and the first Jesuit missionaries arrived to reconvert England. The result was a Parliament, called in 1581 to enact laws against recusants (catholics who would not attend the Anglican Church) and missionary priests. More plots against Elizabeth and, in July 1584, the assassination of the Dutch protestant hero, William of Orange, prompted another Parliament (1584–85) to provide for the queen's safety.

These were all Parliaments called for advice and new laws rather than for money. However, the council rarely missed the opportunity to seek financial assistance too. Only in 1572, when its exclusive concern was 'the great cause' – Mary Queen of Scots – did it neglect to make such a request. When, fifteen years later, Parliament was once again called for advice on Mary's fate, Lord Chancellor Bromley explained in his opening address that it was not summoned 'for Fifteenths and Subsidies, although there were some cause'.[2] This was not a request, but it was certainly a broad hint which was duly taken. Even in peacetime, money could be the sole reason for summoning Parliament, as in 1576. Once England had drifted into its long war with Spain that was certainly the case. In 1589 the costs of the Armada campaign had to be met. Four years later Parliament met again as soon as the last instalment of the 1589 subsidies had been paid. It voted an unprecedented triple subsidy with the final payment due in 1597, whereupon yet another assembly was called for financial aid. Parliaments remained occasional and short (averaging 9 weeks and ranging from 5 to 10 weeks in duration) while Burghley was in the Lords. However, they were essential to his management of the State, equipping the council with the laws to combat the catholic menace at home and abroad, supplementing the Crown's resources in peacetime and funding the Elizabethan war machine. They could also be employed, as we shall see, to coerce his vacillating mistress into action on matters of great urgency. Moreover the very prestige which he brought to the upper house by his presence and activities there, and his use of it to pursue his parliamentary ends, made it the nerve-centre of Parliament and politically revitalised it in the later sixteenth century.

MEMBERSHIP

As we have seen, the growth of the size of the House of Lords continued to be determined by royal action: the creation of peers, the erection of new bishoprics and rapid promotions or appointments to vacant ones. Elizabeth was notoriously dilatory or reluctant in all such matters. She was unwilling to bestow titles on 'new men' and only one – William Cecil – was raised to the peerage. Indeed there were only ten genuine creations during her long reign, and they already possessed peerage connections, noble ancestry or kinship with the queen. In addition there were five titles which were restored, the recognition of Reginald Grey's right to resume the earldom of Kent (which had lapsed in 1523 because of poverty), and two who succeeded through female descent.[3] Elizabeth's sparing use of honours did not compensate for the wastage due to natural causes (fourteen failures of the male line) and State action (six attainders). In consequence the peerage actually declined slightly from fifty-seven to fifty-five during the reign.[4]

Any increase in the number of bishoprics was normally determined by the Crown's awareness of the Church's administrative needs. Elizabeth, however, did not think it necessary to add to them and they remained constant at twenty-six. Therefore fluctuations in the number of bishops at time of Parliament depended on the rapidity with which she appointed replacements to vacant sees. It had been a recognised practice in the past for the Crown to leave sees vacant for a year or more and collect the revenues from them. The queen was particularly guilty of this offence against sound ecclesiastical government, using the income from vacant bishoprics not only to augment her own but also as a source of pensions to those in favour. Sometimes she carried the practice to absurd lengths: Oxford was left vacant from 1558 to 1567, 1568 to 1589 and again from 1592 for the remainder of her reign – a total of forty-one years! Ely had no bishop between 1581 and 1599, nor did Bristol after February 1593. Altogether there were twenty-four vacancies of a year or longer, and in consequence there was never a full complement of bishops when Parliament met.

The net result of royal actions in harness with natural wastage was an undramatic but none the less real decline in the size of the Lords. Between 1571 and 1597, the years when Burghley sat in the Lords, the bishops diminished in number from 25 to 20, the peers from 63 to 57 and the whole house from 88 to 77. There were fluctuations, as when the total rose to 90 in 1572, but the steady erosion is unmistakable.

Moreover some of the peers were ineligible and so denied writs of summons (or at least ordered not to attend) for the usual variety of reasons. Minority was the commonest (e.g., six in 1572) but there were others. Some were on distant royal service (e.g., Scrope and Hunsdon on the Scottish borders, Lincoln and Dacre of the South on an embassy to Paris in 1572, and Lord Burgh in Ireland in 1597). A number had offended the queen or even committed treason. Late in 1560 the earl of Hertford, secretly and without royal permission, married Lady Katherine Grey, a strong claimant for the crown if Elizabeth died childless. For this offence he spent ten years in prison and under house arrest before the queen relented and he took his seat in the Lords in 1572. It was in that session that political disaffection took its greatest toll. Norfolk was executed. Arundel (FitzAlan), Southampton, Cobham and Lumley were all in detention, while Morley had fled abroad. Nor were they the last of the Elizabethan catholic miscreants: Westmorland had already escaped into exile, Lord Paget was to follow him in 1583 and Arundel (Howard) was to forfeit his title in 1589.

Nor were the bishops immune from royal disfavour. Archbishop Grindal of Canterbury was suspended from the spiritual functions of his office in 1577 for refusing to suppress 'prophesyings' (meetings of the clergy which were designed to improve their standards, but which Elizabeth suspected to be platforms for puritan propaganda). Richard Cheyney (Gloucester), who caused great offence by his Lutheranism, virtually seceded from Parliament after 1566, perhaps at the queen's command. The cumulative effect of all these forms of disability was to make the Lords even smaller.

At the same time the Commons continued to grow as the queen gave way to importunate suitors. It can be no coincidence that boroughs in the Isle of Wight, where her relative Sir George Carey was governor, received six new members. The earl of Huntingdon, her cousin, and Leicester, her favourite, secured the enfranchisement of five Hampshire boroughs. So the Commons inexorably grew: from 420 in 1563–66/7 to 438 in 1571, just two more in 1572 and then another twenty in 1584. The enfranchisement of Andover, a gesture to Leicester in 1586, was the last new parliamentary borough of the reign. By then the Commons' membership numbered an unwieldy 462, the Lords only 86 – simple facts which go far to explain the council's continuing concern about the inefficiency of the lower house.

Changes in the composition of the Lords were more important than alterations in its size. There were two focal points of such change. At the beginning of the reign, Elizabeth added to the peerage by rewarding her friends, relatives, allies, and those victimised by her sister's regime. Altogether she created or restored six peers,[5] who would not have made a significant impact on the upper house. However, there were also the catholic bishops who, with the exception of Kitchin of Llandaff, would not accept the Elizabethan Settlement and who by

1563 had been replaced by men of moderate protestant persuasion. This was a far more important change, because the bishops constituted almost 30 per cent of the house and, in the past, they had been among its more active members. It only remained for her to raise Robert Dudley to the earldom of Leicester to round off the first important phase of change in the Lords' membership.

The second phase (1568–72) was not of the queen's choosing but was forced upon her by the political crisis inaugurated by Mary Stuart's flight to England and concluded by the discovery of the Ridolfi Plot. This time only the peerage was affected. Norfolk and Northumberland were attainted and executed, while Westmorland and Morley became exiles. Three of the greatest regional nobles in the kingdom disappeared from the political scene and their empires collapsed in consequence. Perhaps Elizabeth was recruiting support when she restored De La Warr, allowed Kent to resume his title, created a crop of new barons (Burghley, Cheyney, Compton and Norris) and summoned two heirs apparent in the junior titles of their fathers. Furthermore, between 1568 and 1572 three peerages became extinct for lack of male heirs and eleven others passed on to eldest sons. The composition of the lords temporal who reassembled in 1576 was very different from that of a decade before. Thereafter, however, change was the simple undramatic consequence of the passage of time and lack of male heirs. The most important change, a qualitative one, had already occurred: Cecil's elevation to a barony in 1571.

ATTENDANCE

It has already been demonstrated that membership of the Lords bore no obvious or intimate relationship to attendance. The majority continued to observe the call of duty but many did so without enthusiasm. Nobles and bishops had a life tenure in the House of Lords, therefore age, as well as residence in distant estates or dioceses, could erode enthusiasm and a sense of responsibility. Others who struggled up to London were soon bored by speeches of interminable length and by the complexities and technicalities of legislation. They found their good intentions overtaken by the seductive pleasures which the court and London had to offer. The usual result was that as before a relatively full house gradually thinned. In the first week of the 1571 Parliament the daily attendance averaged 54, but during the last week it had dropped to 45. In 1572 it fell from 48 to 37, in 1584 from 42 to 35, in 1593 from 45 to 39, and in 1597 from 43 to 33. On the other hand, in 1581 and 1589 it actually rose during the closing days. Clearly it is dangerous to generalise about the attendance record of Parliaments over a lengthy period of time. Members responded to each one according to their own interests, priorities and religious position.

Nevertheless it is possible to make some general observations about the Lords' attendance. As always, members fell into three groups. At one end of the spectrum were the backwoodsmen, who did not turn up at all. At the other were the 'parliament men' who attended regularly, debated Bills, revised them in committee and took upon themselves the lion's share of legislation. In between there was the body of members who put in an appearance, sometimes quite often, and played a supporting, albeit irregular, role in the enactment of Bills. The size and composition of these groups inevitably varied from one session to another. The 'regulars' (those attending three-quarters or more of the daily sittings) numbered only 12 in 1584, about 30 in 1589 and 1593 and 38 in 1571. They were a motley crowd, drawn from the lords both spiritual and temporal, but the bishops and the peers of recent origin were dominant. Some of them enjoyed a long tenure of their seats on the Parliament benches and in the process must have acquired a skill and experience unmatched by most members of the Commons. With almost tedious regularity they were appointed to committees, not only in Burghley's first Parliament in 1571 but in most of the sessions during his long sojourn there: such men as Viscount Montagu, the third earl of Sussex, and Lords Buckhurst, Hunsdon and North. Together they provided a thread of continuity and a pool of legislative skills.

In contrast there were the backwoodsmen who could have contributed nothing to parliamentary business. Like the regulars they fluctuated in number (from 19 in 1571 to 27 in 1589) and always constituted a mixed bag. Nevertheless a number of 'types' can be detected. There were bishops reluctant to drag themselves from distant sees (especially York, Carlisle, Bath and Wells, Chester, Exeter. Gloucester and Hereford, and the incumbents of those remote Welsh fastnesses, St Asaph, St David, Bangor and Llandaff); royal servants engaged on the queen's business; the wastrels, such as Berkeley and Oxford; and those who were just uninterested. Illness, age and all kinds of personal conditions account for many other sessional absences.

Fortunately there were always enough members available to transact business. The regulars usually constituted a sizable group and most of them were active committee-men. Moreover, many others who attended less frequently shared the burden of committee work. In other words, the Lords' labours were broad-based and the house had a healthy record of activity. Nevertheless the privy council kept a watchful eye on attendance and absenteeism. Perhaps, indeed, the activity was a consequence of conciliar supervision – impossible to tell. Obviously there were advantages to be derived when the house rarely numbered fifty and usually ranged between 25 and 47. Every member could have his say and procedures could be applied more flexibly in a small group of men who, especially in the case of the peers, were well-acquainted and often related by blood or marriage.

The daily presence could dwindle alarmingly on occasions, to as low as 16 and 6 in 1584/5, 17 in 1589, and 12 in 1597. That this occurred so rarely, however, is a tribute to the responsibility of both orders and the council, despite the competing claims of convocation and star chamber days. There was no relaxation in the procedure whereby would-be absentees applied for licences and appointed proctors to represent them during their periods away. Indeed, by 1597 the system had tightened up. Inevitably it was Burghley's doing. He moved the house 'that such Lords as were absent from the parliament, and had not sent their proxies, and such others as had made their appearance in the beginning of the parliament, and have since neglected their attendance, may be admonished to reform the same'.[6] There followed a rash of apologies from members who were but briefly absent for a day or two: the bishops of Chichester and Llandaff, the marquess of Winchester, the earls of Huntingdon and Lincoln all excused themselves on the grounds of sickness and, in each case, fellow prelates or peers testified on their behalf.

This may have been the consequence of more careful and detailed recording by the clerk of the Parliaments. Early in the session, on 10 November, Burghley moved that the journals 'kept heretofore ... seemed to have some error in them' and proposed that, in future, they should be 'viewed and perused every parliament, by certain lords of the house . . . and that this order might begin this present parliament'.[7] So the final step was taken whereby the clerk's personal record was transformed into the official journal of the house. The detailed information about absenteeism may be the consequence of this, rather than a novel, more thorough, level of supervision. If that is the case, it still means that little in the house escaped the watchful eye of the lord treasurer, in his seventy-eighth year and the last of his life.

The Commons, not the Lords, remained the serious, even intractable problem: not of opposition, but of absenteeism. Whether at Burghley's behest, or on their own initiative, councillors and their aides attempted to keep it within reasonable bounds. In each session knights and burgesses continued to apply to the speaker to absent themselves on their 'special', 'necessary' or 'great' business. However, they were always a mere handful, a minute proportion of those who stayed away: 6 in 1571, 5 in 1572, 3 in 1576, and 2 in 1581. The house took steps to ensure a larger presence and resolved in 1571 that members who did not attend prayers at 8.30 a.m. should forfeit fourpence to the poor box. The next day the roll was called in order to discover the delinquents. The problem came to a head in 1581, a session vital to the council which, in an atmosphere of growing crisis, sought money and harsher penal laws against the recusants. On the opening day the clerk reported that the number of members present 'was not great' and he went on to explain why. There had been 'sundry' prorogations of the session when its meeting was at hand, with the result that, after so many false alarms, many members did not believe that it would meet or simply could not be bothered to turn up. Moreover, since the last session in 1576, death and 'other Occasions' had left vacancies. Some had not been replaced, while others, newly returned, could not take their seats until they had sworn the oath of supremacy (see below, p. 143).

The replacement of members who were dead, sick or on royal service became a subject of hot debate in this session. A committee was appointed to examine returns of new members and it was finally resolved that the original members 'shall stand and continue for their said several Rooms . . . notwithstanding any such Causes of Sickness, the Queen's Service, or supposed Allegation of being dead'.[8] This served only to diminish the number of knights and burgesses available for parliamentary business. Not that the house was unaware of the continuing problem of endemic absenteeism: in a session of forty-five sittings the Commons was 'called' seven times. Such was the dissatisfaction with the daily presence that finally it was resolved to fine sessional absentees: £20 to be levied on each delinquent knight and £10 on each absent burgess. Those who had put in an appearance and then departed without the speaker's licence were to lose their wages.[9]

It would be rash to assume that, behind all these attempts to ensure a sufficiency of members, there was the hidden hand of Burghley. However, as we shall see, he remained the queen's parliamentary manager-in-chief after his elevation to the Lords. He set an example by his own regular attendance and assiduous attention to business, despite the gout which had afflicted him since his thirties and his increasing absences from court on a bed of pain. His attendance record in the House of Lords speaks for itself: 77 per cent of sittings in 1571; 70 per cent in 1572, 91 per cent (1576), 68 per cent (1581), 72 per cent (1584), 38 per cent (1586/7), 90 per cent (1589), 88 per cent (1593) and 66 per cent in 1597. His one lapse, in 1586/7, was the supposed consequence of a fall from his horse in early February. In March he was still lame, and did not attend Parliament again until the closing session. Perhaps he was in disgrace after Mary Stuart's execution. During the 1590s attacks of gout recurred more frequently, and he was often away from court, yet despite a bout during the Parliament of 1593 he attended regularly. He might describe himself to the upper house as 'an old man, beside his years decayed in his spirits' but he soldiered on, marshalling his troops in the 1597 session within a year of his death.[10] Moreover he remained the indefatigable committee man, nominated to 22 committees in 1571, 7 out of 21 in the following year, and, later, 11 (more than anyone else) in 1584. Ailing and tired though he was in 1597, he was a member of 19 of the 33 recorded committees and joint conferences on all manner of subjects. He remained to the end the devoted royal servant, within Parliament as much as in council and court.

LEGISLATION

A study of law-making represents a particular problem, created by the fact that the Commons' journal – its record of business – for the later Elizabethan Parliaments (1584–1601) have long since disappeared. The only substitute is Sir Simonds D'Ewes' printed edition of the journals of both houses which he compiled in the 1620s – evidence that the journals of the lower house were still available then. He incorporated extracts from private journals, diaries and copies of members' speeches. Together these give a fuller picture than was provided by the clerk, who was after all only interested in the record of business – readings of Bills, committees, amendments and so on. Unfortunately this bonus is offset by D'Ewes' abridgement of business entries. Frequently we learn no more than that 'three bills of no great moment, had each of them one reading'. In the absence of a full journal record there are serious gaps in our knowledge after 1581. Did the inundation of the Commons continue? What proportion of its Bills was abortive? These questions cannot be answered precisely yet[11] and analysis of later Elizabethan legislation must be in part speculative and hedged in with judicious qualification.

This period includes seven Parliaments (including one of three sessions) and covers more than a quarter of a century. We must ask ourselves whether it reveals any long-term trends of continuity or change in the nature, volume and success of Parliament's law-making activity and in the legislative role of the two houses *and* the privy council (for the three are inseparable). A useful starting point and possible commentary on what Neale calls a 'new relationship of the Houses' is the comment which Sir Christopher Hatton made shortly before the parliament of 1589.[12] He wrote to Serjeant John Puckering, the Commons' speaker in 1586/7, about some Bills which had failed to pass because of the time spent on the matter of Mary Stuart. As 'the use of the Higher House is not to meddle with any bill until there be some presented from the Commons' he wanted to revive the 'failed' Bills in the Lords, in order to keep the bishops and peers occupied during the opening days of Parliament. At first glance it might seem that Hatton was right and that the Lords had ceased to initiate Bills. If its journal is to be taken at face value, in the twelve opening sittings of the previous session the house's sole concern was the 'great cause' and on six mornings it did nothing at all. Moreover, when it reassembled in 1589, it read four old Bills in the first fortnight before any came up from the

Commons. On the other hand Hatton had no previous experience of the Lords, and the previous Parliament had been exceptional in the way it pursued Mary Stuart's death to the neglect of private legislation. Altogether only ten Acts had been passed, with the result that the expectations of Bill promoters had been frustrated. Furthermore in 1589 the Lords introduced seven new Bills of its own before one came up from the Commons and it initiated nine of the twenty-four Acts passed – over one-third. In 1586/7 the proportion (40%) had been even higher. Hatton's commentary on the Lords' position must be taken with more than a grain of salt.

However, it may be no more accurate to accept that, with Burghley there, the Lords underwent some kind of legislative regeneration. The role of the two houses must be looked at in several ways in order to reach a realistic assessment, in particular as initiators both of abortive Bills and of Acts. This can be done in a quantitative way.

TABLE 3 – The House of origin of Acts, 1571–1597.

	Acts originating in Commons	Acts originating in Lords	Total Acts
1571	20 (50%)	20 (50%)	40
1572	11 (65%)	6 (35%)	17
1576	20 (54%)	17 (46%)	37
1581	20 (69%)	9 (31%)	29
1584	31 (65%)	17 (35%)	48
1586/7	6 (60%)	4 (40%)	10
1589	15 (62.5%)	9 (37.5%)	24
1593	15 (55.5%)	12 (44.5%)	27
1597	32 (74%)	11 (26%)	43

Thus the Commons originated between one-half and three-quarters of the successful Bills in each session. However, this kind of measurement is unreliable because the passage of some classes or types of Act continued to be a mere formality, such as private estate Bills, which began in the Commons, or general pardons and restitutions in blood which usually – though not invariably – were supported with the sign manual (the monarch's autograph) and entered the Lords first.[13] The simple fact is that not all Bills or Acts were equal. The privy council's measures, which usually included a subsidy, were the reasons why Parliament met and so they deserve a priority of importance. Sometimes they were couched as a proposal (e.g. the recusancy law of 1581) or as a request, especially for a subsidy (which, as we shall see, had usually been carefully prepared and even drawn before the event). Whatever form they took they were the chief, even the sole reason for a Parliament's existence.

However, the council also took the opportunity to enact Bills in the cause of the commonweal and good government, and it might take over a private member's measure and sponsor it, thereby in effect transforming it into an official one. In other words, while there was an identifiable hard core of official legislation, the council's programme was essentially *ad hoc*, fluid and a response to events during the session. Nevertheless a knowledge of the council's own interests, contemporary politics and the technical distinction between conciliar and unofficial Bills[14] makes it possible to identify many of those which they drafted, promoted or favoured. As we know, some of them regularly commenced in one particular house: lay subsidies in the Commons and the confirmation of clerical subsidies voted by convocation, together with the queen's general pardon, in the Lords. One change occurred with the Continuance Act. This regularly renewed important economic statutes which had a limited life, usually to the end of the next Parliament. In 1571 and 1572 it began in the Lords, but from 1584 onwards it was placed in the other house first.

As for the rest of the council's programme, the role of the two houses is not clear-cut. In 1571–72 Parliament provided a statutory response to the disloyalty and foreign threats which had challenged the government since 1568. In 1571 measures against papal bulls and fraudulent gifts made by northern rebels began in the Lords. So did Westmorland's attainder. In contrast the Acts against catholic fugitives and treasons started in the Commons, although the latter required a joint conference in order to mould it into a shape acceptable to the queen. In addition, Acts treating of tax collectors (and especially their abuses) were put into different houses. As for Bill B of the Alphabetical Bills, it was read first by the Commons but had the active support of Burghley, fellow peers and the bishops in the Lords. Other major pieces of official legislation must be viewed in the same light, that is, as collaborative exercises between council, Lords and Commons and especially Burghley and his clients: for example, the Bill against Mary Stuart in 1572, the laws against recusancy and sedition in 1581 (the latter being redrafted by the Lords); the queen's preservation and the Act against Jesuits in 1584. The remaining important government measures in this period include, in 1572, the penal laws against seizure of the queen's castles and the 'enlargement' of prisoners, three Acts in 1576 (concerning letters patent and against clipping coin and fraudulent conveyancing), and another on tax officals (1584) all of which began in the Lords. In contrast, only two official Acts in this period were initiated and hammered more-or-less into their final shape by the Commons. This tedious recitation has its purpose. It demonstrates not only that the Lords was very much to the fore in the important legislation of Parliament, but also that, in much of the crucial law-making activity, the council and the two houses were intermeshed and at one in their ultimate objectives.

In practice the council's legislative role was untidier than the preceding description suggests. Individual councillors pushed particular

Bills and there was never any guarantee of conciliar unanimity. Some of them, for example, repeatedly supported a measure to renovate Dover harbour, but should this be termed an official Bill? Likewise Burghley's old-fashioned hostility to a Bill allowing usury and his obstinate resistance to the repeal of an earlier Act making Wednesday a compulsory fish-day should not be designated official actions. Tudor government was personal and non-doctrinaire, and there was no such concept as 'cabinet unanimity'. In any case official Bills were not the only legislative concern of Parliaments. All Elizabethan assemblies, no matter what the political circumstances, must be assessed in terms of expectations: not only what the Crown hoped to obtain, but also what Bills were carried up to Westminster in the trains of bishops and peers and in the saddlebags of knights and burgesses. Parliament was there to enact laws for the subject as well as for the queen, and the Commons, because of its representative character and its size, continued to be the house into which professional lobbies, economic interests, localities and individuals placed their Bills. However, as its popularity grew so its level of productivity continued to fall: from 21 per cent of its Edwardian Bills to 18 per cent in Elizabeth's fourth Parliament. In the three sessions of that Parliament 83 Acts were passed, but 271 Bills were abortive and only 51 of the Commons' 278 measures became law.

In contrast the Lords' figure was 43 per cent (or 32 out of 75); nor did that situation significantly change. In 1589 the upper house read eighteen of its own bills but also twenty-seven sent up from the nether house. One wonders how many more failed below, by rejection or sheer lack of time. The Lords may have initiated only 37/38 per cent of the Acts in that session, but these constituted half of all its Bills, and it therefore remained the more productive chamber. Under Burghley's supervision it remained the more prestigious one, too. At the closing of the 1571 parliament Elizabeth expressed her opinion through Lord Keeper Bacon:

> [A]s to the Lords here of the Upper House, her Majesty hath commanded me to let you know, that [she] taketh their diligence, discretion and orderly Proceedings, to be such, as redoundeth much to their Honour and Commendations, and much to her Comfort and Consolation.[15]

Ten years later Thomas Norton, an outspoken Parliament-man in the Commons, refused to amend a Lords' Bill concerning a bishop. As he later wrote 'I gave my yea to it in the House, and further cause I had not to meddle with it, for it came ready passed from the Lords . . . and no adverse party to be heard against it'.[16] The upper house remained powerful, persuasive and worthy of the respect of even the most forward and independent members of the Commons.

Its continued importance still owed much to the legal assistants' presence and assiduous attention to business. It is true that, twice, solicitors-general vacated their seats on the woolsacks in order to be elected speaker of the Commons.[17] Doubtless that was at the behest of the council. More significant, perhaps, is the Commons' decision, naturally based on precedent, concerning one of the queen's serjeants. He had been called to the upper house as a legal assistant and, at the same time, he was elected one of the knights for Sussex. The Commons resolved that he 'may have Voice . . . in this House . . . notwithstanding his Attendance in the Higher House . . . as the Place where he hath no Voice, nor is any Member of the same'.[18] Perhaps that was why they sought election to the Commons: that they had no 'voice'. In 1576 one of the masters of chancery, Dr Barkley, 'rashly and indecently opened his mouth, without waiting to be called upon by the lords'. Not only was he personally reprimanded but thereafter 'not one master has ever since been required to utter so much as one word'.[19] The story may be apocryphal or misdated. Whatever we make of it, there may be some connection with the change which occurred in 1597. D'Ewes observed that, in that Parliament, legal assistants were no longer appointed to committees as co-equal members with bishops and peers 'but only as Assistants to the Committees to give their advice if they shall be required, and not otherwise'.[20] If he was right, it meant that the judges, serjeants and the rest were further downgraded in status. It might be an optical illusion: that when the clerk wrote that they were required 'to attend the lords' it was no more than the consequence of Burghley's call that the journals be more carefully and precisely kept. Whatever the explanation, and no matter how their status altered as a consequence, the legal assistants provided a professional stiffening to amateurs and served the house in many ways. If they were now reduced to attendants on their lordships, none the less they continued to be appointed to committees – to every one of the twenty-four recorded in this session. Bills were referred to them for scrutiny, revision and even drawing or re-drafting. They considered privilege cases, conferred together over the principles on which Bills were based, drew up objections to Commons' measures, attended their lordships at their behest and regularly carried Bills down to the Commons. There is no doubt that, to the very end of Burghley's life, the legal assistants rendered a very real service to the House of Lords.

THE POLITICS OF PARLIAMENT

Relations between the members of the parliamentary trinity were determined by three considerations: high political issues, the impact of the court and legislative business. The first was central to parliamentary history between 1571 and 1597, but great issues were not, as Neale portrayed them, a fruitful source of conflict between queen and Commons. In dramatic contrast to contemporary Europe, there existed internal stability and a general accord between Crown and governing class on political and religious fundamentals. There were parliamentary grumbles about administrative abuses such as purveyance (the Crown's right to purchase supplies or requisition transport at rates below the market price) and, in 1597, the queen's misuse of monopolies as a cheap form of patronage (see also Ch. 8, p. 156). There were also, in 1566 and 1576, tactless outbursts from Paul and Peter Wentworth, who charged Elizabeth with breaches of parliamentary liberties, but they were 'loners' without much support.[21] Indeed, apart from catholic and presbyterian minorities, council, Lords and Commons were in agreement on most important matters. Moreover, there were no professed catholics in the Commons after 1566/7, because each member now had to take the oath of supremacy. This did not extend to the Lords, but by 1571 some of the leading catholic malcontents were dead or in exile and in 1572 Arundel, Southampton and others were in detention. Although the surviving malcontents continued to be summoned and to attend, they were a mere handful who created no parliamentary tumults and their numbers were matched by catholic loyalists such as Derby and Montagu. The presbyterians, centred on the Commons, were likewise few in number and lacked widespread sympathy and support. Their published *Admonitions to the Parliament* which, in 1572, attacked the prayer book and government by bishops, was not well received; their parliamentary attempts to legislate a presbyterian Church into existence in 1584 and 1587 were easily nipped in the bud by the speaker and councillors. Certainly there were carefully planned presbyterian agitations, but they never seriously threatened the council's control of Parliament.

When parliamentary confrontations occurred, they were the consequence not of the queen's actions but of her inaction, her reluctance to move on such vital issues as her marriage, the succession, Mary Stuart's fate and Church reform. Furthermore they were not confrontations with a puritan opposition in the Commons, as Neale argued. The great issues of the time concerned the very survival of the national Church and independent English State – and they troubled equally the privy council and the governing class. What may be misread as government–opposition clashes were actually co-operative exercises between the two houses, orchestrated by the council and designed to coerce Elizabeth into action; and usually one can detect the guiding hand of Burghley, combining loyalty to his queen with a determination to force her hand for her own good.

Unlike the early Stuart period, little work has been done on the connection between Tudor court politics and Parliaments. Yet there is no doubt that the connection was there: in the manoeuvres of Cromwell's opponents in 1539–40, Thomas Lord Seymour's intrigues in

1548/9 and the Gardiner–Paget duel in 1553–54. Behind the marriage and succession campaigns of 1563–66/7 were the competing objectives and ambitions of Cecil, Leicester and Norfolk. The unsuccessful court conspiracy against Cecil in 1569, headed by Norfolk, Arundel, Leicester and Pembroke, may have had parliamentary repercussions in the campaign to execute the duke in 1572 (see below, pp. 150–1). In the 1590s those court rivals Sir Robert Cecil and the earl of Essex were also competitors in the hunt for parliamentary patronage. Even the royal veto of Bills which had passed both houses could conceal the activity of powerful court interests: in 1581 Weymouth's parliamentary agent advised the borough not to proceed with its Bill because Sir Christopher Hatton 'would overthrow it when it should come to her Majesty's hands'. [22]

Parliament's business was legislation, not only the queen's essential business but also beneficial laws and the redress of grievances sought by members of the governing class. The privy council's natural priority was the first of these, to secure the money and laws required for effective government and national security. At the same time, however, the volume of private Bills (mainly in the Commons) had become formidable and the council could not afford to frustrate too many of their promoters. Thus there was implicit, in each session, a clash of priorities.

On the other hand inter-cameral relations were essentially harmonious and co-operative. Few sharp disagreements occurred between Lords and Commons (and council too) on important matters of principle and policy. There were disturbed sessions: that of 1566/7 was marked by Paul Wentworth's three resolutions on the Commons' liberties and the failure to renew eleven important statutes which were due to expire. Furthermore a lawyer member proposed that the succession question and the subsidy should be considered together, a tactic adopted again in 1584 when religious grievances were linked with supply. In both instances the manoeuvre was directed against the queen, not the Lords, and in any case they were ineffective. Relations between the two houses were more likely to be ruffled by petty disputes over points of protocol and procedure. Usually it was the Commons which stood on its dignity, but its sensitivity is understandable – it had to cope with the intimidating social superiority of the upper house, especially of the peers. This was illustrated by the procedure at joint conferences when the Commons' delegates stood bareheaded before their seated and covered social betters. In 1581 one of the lower house advised against 'often conferences' which resulted in the 'terrifying of men's opinions'. He did not mean that the Lords' delegates deliberately set out to intimidate, but that knights, and especially burgesses, were obsequious, sought out their lordships' opinions and 'knowing that in the common house nothing is secret', they made those opinions their own when they returned. [23]

The Commons' irritation with this state of affairs was sometimes expressed by an obstinate stand on procedural niceties. When in 1576, the Lords asked why the restoration in blood of Lord Stourton, a grace Bill bearing the sign manual, had been stayed and modified there, it was bluntly informed that the lower house had the right 'to dash any such bill, much more to alter'. The Lords' request for a joint conference was snubbed with the tart advice that only the house which possessed the Bill could seek such a meeting. So they 'will (if they see cause . . .) pray conference . . .; and else not'. Indeed the Commons could be childishly tetchy. On the last day of the 1581 session the Lords, having passed the subsidy Bill, returned it with the casual comment 'that the use is indifferent, either to take it there, or send it hither' – in other words it did not matter in which house the completed tax Bill stayed until the Commons' speaker presented it to the queen during the closing ceremonies. The proprietary pride of the Commons over the subsidy Bill was deeply wounded. It immediately resolved 'that the use thereof is *not* indifferent, but always hath been, and is, that it be sent down into this House, and not left there'.[24]

However, the unkindest cut of all was yet to come. In 1589 the Commons, whose members were ludicrously under-assessed for taxation, voted the exceptional sum of two subsidies. It proposed the same again in 1593, whereupon a smug glow of liberality warmed the house. The euphoria soon vanished when, at a joint conference requested by the upper house, its delegates were brusquely advised by Burghley that the Lords would accept no less than three subsidies, to be paid within three years and not at the customary rate of half a subsidy per annum. Moreover – a sting in the tail this – incomes must be more realistically assessed. This assault on the Commons' constitutional rights engendered heated debate, but in the end it gave way and 'gladly and cheerfully' granted three subsidies over a four-year period.[25]

The Lords too could be sensitive to a fault on points of honour and dignity. Increasingly, however, it adopted one of two alternative positions: as the queen's assistant fulfilling her business, or as the Commons' ally lobbying her to act. It was assuming the role of middleman, a kind of parliamentary broker willing to work with either (or both) of its partners according to the issue of the moment. It was also Burghley's instrument with which he attempted to work his will.

This is not to deny that both houses were sensitive of their privileges. Freedom of speech normally and rightly focuses our attention on the Commons, but not because it was growing in power. Its members were not natural politicians, schooled in circumspection and discretion like the bishops and peers (who in any case could voice their protests through clients in the nether house). They were more inclined to overstep the mark, especially as Elizabeth imposed on them the unhistorical (even unconstitutional) distinction between commonwealth matters (on which they could speak freely) and matters of State (to be debated only with her permission).

Freedom from arrest, too, is normally discussed solely in relation to the Commons, although it should not be. There are two aspects to the subject. First, there was the undoubted right to attend Parliament without fear of arrest at the suit of private persons – usually creditors seeking to collect debts. Certainly the privilege did not give immunity from criminal actions. It did, however, protect a member's servants, who were considered necessary to the performance of his parliamentary duties, and was a privilege obviously open to abuse. At various times, Elizabeth, her lord keeper and council admonished those who had secured election in order to visit London without fear of arrest. A test case in 1542 had established the Commons' right to free arrested members by warrant of its mace. Thereafter a member could procure his own arrest and secure his release as a matter of privilege, after which he could not be seized again for the same offence. Eventually the house, normally self-indulgent in this matter, felt obliged to act when, in 1576, Arthur Hall flagrantly misused the privilege.[26]

Secondly, there was the arrest of members by the Crown for political offences. Once again our attention is Commons-orientated. When William Strickland was sequestered in 1571 for introducing a Bill to reform the prayer book, it provoked uproar in the house. After this Elizabeth was careful to ensure that arrests were for offences committed before the session or outside Parliament. However, attention should be paid to the Lords too. The queen imprisoned two catholic bishops during her first Parliament, and the earl of Hertford, some of the catholic malcontents in 1572 and Archbishop Grindal were all parliamentary absentees as a consequence of her displeasure. While the Lords avoided a confrontation with Elizabeth on this issue, it was as sensitive of its privileges as the Commons. So, when the irascible Henry Lord Cromwell appealed to it in 1572, after he had been arrested for contempt of the court of chancery, he received a sympathetic hearing. The house consulted the judges, disregarded the lord keeper's advice that noblemen were not exempt from the law and condemned his arrest as derogatory to the privilege of peers. Although he had been arrested when no Parliament was in session, it followed that immunity from arrest for contempt would also apply during one. Cromwell's personal victory was the first of a series of decisions which greatly enlarged the peers' freedom from arrest.[27] Nor were the bishops excluded from such privileges: in 1597 Archbishop Whitgift's servant was released and his captor imprisoned by order of the house. The upper house, no less than the Commons, was conscious of its honour and dignity as a member of the parliamentary trinity.

Burghley was the key to the role of the two houses within that trinity. From 1571 he managed Parliament from the Lords. If we reject Neale and Notestein and accept that the Commons was not becoming more powerful and obstreperous, then it was not foolish or shortsighted to elevate him to the upper house. After all, Thomas Cromwell and (less so) Stephen Gardiner had successfully transacted the Crown's business from their places there. Nevertheless it did require Burghley to modify his managerial techniques – what Elton calls 'a new form of conciliar control, called into existence by the departure to the House of Lords of the manager-in-chief'.[28] If we could imagine him drafting one of his characteristic memoranda, it might read thus: to secure a subsidy, but also some necessary laws for the commonweal; to persuade Her Majesty of the necessity to marry or name a successor (or to improve the condition of the Church, punish Mary Stuart, provide severer penal laws against obdurate catholics, or whatever); and to allow time for bishops, peers, knights and burgesses to enact laws beneficial for themselves, their fellows and constituencies. This conjectural summary exhibits the different caps worn by Burghley. Parliament met in order to conduct the queen's business and that was his over-riding concern. He was also the wise male counsellor who had to direct a perverse woman into the right courses. Parliament could be used to this end. Burghley was also one of the governing class and knew its parliamentary expectations in terms of beneficial Acts and wholesome laws for the commonwealth.

Doubtless a Cecilian memorandum would have identified obstacles to these objectives too: (a) when Parliaments are at variance; (b) short sessions; (c) the volume of business; (d) the Commons' inefficiency; (e) Her Majesty's reluctance to proceed in important matters. These difficulties, except for the first, were common and real enough. Elizabeth, no lover of Parliaments, drove council, Lords and Commons on to finish as quickly as possible. At the same time the volume of private Bills in the Commons continued to grow and threatened to inundate a house which was ill-equipped to cope. More than half its members in each Parliament were raw novices, 'in troops making strange noises' and 'out of all order' as an old Parliament man contemptuously put it.[29] They quickly tired of the legislative grind and in any case many were in London only 'to learn and see fashions'.[30] Absenteeism was endemic among not only such young aristocratic fashion seekers but also the men most crucial to the Commons' legislative efficiency, the lawyers, who preferred to practise to their profit in the law courts next door.

Such problems merged together to threaten parliamentary productivity in general and official programmes in particular. Burghley's answer was to monitor Parliament's progress and apply pressure to its legislative bottleneck, the Commons, through the House of Lords. The latter was not beset with the problems which afflicted the lower house, because it was much smaller, more experienced and handled relatively few Bills. Its attendance was more closely and effectively supervised and the legal assistants, unlike their legal brethren in the Commons, were regularly present. Moreover many of the bishops and peers were Burghley's friends, relatives by marriage, colleagues or subordinates in royal administration, political allies, or fellow councillors – thus their support could usually be relied upon. It is no coincidence that, once he had departed to the upper house, the Commons was subjected to a stream of messages from above: to concentrate on commonweal matters and lay aside all private Bills; to hurry business along because 'the season of the year waxed very hot and dangerous for sickness'; and to arrange Bills into an order of priority, giving precedence to the subsidy and other important business. Council measures were sent down with requests for their speedy despatch and messengers demanded 'bills with speed, if any were ready'. The Lords, under Burghley's guidance, maintained a relentless pressure and the Commons, perhaps surprisingly, responded to it in a positive and constructive fashion.[31]

This did not exhaust his arsenal of managerial weapons. Successive lord keepers stressed the urgency of the queen's business, the importance of commonweal matters, and the royal prohibition on Bills of religion. The Commons' speaker was also recruited to strum the same themes. This was easily done because, although he was formally elected by the Commons, he was the Crown's nominee. While the early Tudor speakers had been privy councillors and officers of State, in Elizabeth's reign they were not of such exalted status. Their connection with the Crown remained nevertheless an intimate one: after 1559 they were lawyers and included three solicitors-general and five queen's serjeants. The speaker was a vital instrument of conciliar control, determining the order of business and controlling debates, while those privy councillors who were of the house sat around his chair and fed him with whispered advice and instructions. Doubtless it was they who, in 1581, prompted Speaker Popham's advice to the Commons 'for that the Parliament was like to be very short' not to spend too much time in 'unnecessary motions or superfluous arguments'.[32]

Burghley also looked to his lieutenants, Knollys and Mildmay, to direct affairs in the Commons, but more important than them were his clients who, in the Parliament time, served as his 'men-of-business'. There were always a number of loyalist knights and burgesses who were anxious to advance the queen's business and who looked to the council for a lead. Among them were men connected to privy councillors by ties of kinship and clientage, such as Thomas Dannett (Burghley's cousin) and Thomas Digges (a client of Burghley's brother-in-law, Lord Keeper Bacon), who campaigned for the deaths of Mary Stuart and the duke of Norfolk in 1572. Others rendered more consistent service: careerist lawyers like Robert Bell, Christopher Yelverton and John Popham, for whom a successful parliamentary performance might lead to high judicial office; the clerks of the Commons, especially Fulk Onslow (between 1571 and 1601); and, above all, the members for London.

Harmonious relations between court and City were one of the keys to the success and stability of Tudor government. London was unique in that it had four members and its special relationship was expressed in the fact that they sat next to the councillors around the speaker's chair,[33] whereas the rest of the house 'sat as they came'.[34] Prominent merchants and bureaucrats, such as Thomas Aldersey (1572–89), Recorder Fleetwood (1558–89), Sir Rowland Hayward (1572–81), John Marsh (1547–54, 1555–76), and George Sotherton (1593–97), had business and administrative connections with the council, some attended Court and a number were the clients of councillors. In the Commons they served the interests not only of the City but also of the privy council and especially of Burghley.[35]

Foremost among them was Thomas Norton. He was a lawyer, the lord mayor's first 'remembrancer' (secretary) and so the intermediary between the City and the privy council. He was a moderate puritan, but it was his obsessive hatred of popery which made him a political activist and throughout his career he remained a devotee of queen and council. He established links with prominent councillors such as Hatton, Mildmay and Walsingham, and above all Burghley, who was 'the only man in whom I have and do lay the course of my relief'.[36] As a formidable debater, an inexhaustible committee man, a prolific parliamentary draftsman, and a popular Commons man, he was the lord treasurer's ideal instrument to further his ends there by remote control from the Lords.

Between 1563 and 1581 Norton became the man-of-business *par excellence*, but he was not unique. After his death James Dalton, Digges, William Fitzwilliam (Mildmay's son-in-law), Fleetwood and others continued the good work. In practice, however, they all followed Norton's precept 'to avoid offensive speech and proceeding in the house, to act with reverence towards the queen and to work through her and the council'. Their 'chiefest care was in all things to be directed by the council'.[37]

The managerial services rendered by the men-of-business were invaluable. Burghley needed his eyes and ears in the Commons to keep him informed of what was happening. Speakers (especially Bell in 1572), the clerk, lawyer members and London's representatives, especially Fleetwood, fed him with reports of debates and committee proceedings, lists of Bills and the stages which they had reached.[38] More important for his purposes was the way in which they pushed official business along by drafting Bills, guiding debate on them, and revising them in committee. In 1581, for example, his fellow councillor, Sir Walter Mildmay, and Norton dominated not only the initial debate when the council sought a subsidy and a harsher law against recusants, but also the committee which drew the Bills.[39] Norton was also in the thick of procedural innovation, designed to render the Commons more efficient and speed up business. Joint conferences (to anticipate or iron out disagreements with the Lords at an early stage) were regularised; afternoons were set aside for private Bills (in order to clear the morning sessions for more important business); and specialised committees were appointed to revise or collate the many Bills on such popular subjects as the cloth industry and timber preservation.[40]

The men-of-business were also generous in their advice. One, in 1581, explained how 'to have the session short' by reducing the number of private Bills, especially those of London, avoiding contentious matters which gave rise to 'long argument' and preventing delays to official business. Although Burghley hardly needed such advice, the writer did touch on one important matter, the subsidy, which should be 'ready written both in paper and parchment' when Parliament began.[41] As the lower house alone could initiate money Bills, *it* should have made the initial paper draft and engrossed the final version. Yet in 1566 Secretary Cecil had reminded himself 'to have the books of the subsidy put in a readiness'[42]; in 1576 a Commons' committee had decided the terms of a grant but left the council to draft the Bill; and in 1581 Norton dominated the subsidy committee, proposed the terms, drew them up and possibly even drafted the Bill. Even the Commons' exclusive power to initiate lay taxation may have been reduced to a formality by Burghley and his aides.

The most important political service of the men-of-business was their willingness to apply pressure and overcome Elizabeth's obstinacy: over marriage and succession (1563–66/7), treason and religion (1571), Mary and Norfolk (1572) and harsher penal laws (1581 and 1584). Elton has shown that in 1571 the Bill to apply communion as a religious test was not the work of a puritan opposition.[43] Councillors, men-of-business and bishops supported it and Burghley spoke in its favour in the Lords. The queen vetoed it, but the bishops petitioned for it to pass in 1572, and it appeared in the Lords in the next two sessions, with one draft annotated by the lord treasurer. Similarly the Alphabetical Bills, introduced late in the 1566/7 session and presented again in 1571 along with the *Reformatio legum ecclesiasticarum*[44] were not, as Neale saw them, an opposition puritan programme. Their authorship is uncertain but they were probably sponsored by Burghley and other councillors, their lawyer clients (e.g., Norton, Yelverton, Bell and Dalton), and the bishops. Their efforts received widespread parliamentary support, but Elizabeth allowed only two Bills (B and E) to become law.[45]

The most co-ordinated campaign during Burghley's long supremacy occurred in 1572. Parliament had been summoned specifically to consider the 'great cause' (Mary Stuart's fate). As Elizabeth had placed the problem before it, one might expect the councillors to have been optimistic about the outcome. By then, however, they knew their queen. She was reluctant to act against Mary or execute Norfolk, and it was the council which had persuaded her to call Parliament, once again in the hope of using it in order to coerce her. The council's objectives were Mary's exclusion from the succession, if possible her attainder, and Norfolk's death, and from the start it stage-managed a remorseless campaign to achieve them. Lord Keeper Bacon and his clients, Speaker Bell, Burghley's men-of-business, the lawyers, bishops and legal assistants in the Lords all participated. The harvest was a meagre one. Elizabeth bowed to the pressure and Norfolk died, but at the end of the session she vetoed the great Bill against Mary.[46]

However, Burghley persisted and, despite the queen's obstinacy, he achieved much of what he set out to do. The Parliaments of 1581 and 1584 passed severe anti-catholic laws. In 1584 Elizabeth approved the 'act for the queen's safety', which excluded Mary from the succession and empowered commissioners to investigate any conspiracy against the queen and reach a verdict. Two years later, after the Babington Plot, it was enforced in order to bring the Scottish queen to trial. Burghley then secured a Parliament in order to exert irresistible pressure on Elizabeth if she proved reluctant to authorise the execution. During the war with Spain his prime parliamentary objective was money and, in 1593, he clumsily but effectively used the Lords to obtain an unprecedented grant.[47] Even during the 1590s the ageing, ailing lord treasurer was still capable of significant successes.

However, at court he gradually transferred work, responsibility, and therefore authority to his son, Sir Robert Cecil. Indeed, the entire political spectrum was changing as a generation of politicians and bureaucrats died: Leicester (1588), Mildmay (1589), Warwick and Walsingham (1590), Knollys (1596), and finally Burghley himself (1598). Although Leicester and Burghley were rivals for power for thirty years, they were moderate men, often collaborated, and neither monopolised authority and patronage because Elizabeth would not allow it. However, their political heirs and successors were their step-son and second son respectively. The rise of the earl of Essex and Sir Robert Cecil was marked by a decline in political morality and a novel, abrasive quality in politics. Their factions split court and country. When Parliaments were summoned they laboured to return their clients, especially by the acquisition of borough stewardships.[48] There is no evidence that they used Parliament in their power-struggle and perhaps they were just competing for prestige, though it pointed the way to early Stuart patrons who would manipulate their parliamentary clienteles to attack opponents at court.

As for the Lords, its prestige and authority were significantly affected by Burghley's presence. It recovered some of the ground which it had lost in the 1550s and became the motivating force in Parliament, simply because he was a member. The house lent him the collective weight of its support as the social élite and the assistance of its clients in the Commons. It would be wrong, however, to assume political unanimity in an assembly which housed both Burghley and Leicester, Whitgift and the 'puritan' nobles, an anti-clerical laity and acquisitive, competing peers. On some issues unity was impossible, but at least, unlike the Marian and early Stuart Parliaments, conciliar divisions did not erupt into public, parliamentary conflict. Instead the Lords generally responded to Burghley's guidance, pressuring the Commons and the queen whenever necessary. In the 1590s, however, the pendulum of power slowly swung back to the Commons where his successor, Robert Cecil, sat.

REFERENCES AND NOTES

1. Trinity College Dublin MS 1045 (Thomas Cromwell's journal for the parliamentary sessions of 1572–84, hereafter cited as 'Cromwell'), fo. 4; Anonymous journal, Bodleian, Tanner MS, 393, fo. 45v.
2. Sir Simonds D'Ewes, *The Journals of All the Parliaments during the Reign of Queen Elizabeth* [D'Ewes, *Journals*], London, 1682, p. 377.
3. *H.P.T.*, 1558–1603, II, p. 224; L. Stone, *The Crisis of the Aristocracy, 1558–1641*, Oxford, 1965, p. 756.
4. Ibid., pp. 98–9, 758.
5. Marquess of Northampton (William Parr), earl of Hertford (Edward Seymour), Viscount Bindon (Thomas Howard), and Barons Dacre of the South, Hunsdon and St. John of Bletsoe.
6. *L.J.*, II, 196.
7. Ibid., 195.
8. *C.J.*, I, 115–17, 129, 135–6.
9. Ibid., 115–36.
10. B.L., Lansdowne MS, 104, ff. 78–9.
11. David Dean, who is investigating later Elizabethan legislation, will provide a fuller picture.
12. Neale, *E.H.C.*, p. 373.
13. Elton, 'Functions and Fortunes', 260.
14. Elton, 'Enacting Clauses', 183–91.
15. D'Ewes, *Journals*, p. 151.
16. W. D. Cooper (ed.), 'Further particulars of Thomas Norton, and of state proceedings in matters of religion, in the years 1581 and 1582', *Archeologia*, XXXVI (1885), 110.
17. John Popham (1581) and Edward Coke (1593). In 1566 the solicitor-general, Richard Onslow, had been chosen to fill the vacancy caused by the death of the Commons' speaker, Thomas Williams.
18. *C.J.*, I, 106.
19. 'A Treatise of the Maisters of the Chauncerie', in F. Hargrave, *Collec-*

tanea Juridicia, consisting of Tracts relative to the Law and Constitution of England, 2 vols, Dublin, 1787, I, p. xl and Chapter III.

20. D'Ewes, *Journals*, p. 422.
21. Neale, *Eliz. Parls*, I, 152, 318–29.
22. Elton, 'Functions and Fortunes', 276–7; Neale, *E.H.C.*, pp. 388–9.
23. B.L., Harleian MS, 253, ff. 32–6.
24. Elton, 'Functions and Fortunes', 261; 'Cromwell', f. 130v; *C.J.*, I, 114–15, 136.
25. Neale, *Eliz. Parls*, II, pp. 302, 310.
26. Elton, *Tudor Constitution* (1982), pp. 261–2; ibid., 'Arthur Hall, Lord Burghley and the Antiquity of Parliament', in *History and Imagination*, H. Lloyd-Jones, V. Pearl, and B. Worden (eds), London, 1981, pp. 88–103; ibid., 'Functions and Fortunes', 270.
27. M. A. R. Graves, 'Freedom of Peers from Arrest: The case of Henry Second Lord Cromwell, 1571–1572', *American Journal of Legal History*, XXI (1977), 1–14.
28. Elton, 'Functions and Fortunes', 267.
29. B.L., Lansdowne MS, 41, f. 45, Fleetwood to Burghley, 29 Nov. 1584.
30. B.L., Harleian MS, 253, f. 32.
31. For example, *C.J.*, I, 85–6, 96, 100, 102; Hooker's Journal in T. E. Hartley (ed.), *Proceedings in the Parliaments of Elizabeth I*, Vol. I, 1558–81, Leicester, 1981, p. 248.
32. *C.J.*, I, 118.
33. So did the two members for York, the second City of the realm.
34. Neale, *E.H.C.*, p. 365.
35. For the government and governing élite of the city, see F. F. Foster, *Politics of Stability. A Portrait of the Rulers in Elizabethan London*, London, 1977.
36. Graves, 'Thomas Norton', p. 18 and n. 48.
37. For Norton and other men-of-business, see Graves, 'Thomas Norton', 28, 34; ibid., 'Council's Men-of-Business', 11–38. Much work remains to be done on the Parliaments of 1584–1601.
38. Elton, 'Functions and Fortunes', 265–7.
39. Graves, 'Thomas Norton', 31–2.
40. Ibid., 24–5.
41. B.L., Harleian MS, 253, ff. 32–6.
42. P.R.O., S.P. 12/40/68.
43. Elton, 'Functions and Fortunes', pp. 273–4.
44. See above, Chapter 1, note 4.
45. Neale, *Eliz. Parls*, I, pp. 193–217; Elton, 'Functions and Fortunes', 274; Graves, 'Council's Men-of-Business', 12–13, 24.
46. Ibid., 24–8.
47. Neale, *Eliz. Parls*, II, pp. 298–312.
48. Neale, *E.H.C.*, pp. 233–43; *H.P.T.*, 1558–1603, I, pp. 63–5.

Chapter eight

EPILOGUE

The Parliament of 1597–98 had granted a triple subsidy, the last instalment of which was due in October 1600. However, the yield from each subsidy continued to fall, the war dragged on and the Crown's debts mounted. The later 1590s were years of social, economic and military crisis: soaring prices, growing unemployment and vagabondage, bad harvests and alarming public disturbances. Nor did the Spanish threat diminish. There were Armadas in 1597 and 1599 and descents on the south-west coast, while in 1601 an expeditionary force landed in Ireland to assist catholic rebels. By 1601 the war had lasted fourteen years, yet England remained as beleaguered as ever, so the air of war-weariness which pervaded the last Elizabethan Parliament is not surprising. Domestic developments, however, transformed weariness into irritation, even anger. Elizabeth's war economies included a reduction of patronage and a preference for financially painless grants. Monopolies empowering favoured courtiers and servants to manufacture such items as glass, steel, paper, cards, tin and saltpetre cost the queen little, but they could harm her subjects who might incur higher prices for inferior products. Moreover a military administration, hastily assembled in wartime without effective royal supervision, bred corruption. Meanwhile the bitter faction conflict between the Cecils and Essex tore the court apart and tarnished its public reputation. In February 1601 the climax came with Essex's abortive rebellion and execution, which probably deferred Parliament until late in the year. By then the need for money was desperate.

As if in defiance of her previous record of ecclesiastical mismanagement, Elizabeth was able to summon twenty-three lords spiritual to her last Parliament. Only Bristol, Oxford and Llandaff remained without bishops (though two of them had been vacant for eight years or more). Nevertheless the lords spiritual still constituted less than one-third of the upper house. Despite minorities and the failure of male lines since 1597 just over fifty peers received writs. However, some bishops and peers were licensed sessional absentees, while the earl of Southampton had been imprisoned for life and five peers were ordered to stay away because of their involvement in Essex's rebellion. Only nineteen lords spiritual and thirty-four lords temporal put in an appearance during the session and the daily attendance fluctuated between 29 and 44. As so often before the lords spiritual had the more creditable record, with an average daily presence of seventeen compared to the peers' twenty-two.

The Lords' average attendance of 39 out of 74 (or 53 per cent) was not an impressive performance, but it still contrasted favourably with the Commons where, in fifteen divisions, only 44 per cent voted.[1] Absenteeism continued to trouble concerned members of the lower house. Sir Robert Cecil might be gratified 'to see the Parliament so full, which towards the end used to grow thin', yet he uttered these words just after a division in which 310 voted but a third of the members were absent.[2] Indeed, the house was remarkably lax about attendance as William Wiseman pointed out when he 'moved the House to remember . . . that it had been an ancient custom in Parliament, sometimes to call the House, which as yet was not done.'[3] To the very end of Elizabeth's reign the Commons had an inferior attendance record. This is not surprising. Parliaments meant time, tedium, labour and expense. Henry VII promised not to burden subjects with frequent assemblies, and Sir Thomas Smith said 'What can a commonwealth desire more than peace, liberty, quietness [and] few Parliaments?'[4]

Parliament met on 27 October 1601 and the queen dissolved it just six days before Christmas. As the crucial business was taxation, the Commons held centre stage and obliged with four subsidies and eight fifteenths and tenths, after extended discussion as to whether the 'three pound men' – the poorer sort – should be assessed. This apart, however, the absence of a Commons' journal renders it impossible to provide a precise and detailed assessment of the legislative role of the two houses. Even so, all the signs point to an overburdened Commons and a leisurely Lords. The latter conducted business on twenty-eight mornings and six afternoons, whereas the former's comparative figures were forty-two and ten. Sometimes dedicated knights and burgesses sat through four-hour sessions and twelve-hour days.[5] The government, desperate for money and fearful of competing, time-consuming private Bills, served notice through the speaker 'that this Parliament should be a short Parliament', and so members 'should not spend the time in frivolous, vain and unnecessary Motions and Arguments'. Secretary Cecil warned against 'fantastic speeches or idle Bills' and later scolded that 'we consume our time now in unnecessary disputations' while the queen advised of a pending dissolution.[6] As always the threat came from unofficial Bills. Indeed, Robert Wingfield asked that 'seeing the Subsidy was granted . . . it would please her Majesty not to dissolve the Parliament till some Acts were passed'.[7] Concerned members did what they could – attempting to refer a Bill back to London and obliging promoters of successful private Bills to pay sizeable sums for poor relief[8] – but with little success. Forty of the fifty-nine bills before the Lords originated in the Commons and (as Robert Cecil superseded his father) so did most of the Acts: 56 per cent in 1593, 74 per cent in 1597 and 90 per cent in 1601. Yet the small upper house of experienced legislators, assisted by the legal assistants, remained the more efficient chamber. Furthermore, despite the deficiencies of evidence, it is clear that procedural refinement and experimentation were going on apace in *both* houses. The Commons frequently resorted to the 'committee of the whole house', a more time-saving, efficient device than formal debate.[9] It was also making more effective use of its specialists, the lawyers, who were appointed *en bloc* to twenty-four committees in 1601.[10] In the Lords procedural aberrations were giving way to procedural uniformity:[11] thus only one of the fifty-nine Bills before it was committed after the first reading. In the organisation of its business Parliament had come a long way since 1485.

Although there was no organised 'opposition', this was a fractious Parliament. Privilege cases abounded: a printed libel and members served with subpoenas or arrested for debt. Elections were challenged on various grounds. The Commons 'hemm'd and laughed and talked' during Serjeant Hele's speech and 'hawk'd and spat' during another's address. There were complaints about the misconduct of pages and servants, gentlemen '[who] stand before the Door, which breeds a confused sound' and members wearing boots, spurs and rapiers. The famous monopolies debate must be seen in this context and certainly should not be underestimated. The Commons' explosive protest against Elizabeth's grants occupied its attention between 18–24 November, in a Parliament of almost eight weeks. One member spoke out 'for a Country that groaneth and languisheth' and he described monopolists as bloodsuckers; another complained that the price of salt had multiplied elevenfold; and a third that, unless they acted promptly, 'Bread will be there before the next Parliament'.[12]

Nevertheless this was but one episode in an irascible Parliament. There were heated exchanges between members, a fractious joint conference, criticisms of the speaker and rejection of his choice of Bills to be read. Sir Robert Cecil was partly responsible. After Essex's death he had no rival in government, but he was tetchy, censorious, even tactless. Consequently he sometimes lost control, found himself isolated and even over-ridden by the house. Indeed the Commons was often out of control, as when Cecil expostulated that he had never seen it 'in so great Confusion', and when the recusants Bill ended in scenes of disorder. In contrast the Lords was decorous, leisurely and orderly, and moreover continued to wield the influence of a social élite: – an MP could introduce a Bill at the prompting of Lord Cobham's brother and with the speaker's support. The lords in Parliament continued to reflect the place which they occupied in society, even though the Commons had become, since Burghley's death, the political centre of parliamentary gravity.[13]

Between 1485 and 1601 much changed, but the changes were less substantial than was once thought. Parliaments remained irregular, brief and, apart from the Reformation 'crisis' of 1529–59, infrequent. They remained an occasional supplement to royal government and their life continued to be determined by the monarch's fiat. Of course there were important, even fundamental, changes, but their significance should not be misread. Late fifteenth century assemblies were still occasions when kings met the governing class to promote and negotiate their separate and mutual interests. King *and* Parliament best describes them. The Lords remained the more powerful and prestigious chamber, a fact reflected in inter-cameral procedure. The Commons, however, exercising the sole right to initiate lay taxation, had also progressed from a mere petitioner to a full legislative partner, even if this still needed judicial confirmation. Nevertheless the law-making competence of Parliament was strictly circumscribed, with matters spiritual and the sanctity of property still generally beyond its purview.

Even before the Henrician 'revolution' of the 1530s, however, an important constitutional process had reached its conclusion. King *and* Parliament had become king-*in*-Parliament. In other words the monarch had become an integral part of Parliament which consisted of a trinity of king, Lords and Commons, in that order of importance. Then, in the 1530s, king-in-Parliament became the constitutional sovereign and the limitations on statute fell away. The Edwardian, Marian and Elizabethan religious changes confirmed and clarified this. In the process Parliament became a popular clearing-house for the business and interests not only of the Crown but also of the governing class. However, this created problems, especially for the Commons. It grew in size (from 296 to 462), partly due to the incorporation of Wales into the parliamentary system in accordance with the Act of Union of 1536, but especially because successive monarchs acceded to the importunate suits of aristocratic patrons. 'Carpet-bagging' gentry invaded the boroughs, often sitting but once as part of their political education. Organisational problems grew with the size of the house, its many parliamentary novices, and its inundation with private Bills. The council responded with procedural experiments and improvements, preparation of official business, and the refinement of managerial techniques.

The relationship of the two houses was determined by political circumstances and the location of the chief minister. However, there occurred a turning-point in 1553–55, when conciliar factions used the Lords in the furtherance of their own interests. The house suffered a temporary eclipse, recovered some lost ground in Elizabeth's reign but never recovered its former legislative initiative, at least in strictly quantitative terms. By the end of the century the Lords had become a parliamentary broker, though never a cypher. Its invisible social influence, greater experience and its legal expertise made it a continuing and formidable parliamentary force.

By 1601 much had changed, but all within a recognised framework. The essential crown/governing-class harmony survived intact, though not without stresses and strains. Opposition to royal policies, even during the Edwardian Reformation, in Mary's reign, or in the long war of 1587–1604, never seriously jeopardised that harmony. Although Parliament had dramatically enlarged its authority, so long as the harmony survived intact the Crown, an integral part of Parliament, was the chief beneficiary. It continued to obtain money and laws and to sound out public opinion. Of course harmony was not, in itself, a guarantee of success. Parliamentary management was always an official priority, even if techniques changed from overt conciliar control to the use of 'men-of-business' during the century. Managerial controls were seldom seriously tested by expressions of political discontent in Parliament. Despite the growing war-weariness of the governing class, the divisions in court and council, and the unprecedented period of annual taxation, Parliament continued to be a source of strength to the Tudors until the death of Elizabeth, the last of the line.

REFERENCES AND NOTES

1. *H.P.T.*, 1558–1603, I, p. 100 muddled the figures for one division and omitted five others.
2. D'Ewes, *Journals*, p. 675.
3. Ibid., p. 661.
4. John Strype, *The Life of the Learned Sir Thomas Smith*, Oxford, 1820, p. 192.
5. *H.P.T.*, 1558–1603, I, p. 100; D'Ewes, *Journals*, pp. 632, 667, 675.
6. Ibid., pp. 621, 623, 675, 676–7.
7. Ibid., p. 632.
8. Ibid., pp. 665, 680–1.
9. *H.P.T.*, 1558–1603, I, p. 99.
10. Ibid., p. 98.
11. The flexibility and self-confidence of a small assembly of the social élite should not be confused with procedural sloppiness. See E. R. Foster, 'Procedure and the House of Lords in the Seventeenth Century', *Proceedings of the American Philosophical Society*, **126**, No. 3 (1982), 184.
12. D'Ewes, *Journals*, pp. 623–5, 629, 633–5, 637–40, 642–54, 672–3, 675, 677, 680, 685–6.
13. Ibid., pp. 627, 630, 651, 673–9, 683–4.

PARLIAMENTARY SESSIONS, 1485–1601

Parliament	Dates of sessions	Date of dissolution
Henry VII		
1485	7 November–10 December 1485	March 1486
1487	9 November–December 1487	December 1487
1489	13 January–23 February 1489	27 February 1490
1491	17 October–4 November 1491	5 March 1492
1495	14 October–21/2 December 1495	21/2 December 1495
1497	16 January–13 March 1497	13 March 1497
1504	25 January–(?) April 1504	April 1504
Henry VIII		
1510	21 January–23 February 1510	23 February 1510
1512–14 (1)	4 February–30 March 1512	
(2)	4 November–20 December 1512	
(3)	23 January–4 March 1514	4 March 1514
1515 (1)	5 February–5 April 1515	
(2)	12 November–22 December 1515	22 December 1515
1523	15 April–29 July 1523	13 August 1523
1529–36 (1)	3 November–17 December 1529	
(2)	16 January–31 March 1531	
(3)	15 January–14 May 1532	
(4)	4 February–7 April 1533	
(5)	15 January–30 March 1534	
(6)	3 November–18 December 1534	
(7)	4 February–14 April 1536	14 April 1536
1536	8 June–18 July 1536	18 July 1536
1539–40 (1)	28 April–28 June 1539	
(2)	12 April–24 July 1540	24 July 1540
1542–44 (1)	16 January–1 April 1542	
(2)	22 January–12 May 1543	
(3)	14 January–29 March 1544	29 March 1544

The Tudor Parliaments

Parliament		Dates of sessions	Date of dissolution
1545–47	(1)	23 November–24 December 1545	
	(2)	14–31 January 1547	31 January 1547 (automatically dissolved by the king's death)
Edward VI			
1547–52	(1)	4 November–24 December 1547	
	(2)	24 November 1548–14 March 1549	
	(3)	4 November 1549–1 February 1550	
	(4)	23 January–15 April 1552	15 April 1552
1553		1–31 March 1553	31 March 1553
Mary I			
1553		5 October–6 December 1553	6 December 1553
1554		2 April–5 May 1554	5 May 1554
1554/5		12 November 1554–16 January 1555	16 January 1666
1555		21 October–9 December 1555	9 December 1555
1558	(1)	20 January–7 March 1558	
	(2)	5–17 November 1558	17 November 1558 (automatically dissolved by the queen's death)
Elizabeth I			
1559		23 January–8 May 1559	8 May 1559
1563–67	(1)	11 January–10 April 1563	
	(2)	30 September 1566–2 January 1567	2 January 1567
1571		2 April–29 May 1571	29 May 1571
1572–81	(1)	8 May–30 June 1572	
	(2)	8 February–15 March 1576	
	(3)	16 January–18 March 1581	19 April 1583
1584/5		23 November–29 March 1585	14 September 1585
1586/7		29 October–23 March 1587	23 March 1587
1589		4 February–29 March 1589	29 March 1589
1593		19 February–10 April 1593	10 April 1593
1597/8		24 October 1597–9 February 1598	9 February 1598
1601		27 October–19 December 1601	19 December 1601

BIBLIOGRAPHY

For two reasons this is a bibliographical note rather than a comprehensive bibliography. In the first place, many of the most important books and articles on Tudor Parliaments have been cited in full in the references for Chapter 1, which deals specifically with the historiography of Tudor Parliaments. Secondly, current economic realities make a selective bibliography more viable and realistic than a comprehensive one. The items listed below have been included because (1) they are primary sources essential to a study of Tudor Parliaments; (2) they are books or articles which have been cited in chapters 2–8 or utilised (though not cited) in the preparation of this book.

PRIMARY SOURCES

D'Ewes, Sir Simonds, *The Journals of All the Parliaments during the Reign of Queen Elizabeth*, London, 1602. Omits the Lords' attendance record and abridges entries in the Commons' journals but, at the same time, supplements the latter with private journals and diaries.

Halle, E., *The union of the two noble illustre famelies of Lancastre and York*, London, 1550, reprinted Menston, 1970. Hall was an MP in the Reformation Parliament and his chronicle contains eye-witness accounts.

Hartley, T. E. (ed.), *Proceedings in the Parliaments of Elizabeth I*, Vol. I, 1558–71, Leicester, 1981.

Historical Manuscripts Commission Reports. A goldmine of information on borough and other local parliamentary interests, e.g., City of Exeter MS (1916).

House of Lords Records Office, Original Acts. The manuscript text of Acts passed by the Tudor Parliaments.

Brewer, J. S., Gairdner, J., Brodie, R. H. (eds), *Letters and Papers, Foreign and Domestic, of the Reign of Henry VIII*, London, 1862–1932. Especially important for Henry VIII's reign, above all the 1530s.

Journals of the House of Lords, vols I, II, London 1846. They include attendance registers of bishops and peers, but otherwise they constitute only a brief record of business.

Luders, A., Tomlins, T. E., Raithby, J., *et al.* (eds), *Statutes of the Realm*, 11 vols, London 1810–28, Vols. I–IV. The text of public Acts.

Smith, Sir Thomas, *De Republica Anglorum*, ed. M. Dewar, Cambridge, 1982. The classic Elizabethan description of Parliaments.

Townshend, Hayward, *Historical Collections, an exact account of the last four parliaments of Elizabeth*, London, 1680.

Vardon, T. and May, T. E. (eds), *Journals of the House of Commons*, Vol. I (1547–1628), London, 1803.

SECONDARY WORKS

Bond, M. F., 'Acts of Parliament', *Archives*, III, no. 20 (1958), 201–18.

Bond, M. F., 'The Archives of Parliament', *Genealogists' Magazine*, **11** (1953), 338–48.

Bond, M. F., *The Records of Parliament*, Canterbury, 1964. The works of Maurice Bond, clerk of the records and for long the presiding officer of the House of Lords Record Office, provide an excellent working manual for students of parliamentary legislation.

Bush, M. L. *The Government Policy of Protector Somerset*, London, 1976. Useful for the parliamentary sessions of the Protectorate (1547 and 1548–49).

Chrimes, S. B., *Henry VII*, London, 1972. Ch. 7 is essential for the Parliaments of the first Tudor.

Cooper, J. P., 'Henry VII's last years reconsidered', *H.J.*, **2**, no. 2 (1959), 103–29.

Elton, G. R., 'Henry VII: Rapacity and remorse', *H.J.*, **1**, no. 1 (1958), 21–39.

Elton, G. R., 'Henry VII: a restatement', *H.J.*, **4**, no. 1 (1961), 1–29.
The above three articles are concerned with the myth or reality of Henry VII's rapacious financial policy, but they also shed light on the parliamentary backlash against his practices in 1510.

Elton, G. R., *England under the Tudors*, London, 1974. First published in 1955, it was reprinted eleven times in the next 16 years. Finally a 'new' edition appeared in 1974. This did not amount to a re-writing of the original work – only an amended and extended bibliography and the addition of a chapter of 'Revisions' in which pp. 482–84 are significant for the history of Parliaments in the 1530s.

Elton, G. R., *Reform and Reformation, England 1509–1558*, London, 1977. A rich mixture of synthesis and original research, which provides the most up-to-date history of England in this period.

Elton, G. R., 'The Law of Treason in the Early Reformation', *H.J.*, **11**, no. 2 (1968), 211–236 (see also Lehmberg below).

Elton, G. R., 'Arthur Hall, Lord Burghley and the Antiquity of Parliament', in *History and Imagination*, H. Lloyd-Jones, V. Pearl, and B. Worden (eds), London, 1981.

Foster, F. F., *Politics of Stability*, London, 1977. A study of the government of Elizabethan London. Important for an understanding of London's parliamentary activities.

Graves, M. A. R., 'Freedom of Peers from Arrest: the case of Henry Second Lord Cromwell, 1571–1572', *American Journal of Legal History*, XXI (1977), 1–14.

Hoak, D. E., *The King's Council in the reign of Edward VI*, Cambridge, 1976. Important for such aspects of Parliament as the Protectorate and parliamentary management.

Lander, J. R., *Crown and Nobility, 1450–1509*, London, 1976.

Lander, J. R., *Government and Community. England 1450–1509*, Cambridge, Mass. 1980.

Lander's works should be used with Chrimes' *Henry VII* for the first Tudor's Parliaments.

Lehmberg, S. E., 'Parliamentary attainder in the reign of Henry VIII', *H.J.*, **18**, no. 4 (1975), 675–702. (See Elton on 'The Law of Treason' above.)

Loach, J., 'Conservatism and Consent in Parliament, 1547–59', in *The Mid-Tudor Polity, c. 1540–1560*, J. Loach and R. Tittler (eds), London, 1980. Interesting but slight. To be used with caution, because it takes little account of the 'revisionist' work which has appeared since the completion of her doctoral thesis ten years ago.

Loades, D. M., *The Reign of Mary Tudor*, London, 1979. Solid but, so far as Parliament is concerned, he has little to offer that is new and, at one crucial point at least, he relies heavily and uncritically on Loach.

Miller, H., 'Subsidy assessments of the peerage in the sixteenth century', *B.I.H.R.*, xxviii (1955), 15–34. Important as an illustration of the declining 'financial productivity' of Tudor Parliaments.

Roskell, J. S., 'The problem of the attendance of the lords in medieval parliaments', *B.I.H.R.*, XXIX (1956), 153–204. Weakest on the early Tudor Parliaments.

Scarisbrick, J. J., *Henry VIII*, London, 1968. Essential for Parliament, its legislation and political context in Henry VIII's reign.

Snow, V. F., 'The Evolution of Proctorial Representation in Medieval England', *American Journal of Legal History*, 7 (1963), 319–39.

Stone, L., *The Crisis of the Aristocracy, 1558–1641*, Oxford, 1965. Rich in biographical detail, especially on the peers.

Storey, R. L., *The Reign of Henry VII*, London, 1968. Useful on the Parliaments of the first Tudor.

Thorne, S. E. (ed.), *A Discourse upon the Exposition and Understanding of the Statutes*, San Marino, 1942. An important work on the authority of statute.

Wedgwood, J. C. and Holt, A. D., *Biographies of the members of the House of Commons, 1439–1509*, 2 vols, London, 1936, 1938. A precursor of the History of Parliament Trust biographies. Not always reliable.

Wilkinson, B., *Constitutional History of England in the Fifteenth Century, 1399–1485*, London, 1964. A valuable collection of documents on the immediate antecedents of the early Tudor parliaments.

INDEX